Dr. Christoph S.

From Islam to Islamism, from Islamic Fundamentalism to Jihadism.

After World Youth Day [...] drunken young Muslims paraded past Cologne Cathedral and shouted: In forty years it will be ours. (From the interview of Auxiliary Bishop Heiner Koch in the RP of 30.08.2006,[1] *Christians must become bolder*" A4).

Dr. Christoph S.

FROM ISLAM TO ISLAMISM, FROM ISLAMIC FUNDAMENTALISM TO JIHADISM

AN ATTEMPT AT IDEOLOGY-CRITICAL ENLIGHTENMENT.

Written in 2007, published in 2017 in German language.

Translated to English in 2024.

---

[1] Rheinische Post: http://www.rp-online.de/politik/deutschland/christen-muessen-frecher-werden-aid-1.2315368

Impressum

Bibliografische Information der Deutschen Nationalbibliothek: Die Deutsche Nationalbibliothek verzeichnet diese Publikation in der Deutschen Nationalbibliografie; detaillierte bibliografische Daten sind im Internet über http://dnb.dnb.de abrufbar.

Die automatisierte Analyse des Werkes, um daraus Informationen insbesondere über Muster, Trends und Korrelationen gemäß §44b UrhG („Text und Data Mining") zu gewinnen, ist untersagt.

Verlag: BoD · Books on Demand GmbH, In de Tarpen 42, 22848 Norderstedt

Druck: Libri Plureos GmbH, Friedensallee 273, 22763 Hamburg

ISBN: 978-3-7597-7469-9

MIX
Papier aus verantwortungsvollen Quellen
Paper from responsible sources
FSC
www.fsc.org
FSC® C105338

Table of contents

Foreword

Bertrand Russell, in his history of philosophy *"A History of Western Philosophy and Its Connection with Political and Social Circumstances from the Earliest Times to the Present Day"*, represents a new conception of the history of philosophy, whose programmatic intentions he already underlines in the subtitle. According to it, philosophy and its history is not a self-reflection of the human mind, detached from time and human society; but "philosophers are both results and causes: Results of their social circumstances, of the politics and institutions of their time; causes (if they are lucky) of the beliefs that give form to the politics and institutions of later ages" (Köln 2002). This general thesis is followed by the analysis. It is argumentatively confirmed in the main section by indisputable references to the Golden Age of Islamic philosophy. In the concluding part, a prognosis is ventured as to how a confrontation of Islam with its own and that of modern times can have socio-cultural effects.

The previous century in Europe was characterized by three major ideologies: Imperialism, National Socialism and Communism. Imperialism and National Socialism have raged in two world wars with tremendous loss of people and material; Communism, which has kept rich harvest of human lives especially in the gulags of the Soviet Union and had about 70 million people murdered in China under Mao, has buried itself in its own contradictions, articulated by President Gorbachev. What unites all three ideologies[2] is their structurally similar value system, which grants man only an instrumental existence, with which these ideologies could play their power game.

But the world's sigh of relief is visibly weakening, because the ideological vacuum created by the largely bloodless demise of the Soviet empire is already beginning to fill again. The religion "Islam" is coming more and more under the political influence of the ruling idea of Islamism, a fundamentalist ideology of liberation[3] with missionary zeal and zealots who take their worldview

---

[2] The embedding of this concept in a negative context, which becomes clear here, is content for the time being in its use to be a deficient social theory with an incorporated rigid practical reference.

[3] This term, too, is initially intended to serve phenomenologically as a collective term for the manifestations that can be grouped together under this dazzling term in everyday life, especially through the use of the media. In doing so, it is assumed that the term "Islam" can initially

from a literal interpretation of the Koran and plan a Muslim state of God with global scope, whose enemy image, the West, is being demonized more and more, so that the Christian Occident, according to this account, is becoming more and more like Sodom and Gomorrah, whose extermination is a work pleasing to God.

Just as the already mentioned major ideologies have developed their enemy images, imperialism the merciless competitor, national socialism the 'inferior races', especially the international Jews tum, communism the 'class enemy', who were demonized and 'demonized' beforehand for easier annihilation, so today Islamism presents its enemy image of the 'crusading West' with the USA and Israel as protagonists.

Here, too, it is striking that the Other (we) pass successively through the roles of fellow citizen, then of adversary, then of enemy, then of diabolical emissary of hell, then finally of beast, inhuman and unbeing (incarnations of evil), so that it must be the duty of every good citizen, as a member of a truly godly worldview, to finally 'dispose' of the 'Other' (us) as 'human waste'. The terrorist wing of Islamism, unmoved by the admonishing voices of some of Islam's religious leaders, has committed itself to this 'disposal' program. It is the cynicism of power that here, as in the other ideologies mentioned, reduces the existence of the human being to a smooth functioning and allows it to be regarded at most as a means.

Inhuman Islamism, which now marches in lockstep in the ranks of "fascism," "communism" and "national socialism," is an attack on all civilized nations, which leads me to expose this terrorist ideology argumentatively and thereby to fight it, not least from my painful experience with communism. "Change through enlightenment" - this is how I would like to summarize my program laid down in this book in a striking way. The argumentative unmasking of Islamism as a negative caricature of an abused religion of redemption (I constantly see before me the two collapsing towers of the World Trade Center in New York) does not leave me emotionally cold, so that I will represent my point of view in normative evaluations in a committed and linguistically unambiguous manner; the postulate of objectivity applies to the factual

---

be clearly separated from the phenomenon of "Islamism": the former means "life according to the holy scripture of the Koran," the latter "life according to its message instrumentalized and deformed by ideologues.

presentation. The reader can always distinguish between normative subjectivity and descriptive objectivity.

That there is much to be said for a military confrontation between the West and Islamism in the future is the opinion of Huntington (1996)[4] . In his controversial book *"Clash of Civilizations"* he argues: 'There are two world cultures (better civilizations), that of Islam and that of the West. Both claim universal power.' The Muslims believe that they have the right and thus the power to spread their culture with physical vigor throughout the world; the Europeans are convinced of the superiority of their rational civilization and want to maintain a Western world civilization despite dwindling power. The latter hope that through the globalization of human concerns a world culture transcending individual culture will emerge. Basically, the sole claim to power means a new edition of the bipolarity between Soviet communism and American capitalism as a struggle between Islamism and the free West.

I would like to bypass the clarification of the disputed terms "civilization" and "culture" here by using the term "system". The objection that there is no unified Islamic system, but only many Islamic states with their own interests that can never form a unity, is well supported historically and in fact, but so is the counter thesis[5] , because the cartoon controversy has shown that in religious matters Muslims have a unified consciousness and because Islamism is preparing to become the common foundation of political Islam across countries. There is also the utopia of a common God-state, which united all or many

---

[4] American" citations are used, i.e. the author, year of publication of his production and page numbers in the text are marked by brackets. If several citations successively refer to the same publication, they appear only as bracketed page numbers.

[5] This is where the particular approach is distinguished from the global approach. By decomposing a problem into many partial problems, one comes very close to the reality, but loses the view of the causative backgrounds, so that an evaluation of the whole is no longer possible. By placing a problem into global contexts, one distances oneself from the concrete reality of the individual data, but gains general structural insights, which for this only allow a general prognosis. Both perspectives have their justification and can complement each other. This work is more oriented towards the globalizing method, which cannot take every detail into account, so that a simplified picture emerges. However, the argument, repeated ad nauseam, *that* Islam as such does not exist, so that each individual case must be examined, only serves to rhetorically confirm all sorts of theories, so that factually existing common goals of Islam can be denied. The aim is to generalize the results of the study with a high degree of hypotheticality. It is also conceded without reservation that Christianity has also gone through historical phases of fundamentalism, but has overcome them on its own.

Muslims in a historically existing empire under Muhammad, the four "rightly guided caliphs," the "Umayyads" and the "High Gate," and can thus become reality again if it is seriously pursued because the basis of faith has not changed. Pan-Arabism is also still an option politically, despite its defeat in the Six-Day War.

German domestic and foreign policy has long ignored, then trivialized, then clumsily addressed this looming global confrontation between two systems. For decades, Muslims were allowed to settle in Germany unchecked. Anyone who saw a coming problem in this unlimited immigration was denigrated as a racist, called a neo-Nazi, ironized as a German Turk, indexed as a right-wing radical. An integrative society was supposed to form on the multi-cultic playground. The European migrants succeeded in this; for there was no political tension with Italians, Spaniards, Greeks, Portuguese, Yugoslavs (as a collective term).

But the Muslims remained among themselves because of their completely different value system, which they brought with them to Western Europe, were not very socially engaged and were strangers who often only had a broken command of the German language[6] . This was not so bad, because in the meantime a Muslim parallel society had formed, which was visibly visible in the emergence of ghettos. This was not so bad, because in the meantime a Muslim parallel society had formed, visibly visible in the emergence of ghettos, in which, reinforced by the media in Turkey, a Muslim social structure influenced by militant Turkish nationalism[7] was formed, in which Turkish is the

---

[6] In the former GDR, all students had to learn Russian; however, because of the low prestige of Russian culture, which stemmed from World War 2, hardly anyone mastered this language. Because of the high prestige of English and French, Muslims living there do not stand out for their lack of mastery of the national language. I attribute the deficient language skills of many Turkish immigrants to a similar phenomenon, the lack of authority and low prestige of the German state, which creates an emotional language barrier.

[7] The nationalistically acting Turkey, which simply ignores the European practice, may be mentioned here. About fifty thousand Turks living in Germany have, in spite of the ban on the 'double passport', subsequently re-accepted Turkish citizenship, even though they knew that their German citizenship would automatically expire when it became known. The Turkish state, which has lent a hand here, refuses to disclose the names, so that we can no longer rule out the possibility of non-German citizens voting unconstitutionally in any election, i.e. committing electoral fraud.

According to the Hartz laws, citizens who apply for state support must disclose their financial circumstances. Now, many Turks who have applied for support under Hartz have assets in

colloquial language. A state-within-a-state that is separating itself from the German state system is gradually beginning to establish itself. The "diaspora syndrome," inadequate educational qualifications, the often propagandistic influence of the Turkish media, whose fomentation of prejudice determines old patterns of thought and behavior of many Muslims, not only Turkish Muslims, the bleak situation on the job market, but especially the feeling of superiority as God's privileged people, which does not correspond to reality, additionally ensure isolation from German society and also rejection of this culture. Despite the many Turks and Muslims living in Germany in conformity with the constitution, the reservation remains that a development is taking place here whose direction can hardly be recognized and controlled. Low commitment to German concerns and emphasis on one's own otherness is causing dwindling acceptance among the German population. We are experiencing world Islam and militant Islamism in the coded form of seismic shocks in our culture, which are difficult to interpret and therefore do not seem to be entirely safe.

Turkey. But the Turkish state refuses to provide administrative assistance to the German authorities, so many Turks are financially better off than Germans.

Introduction

The topic of the work suggests as if a seamless path leads from Islam via Islamism to the terrorist concept of "jihad"[8], that is, with a certain consistency, Islam is to be seen as the starting point of a development that indirectly becomes the basis of jihadist terrorism[9]. Islam itself is assumed to have a high potential for ideologization, which is permanently activated in the present. The three terms, it is assumed here, therefore do not describe three discrete states, but rather a gradual transition that makes a clear classification difficult. In the course of the investigation it must become clear whether this general suspicion is justified, is wrong, or must be modified and differentiated. That religions, insofar as they believed to proclaim the only authoritative truth, were and are to a particular extent the cause or co-cause of ideological conflicts, i.e. susceptible to fundamentalism, is taken as a strong premise. The Thirty Years' War is one such example, in which, in the name of God and Christian religions, religious motives and secular as well as spiritual strivings for power led to an extensive depopulation of the German Empire. The public burning of the pantheist Giordano Bruno by the Inquisition and the reprimand of Galileo Galilei by this institution prove an intolerant fundamentalism of Catholicism at that time.

Tepe's model of hermeneutics serves as an analytical treatment of the problem of fundamentalism. In his stage model of literary text interpretation, he distinguishes between two levels, the cognitive and the reflexive. The cognitive level is characterized by an objective and thus historically resistant sense of the text; the reflexive level poses the question of why the text is the way it is, that is, of the reason for the text's conception (Tepe 2001, 118-124).

---

[8] The term jihad is used here mainly in the meaning "holy war. As a reason for this can be given: "Unfortunately, our Muslim friends have now also adopted it and have drawn a false picture of Islam, which has contributed to many misunderstandings" (Schimmel 1996, 12). Its actual deterioration in meaning is not noted by many authors, so that they translate this term with the "great jihad" that requires inner purification from the believer.

[9] Under the chapter heading "Vom klassischen Djihad der Eroberung zum Djihadismus des irregulären Krieges," Tibi (2004) sufficiently demonstrates the semantic degradation of meaning of this term, which also corresponds to an actual one.

The author would like to apply this model also to the interpretation of cultural phenomena and add to this stage model a third and last one. What presents itself as most real in a culture is its surface with the free play of economy, society, art, individuality, trends, values. At first sight, this agile set of relations seems to be without rules, random and aimless, i.e. chaotic. But with the premise that every effect is preceded by a cause, the question can be asked: Why are the phenomena the way they are?

The analysis of the object level thus brings to light the forces by which the contradictory surfaces are caused: contradictory or reinforcing value systems, convictions, theories. In the case of literary texts, this is the author's formative art program and value system, which determine the text structure as a causal background, so that the author's artistic and worldview intentions are reflected in the text. But the interests of the political actors can be questioned even further. The regress ends where assumptions, theories, value systems cannot be justified by any reasoning in turn. These founding premises are provided in their most comprehensive form by philosophy, religion and myth and directly determine the deep structure of a culture and thus indirectly its multifaceted reality.

Culture and history can be analyzed according to this three-layer theory. Thus, according to this theory, the topic demands a step-by-step approach. Islam as a religion with its unquestionable value system, which provides the ontological premises of the theological and profane superstructure, is first called "Islamism" in a value-neutral way, which in turn provides the theoretical justification for the confusing section of reality called "jihad.

If we compare the deep structures of the Western world with the Islamic world, it turns out that there is a deep, seemingly unbridgeable ontological difference between the Western and Islamic worlds. Islam assumes a world that was created by Allah and is therefore recognizable only through him. The Koran as *sola scriptura* describes objectively, binding for all times, absolutely true, what it is about this world and the role of man. The form of government that results from this is what Prenner (2005, 128) calls "nomocracy," a primary rule of God's word from which reality follows analytically. One can imagine this act of creation as an illocutionary speech act, which at the same time performs the corresponding action to the linguistic in formation, for example: 'I baptize you [...]'

By receiving the Koran, the Muslim learns about God's intention, but also about the nature of his world. The Koran is thus the mediator of objective knowledge, to which the Muslim must adapt: a direct path to knowledge of God and the world is not possible. Truth thus means "conformity of thought and action to the statements of the Koran" because it is semantically valid as God's word and therefore factually objective. The highest commandment of Islam is hidden in the term "surrender to God's will," which means monarchical and theological absolutism of Allah, to whom man is only an insubstantial shadow. Islam defines itself and its world from God, the almighty ruler.

The West represents the ontology of subjectivity according to the motto of Protagoras "Man is the measure of all things". The doubt about the objective world of the Middle Ages, which is understood as a reflection of the divine one, comes to its methodical expression in Descartes. At first everything is doubtable, even the existence of one's own person. But if one imagines the non-being of one's own person, then there must be an imaginer who imagines his non-being, the I, the self-consciousness, which already precedes all individual knowledge. So the universal doubt goes wrong, because to be able to doubt always presupposes already knowledge. Thus, skepticism does not lead to abstinence from knowledge, but to unquestionable knowledge. Descartes' method, then, is to arrive at doubt-free knowledge through doubting. Human reason, he concludes, is the locus of unconditional knowledge, while the object world can at any time feed skepticism because of its contingency. Subjectivism, then, by negating doubt, determines at the same time the indubitable thinking and being subject, no longer an idea of God's existence conceived as absolute objectivity. The power of imagination, reason, ratio are the conditions for the I to be certain of itself as well as of the world.

Thus, modern times represent an anthropocentric worldview, while Islam follows a theocentric basic concept. For him, God and his creation are the absolutely real, to which the human functions of being and cognition must be aligned. Both are diametrically opposed and constitute the fundamental difference between the two worlds. Basic positions, here the relation between religious objectivism of Islam and secular subjectivism of the West, determine the problems of today's world. Thus arises the objective of this thesis: From the philosophical position of realism (value-neutral understood as a collective term for many philosophical currents), which assumes the existence and at least partial recognizability of an extra-subjectively existing external world, the "supra-naturalistic value system"[10] (Tepe 1988, 11) of Islam shall be critically reflected.

First of all, there are two directions of the ideology-critical analysis, the epistemological and the socio-critical: Ideology[11] , now used in a comprehensive sense neutral to positive, changes according to the theory of "location-bound thinking" of cultural sociology (Mannheim 1984) on the one hand the philosophical and profane thinking and perception of reality, on the other hand also the perception and shaping of political-social reality. The former asks about the anthropologically attributed abilities of all human beings to absorb and process data, about the ability to think: about its conditions, possibilities and limits and criticizes attempts to influence the criteria of cognition and thus the ability to cognize on the basis of any pursuit of interests, prejudices or indoctrinations. The other criticizes social designs that pretend to be able to orient a society according to true, i.e. universally valid and binding values.

Birnbacher (1996) has proceeded according to a similar method of *ideology criticism in the* essay *"Schopenhauer as* Ideology Critic". An ideological complex is first subjected to a theoretical critique of the falsity of the statements, then the reason for this "distortion of truth" (51) is determined: political functions and moral intentions of the new doctrines of salvation that have bent the facts of the matter to suit their goals, to be critically evaluated, and finally the behavior of the actors who have produced an ideology or blindly follow it is exposed.

This critique of ideology has already been carried out on a theoretical level. I mention here only Lieber, Tepe, Salamun. Ideology formation takes place according to scientifically researchable laws, whose criteria can be documented scientifically-descriptively. Here I base myself on Salamun (2005),

---

[10] A "supra-naturalistic value system" reckons not only with the existence of a physical reality but also with that of an otherworldly, metaphysical reality.

[11] Mannheim (1984) distinguishes two approaches to thinking: "from within" and "from being" (1982, 213). He calls the former "idea," the latter "ideology" (213). It is not so much the **what of** ideas that Mannheim wants to determine; he wants to consider the mental entity as a function based sociologically on certain conditions. In a broad sense, it is a matter of the underlying socio-cultural value system that makes it comprehensible why the resulting intellectual product is the result of thinking from a certain position of interest, from an "ideology," a certain zeitgeist. This concept is here called **"ideology(+)"** (Tepe 1988, 8). This view largely coincides with Russel's conception of the philosophy of history.

who points to the already elaborated criteria of a critique of ideology and totalitarianism, which can fruitfully contribute their "explanatory approaches and interpretive hypotheses" (9) in the analysis of fundamentalism. Surprisingly, it emerges that all fundamentalist movements develop in a structurally very similar way, so that they can presumably be based on the same, super historical structural model. The individual fundamentalist worldviews are then only individuations of a super historical structure, so that the goal of the work must be a determination of the individual characteristics of Islamic fundamentalism[12] on the basis of these general structural features. But such descriptive accounts - we think of imperialism, National Socialism and communism - are not enough. If a dire calamity can be predicted, it can be effectively combated already, or better: only in its early stages.

Salamun, however, forgets to point out not only the scientific value but also the pragmatic aspect of such analyses. Here the author represents an enlightenment pathos that does not shy away from rhetorically aggravating formulations and yet is based on good reasons, because the principle "*principiis obsta*" (Resist the beginnings) applies; once an ideology has established itself in the negative sense, it gains a momentum of its own that can hardly be slowed down by criticism, because it 'disposes' of its critics until there are none left. The changes in theoretical cognition and practical social action caused by ideology in the deficit sense, **ideology(-),** must be exposed by an ideology-critical analysis. However, this exposure of ideologically deficient structures - another aim of this work - does not pursue an end in itself, but the strategy of bringing about a change in the reader's behavior. According to the logical relation "if **p,** then **q**", if I do not want **q**, the result is the setting of **non-p**; i.e. the emergence, flourishing and decay of an ideology run according to predictable historical phases, but can be influenced by man.

When the purpose of a fundamentalist ideology is exposed as false or inhuman, means must be sought to promote a different purpose in the sense of humanization. This work therefore pursues the concern to prevent the world from stumbling into a Third World War by means of an ideology-critical analysis of Islamic fundamentalism. The argument "*Nobody could know that*", which in reality should be "*Nobody wanted to know that", which* irrationalized the outbreak of the First and Second World War as well as the reign of

---

[12] Islamic fundamentalism is a deficient worldview because it pretends to be able to impose politically from the holy Koran an ideal world whose reality is attainable in the near future.

terror of communism, starts again today to promote thoughtlessness, but also wishful thinking, as an "inherently tolerant and peaceable Islam". If no balance between Western and Koranic thinking can be achieved, the worst must be expected!

The theoretical basis of this work is Tepe's theory of ideology, which he has summarized in two studies, among others[13] . Since the other two world religions are structurally and functionally related to Islam, they are largely excluded from this sub search for editorial reasons, although historically similar circumstances are conceded. Christianity, shaped by various fundamentalisms in its past, has purged itself of its susceptibility to fundamentalism in a painful phase of enlightenment and textual criticism.

But Islam vehemently resists a historical-critical analysis[14] of the Koran. Subsequently, Islamism is subjected to a critical view, as is jihadism, from which consequences can be drawn for one's own political thinking and actions.

---

[13] Tepe, P.: Theory of Illusions. Essen 1988. Same author: Illusionskritischer Versuch über den historischen Materialismus. Essen 1989.

[14] According to the intersubjective experience that "the spirit did not fall from heaven", as a book title of v. Ditfurth negatively paraphrases the metaphysical thesis of *creatio ex nihilo, it* is claimed that a linguistically composed message, even if the bearer passes it on literally and without any additions of his own, has uncritically simply taken as a basis the nature of the language at that time with all the implications brought forth by man. It is indisputable that, since the Qur'anic Arabic is a human creation that has undergone a more or less long development, it is a condition for understanding the message of salvation that Allah has been able to proclaim only under the condition of the existence and mastery of a man-made and constantly changing linguistic system of meaning. Allah cannot speak to man in any other way than in human language. He had to become "human.

The question may be allowed here, how Mohammed could have read the original Koran by an act of God, if he was illiterate according to general judgment.

1. Islam

The number of publications on Islam is legion, making it easy for any interested reader to gain access to this religion, which forms the third strongest denomination in Germany. Therefore, an already differentiated prior knowledge about this world-spanning faith in one God, Allah, is factored in here and only a first summary presentation is prefaced. In the course of the discussion, the developing problems require a more detailed examination of individual sub-areas.

Descriptively (in terms of religious studies), Islam is a creation of the Prophet Muhammad (born around 570 A.D.), who believes himself inspired by Allah to proclaim God's will to mankind. Muhammad lives as a merchant and trader in Mecca and learns about Christianity and Judaism as a caravan leader; he himself is a follower of polytheism, which is practiced by Arab tribes. The Kaaba in Mecca, today the highest sanctuary of Islam, is held in high esteem as a religious shrine by many polytheists. The many often feuding tribes also correspond to various polytheistic systems, so that Muhammad comes into contact with an abundance of deities, many of whom are also feuding with each other. He retreats into the desert and meditates, because he feels like a true seeker of God in this contradictory world of gods.

In the year 610 A.D. his prophetic phase begins; in the form of the angel Gabriel he perceives the voice of his, the one God, which, after a glimpse into the original Koran, imposes on him the true doctrine of God and also the order to proclaim it to all people. After his death, since Muhammad himself is illiterate, his visions, which have already been set down individually in writing, are summarized in the "book", in the Koran, unfortunately not chronologically, but according to the length of the suras, which shorten more and more.

Islam can refer to two sources; the Koran, the word of God, and the Godly life of the Prophet. The "book" written in Arabic, the "language" of God, cannot be translated into other languages according to its divine origin; it is the truth par excellence, valid beyond time, and a binding guideline for every Muslim in all areas of life. According to Muhammad's will, the text of the Koran is the direct word of God; he himself is only "the seal of the prophets" (33:40). Thus, hermeneutically, the Qur'an consists only of a single-layered text whose truth is openly available and not of layers of different levels of truth, so that a depth interpretation is not necessary. This opinion is strongly contradicted by hermeneuticists, because they can prove that the Koran contains very misleading and contradictory texts in many places, which can have their reason only in contradictory background premises and historical influences. Therefore, the faithful follower of Islam (surrender to the will of God) should not reflect, analyze and interpret the Quran, but should transfer God's word into the intended meaning one to one. And this is best done by learning the text by heart.

The godly life of the Prophet, who must, however, be denied any divinity, provides a second basis for the teachings of Islam, because this godly life is a model for every Muslim, but in its truth-guided stringency it can be classified under the Koran. Sayings, actions, questions, many of them concerning everyday life, on which the Prophet took a stand, were collected from those around him and commented on by the first four caliphs. Thus, in addition to the Scriptures, there is a short tradition in Islam in which these instructions are collected, the importance of which is, in my opinion, much too high, since they are not God's words and have not been authorized by the Quran. Such a self-contained instruction is called *Hadith*, of which "up to a million [...] circulate in six canonical books" (Barth 2003, 63), which allows for an abundance of variants of interpretation that cannot be overlooked, even though only about 9000 *Hadiths* are recognized and lead to multiple causes of dispute within Islam.

At the moment, it seems as if Muhammad enjoys a higher standing than God among Muslims. The instructions contained in the *hadiths, which* find their applications where the Qur'an has not provided a regulation, together with the Qur'an form the *sunna,* which has become "custom" according to the example of the Prophet.

The ummah, the "community of all Muslims" (Tibi 2001, 30), as established by Muhammad, is to be distinguished from this. It is the incorporated state idea of Islam and states that all Muslims should live in a state community. The head of such a universalist state should be a caliph or a righteous imam in the succession of Muhammad. In modern times, such an *umma exists* only as a utopia, because only Islamic nation states exist, but no overarching association of states is yet a reality. For Islam, however, the universalistic idea of an *umma*, a "world power Islam," (38) is subliminally always a political program.

It remains to introduce the controversial institution of "*sharia*," for many Europeans a negatively connoted irritant. It is "the collective term for Islamic rules of life, religious duties and the religiously based law of Islam, which is traced back to revelation" (Barth 2003, 67). Regional modifications or misogynistic rules of life and dress have also found their way into this religiously legitimized body of law, which encompasses the entire life of the Muslim. Muhammad's downgrading of women to the second rank has fostered a macho mania for masculinity that we often perceive among young Turks and youth of other Muslim states. Women's rights have been increasingly reduced throughout the history of Islam. It becomes an existential problem when the *Sharia* is imposed on minorities of other faiths. It is the sum of the Koran, Sunna, Hadith, consensus and analogy. We have here a comprehensive legal system that encompasses all of human life; it is total because it regulates all areas of life, thus conveying a great security of life; it is totalitarian for those who perceive the *sharia* as paternalism.

Thus, in Islam there is a pyramid of truth that can be thought of in a stepwise manner. At the top are God and the Koran, followed by the sayings of Muhammad, the *hadiths*, summarized in the sunna, the conclusion by analogy, in which questions that are not explicitly listed and resolved in the Koran and the *hadiths are* decided according to similarity with them, and the consensus, the unanimous opinion of Islamic theologians, which enjoys the reputation of a *fatwa*. The *Shari'ah* encompasses all of these stages to the extent that they incorporate rules from the four sources of law.

Islam's beliefs, which have assimilated Christianity, Judaism, and polytheism, can be divided into two areas: beliefs and practices.

Essential **beliefs** are "the unity of God (monolithic monotheism), the power of angels, revelation, prophethood, the existence of the afterlife and belief in predestination" (76). The five pillars of Islam are considered to be the **practices of faith**: the profession of faith, the five times daily prayer, almsgiving, fasting and the pilgrimage, the *Hajj*.

Before the thesis 'Islam possesses an implicit ideological potential which is particularly easy to activate and which, as Islamism, determines Islam and its basic political lines today' can now be examined, a separate determination of the position is necessary which is based on anthropology, namely because the term 'ideology', according to Tepe's theory, becomes the actual constituting determination of man's being. His definition of man as an "illusion-prone animal" (1988, 7) needs explanation because of its at first seemingly strange choice of terms.

2. Presentation of one's own ideology-functional point of view from the point of view of cultural anthropology in comparison to the Islamic image of humanity

As was to be expected, there are fundamental differences between the Islamic conception of man as laid down in the Koran and that of scientific cultural anthropology. These differences have become even more pronounced in recent decades because of Muslim immigration to Europe, which has led to parallel societies instead of assimilation. Thus, spatial proximity has not brought the two value systems together, but has increasingly alienated them from each other.

Through satellite television, Muslims are connected to their homeland on a daily basis and perceive the reality surrounding them mainly from this perspective. They are "with their head in their homeland, with their body in Germany"; but as these different value systems drift further and further apart, they threaten to tear apart the personal identity of Muslims and the political identity of immigrant states. The difference between the human image of cultural anthropology and that of the Koran must now be named.

2.1 Cultural Anthropological Premises

According to this theory, man is not a being that is safely guided by God through this world, he is an instinct-reduced being with open genetic programs that allow learning. The animal is adapted to its world a priori by ITMs (Innate Triggering Mechanisms) that allow little room for modification. A creature's instinct repertoire, a genetically anchored prior knowledge for characteristic actions and reactions, adapts it in advance to its habitat in such a way that it can survive.

But in the evolution of humans an instinct reduction has taken place; the anticipatory knowledge of the external world stored in the genes exists partly only in open learning programs. While ITMs, for example 'enemy images', which compel to flee, only appeal very selectively and in an attractive way, very strongly extended forms of knowledge anticipation have developed in humans, the categories discovered by Kant and interpreted by Lorenz (1997) in terms of natural history, which contain, as it were, rules of object recognition, and do so a priori. What can be a possible object of experience is already known in advance by man, and in every concrete imagined object the forms of perception space and time as well as the categories quantity, quality, relation, modality are co-represented. They work by anticipating in advance a system of order by which the incoming quantity of data is structured. This makes man a "cosmopolitan animal" (Tepe), capable of perceiving, describing, and responding to an infinite number of possible objects. But this evolution towards flexibility and simultaneous stripping away of instinct-guided behaviors must be paid for by man with dismissal from the security of this protective umbrella and shield.

Thus he gets a problem: He is, paradoxically speaking, forced to be free. (It is no counterargument that many people give up this freedom in favor of institutional securities and place themselves under their protection. Religions, for example, offer the insecure person a sense of his own security). His self-knowledge makes him feel incessantly that he is a constantly endangered, constantly suffering mortal being, since there are no longer any guiding instinctual programs. "Reality and suffering pressure" (Tepe / Topitsch) inhibit any coping with life. Now even the open learning programs don't help him; for what should man learn something for?

He is first of all forced to create a substitute of instinct, which guarantees him the vital security of his life execution. This is necessary, because the normal human being is no Romulus and Remus and also no Robinson, which can grow up in isolation, but a being, which is embedded in culture. Man is a "cultural being by his nature" (Gehlen / Lorenz), i.e. a human nature as a species determination does not exist, which does not contradict a common biological basic equipment, because his 'nature' consists in the necessary absorption of culture, so that he becomes a being created by culture for the second time, which itself can produce culture again, which presents itself in an unmanageable variety.

This culture meets man in an immense abundance of designs, but means stabilization of his needs by "institutionalization" (Gehlen). It fulfills similar tasks as instinct: man is born into a certain culture whose aprioris and values he assimilates. State and social institutions, rules of coexistence established by tradition, sanctions and morals, mythical and religious customs, common language and common past are the cement that now makes possible a meaningful fulfillment of life. One can therefore even speak of a metaphysical need of man for eternally valid values; but human history, on the contrary, consists of a succession of value systems that become detached. While the three basic behavioral capacities cognition, emotion and will shape animal life as behavior, as a unity of knowledge, feeling and readiness to act, these capacities have differentiated in humans. The brain as an organ of survival has evolved into an additional organ of knowledge, which can judge relatively independently of feelings and personal interests. In the knowledge acquisition there is objectivity, it (the knowledge) cannot be completely wrong, although it originates from different cultural and personal sources; because life needs security. Our ratio, according to the realist premise, is capable of representing reality, albeit modestly.

What remains hidden to the people by the "objective spirit" (Hegel), called culture, for a very long time, is that this is in reality only a product of the "subjective spirit", product of the human mental creation which arises with it, changes and passes away. As long as mythical and religious things are understood as eternally lasting things together with a rationality of the perception of nature, which is close to life and fits to it, as reality, a psychic existential security is given, which, however, already starts to falter, when myths and religions are written down and thus have to allow a hermeneutic questioning about their truth content. They are - so the result of the questioning - no objectivations of the divine or spiritual, but only symbols of a reality lived before, which now becomes a fiction. They are only vital deceptions (if they claim an objective truth), they make a personally fulfilled and socially supported life possible for the one who believes, so that Tepe can speak of man as the ideology-decayed being, whose anthropological constant describes the dependence on essentialized illusions (culture-preserving institutions).

It can be called a tragedy that the study of the mythical and religious value systems destroyed the naive belief in the truth of the identity-creating symbolic world. For it soon turned out that these ontological designs are not true, that they are collective projections of the human will, so that what in man as hope, wish, utopia, ideal, illusion pushes for reality and realization, also exists in truth as it should exist.

One's own nothingness can be compensated with these often twisted projections: the slave on earth becomes a master in heaven, earthly mortality is transformed as eternal life after death, in which one firmly believes, so that precisely the one whose earthly fate is lamentable is rewarded for it in heaven with eternal joys. This self-imagined and then rationalized consolation potential, that what is supposed to be is, transforming subjective desires into objective reality, has produced invaluable cultural goods, but at the same time is a source of inadmissible objectifications.

But what would happen if there were a possibility to let mankind exist without illusions? This question touches the permanent crisis mood of modernity; because just by cognitively questioning basically all values for their truth content in the sense of positive natural sciences, it has to state that everything what our culture has produced, namely values, in itself cannot claim a supratemporal validity like laws of nature. In the knowledge that every understanding of values and value behavior yields only a temporary benefit for mankind, that every historical epoch is determined by changing values, the thesis of nihilism, most radically represented by Nietzsche, is based on the fact that even the creation of new values already means a priori their destruction. To seek salvation in the truth of natural sciences fails because nature can in no way give answers to the questions of our life, because it itself exists value-free and can only be investigated scientifically in a value-neutral way.

The world of the intellect is cold; it does not grant a warming feeling of life. The absolute but narrowed claim to truth of the positive sciences, which is imposed from the outside as scientific belief and affiliation, ensures a backyard existence of values, emotions, experience, spiritual experiences: the metaphysical need for existential security is no longer served. Yet it is precisely these that feed the human need for art, culture, moral self-worth, and existence-affirming religions that, through traditions and institutions, provide it with a meaningful life. As a being dependent on social and cultural relations (prolonged childhood, "physiological prematurity", "secondary nest-feeder") (Portmann), culture offers man the protective space for his development, so that he can sublimate the "pressure of suffering and reality". However, the existential anxiety tamed by this can then break out again without restraint when man reflects the mere construct character of this cultural world, which is the case today, so that many people suffer from modernity.

Every human being is shaped in advance by quasi-transcendental constants of his culture. which we can translate with "value-boundness" and with "world-conception-boundness" Tepe 1988, 10). The latter limits our cognitive horizon of expectations to what is conceivable in this time, the former serves as compensation from the pressure of suffering, but assigns even more a social horizon of meaning to lead a good life. But when the construct character of human cultural values has become transparent, when man has become painfully aware of his meaninglessness, he looks for safe, convincing values and in reality finds only utopias, **ideologies(-)** (see next section), illusions assumed to be true, intoxicating transfigurations of existence, fantastic houses of cards, if he does not metaphysically exaggerate them, i.e. endow them with 'higher consecrations'. At this point we come back to Tepe's *theory of illusions* (1988), in which he starts from the "irrevocable ideology-ness" (8) of human existence. Thus, he conceives this concept very broadly, as "dependence on value orientations" (8). The initial biological disorientation caused by instinct reduction is initially more than compensated by the cultural value system in which the young person grows up embedded.

From this comprehensive and value-neutral to value-positive concept of ideology, which can also be translated as culture-boundness or "value-holding" (8), Tepe develops his two concepts of ideology **(+)** and **(-)**, whose content determination and labeling the author would like to adopt, if the context does not allow a clear assignment. In general, man is determined by **ideology(+)**, by value attitudes that basically guide human life often unconsciously and unnoticed like an apriori. **Ideology(+)** is the cultural anthropological term for man's struggle against the paralyzing pressure of reality. But when this explicitly projectively transforms things in such a way that desires and wills become ontologized cognitive and rational being, then the narrower concept of **ideology(-) is** authoritative because something that is only normative in character is made into a descriptive object with the consequence that a cognitively universal claim to truth can be and is made. This transformation from normative to descriptive is, from an ideology-critical point of view, to be judged as sleight of hand, which leads to a "knowledge deficit" (8).

A short foray in the direction of Islam makes the central problem clear: 'How is the absolute claim to truth of this religion, authorized by God, to be evaluated ideology-critically? Is there a voluntaristic projection here that what is supposed to be, God's omnipotence, also *de facto* carries human existence?'

Islam offers man an eternal life in paradise if he fulfills God's will, proclaimed by Mohammed, it promises eternal existential security without being able to prove it empirically; our claim to knowledge, committed to positivism and critical rationalism, sees in man a being that is in principle excluded from any transcendence, so that he must create a substitute for himself through the creation and participation of culture, which as such is always already seen through, can only fulfill itself as a temporally limited value function. It is, in Nietzsche's sense, a "life lie".

Western anthropology can be summarized in the sentences: Man is a being who has come into being through biological evolution and has created himself through cultural evolution and is constantly creating himself through bringing forth culture. He is master of himself, but constantly threatened by sense emptying of being, so that he longs for the security of transcendent powers.

2.2 The image of man in Islam

While the philosophical anthropology of Western culture makes use of all sciences in its argumentation, in Islam there is only one religiously defined one, and that is canonized in the Koran. What is man in the sense of Islam? The answer becomes clear when one sees Muslims praying in the mosque. Not only do they kneel before God, no, they virtually throw themselves on the ground before him, i.e. they are only a speck of dust in Allah's creation. Compared to their God, they are almost nothing and therefore totally submit to him, they are God's completely compliant tools. God is the absolute autocrat.

But by placing themselves unconditionally under Allah's protection, they receive the guarantee of immortality and abundant life in paradise if they live a godly life. God appears as an absolute monarch who rewards or punishes his ruled according to his absolutely valid laws. This unlimited abundance of power remains incomprehensible to man. If the reality of this promise of salvation is believed to be guaranteed, this gives rise to an almost unstoppable cultural impulse to shape life, society and politics according to these guidelines. Equipped with God's monopoly on truth, Islam can divide the world into true and false without disturbing self-reflection in order to promote the truth, itself, and to brand the untruth (everything non-Islamic). This truth - laid down in the Koran - is to be followed uncompromisingly, so that a binding missionary mandate is inherent in it. As creatures chosen by God, they conceive of themselves as his elect, endowed with the privilege of possessing the complete truth. However, this also enforces a certain conservative and rigid way of life that struggles when problems arise that cannot be anticipated religiously, so that it cannot channel contradictory impulses in the time-honored way. An Islamic anthropology, therefore, cannot be empirically supported by one based on natural science. A Darwinian evolutionary one, although it is empirically proven many times, is also frowned upon in Islam. What man is, therefore, can only be explained from Allah, from Islam.[15] And since man is defined only from Allah, he is as himself, as an individual: nothing.

Every human being is a creation of God. "It is He Who forms you in the womb as He wills [...]": Sura (3:6)[16] . Thus, man owes gratitude to Allah for his life, trust as to a father, respect for His omnipotence. In God all threads of the human, animal, vegetable and mineral being run together. We can speak here of a "condensation of being" that can no longer be increased, God, "whose transcendence is absolute, whose will dictates his decrees in unquestionable sovereignty, yet is guided by his wisdom and mercy" (Khoury 2001, 90). God, then, does not impose unfulfillable standards on believers because he exercises contractual loyalty to his creatures, whose welfare he has at heart. In Allah's 'reckoning', then, human incapacities are already priced in, so that the believer can be sure that if he fulfills Allah's commandments 'tolerably', he will enter paradise. The patriarchal element of care for the subjects thus finds its way into the relationship between God and man.

Man is not only symbolically a creature of God, which he created from "dry, sounding clay, from black mud formed into shape": Sura (15:26), but in this Sura there is also a view of the essence of man. He is like everything created, indeed a work of God, "perfectly formed, into which I breathed of My Spirit": Sura (15:30). Nevertheless, the Koran emphasizes God's radical difference from man. Any idea of development is excluded; the perfectly created man, except for a 'construction error', corresponds to a perfectly created nature,

---

[15] We shall only recall here Feuerbach's thesis of religion as a projection of man, in which he "first [misplaces] his being *outside himself* before he finds it in himself" (1994, 33). This "outside himself," God, is himself without knowing it. If man wants to know his essence, he only needs to translate the attributes of God into anthropological *essentials*.

[16] The Koran is quoted according to the edition *Der Koran*, Munich 1992. This edition also considers the introductory formula to a sura with a separate verse, so that there is a difference of one in the numbering of the verses in other editions.

which is directed to his needs. This construction error is called "weakness"[17].
Has God in his omnipotence made a mistake?

I believe that this question is wrongly asked, since it is about the faith bases
of the Islamic revelation, which is not questionable itself: it is just so. A rationalist, however, discovers in this construction the reason why man needs
God at all. What is it about the natural weakness of man? Why is he not created
as perfect as everything else? He is, as already said, a "misconstruction" of
God, because man could not live without God's grace and help. Here cultural
anthropology and the conception of man of Islam touch each other. Man is a
biopsychically weak creature; however, seen from Islam, it is not primarily
culture that compensates for this deficiency, but God in his goodness. However, if Allah had created man perfectly, he would not need God. Why is man
an exception in Allah's creation? Is it therefore selfish motives to justify the
necessity of a redeemer God from the neediness and weakness of man? Does
God need a humanity kneeling in the dust before him to demonstrate his unlimited power?

The Islamic view of man is based on Manichaeism, the struggle between
good (Allah) and evil (Satan). Both principles do not fight each other 'personally', because Allah has already won the fight against Satan *a priori,* but the
"weak man" is the venue of this fight. Here, therefore, a "proxy war" takes
place. Although everything happens according to Allah's will, there remains
the contradiction that man can do evil, which will lead to eternal damnation.
Thus, only the approach of subjectivity of a human development and unfolding of his individuality can be seen. The weak man falls into temptation, lets
himself be guided by God and wins paradise, an eternal, very enjoyable life.

But what happens to the non-Muslims? As representatives of the book religions they are close to Islam, as animists, atheists, positivists they are *de nature* doomed to eternal damnation; unless they would renounce their 'false
doctrines'; because all human beings are Muslims by birth, because they are
descended from the first man created by God's hand, Adam; all other religions
are misconstructions, which have gone different distances from the 'true' faith.

Our rationalism, in which the human reason, the subject, contains the criteria
a priori, with which it examines objects according to these and can allow only
that which does not contradict them, does not stop even before God. God must

---

[17] "Man is weak by nature" (4:28).

let his existence be authenticated by man, if he should not remain a phantom. The true lord of the world is therefore, in the sense of rationalism, the autonomous man, to whose mode of cognition everything that exists is subject. If God exists, then his rationality must be the same as that of man. In the eyes of a Muslim, this subjectivism of being intellectually "like God" is tantamount to blasphemy; for God is for him the absolutely first, existent and objective. In the sense of rationalism, man is the highest, self-supporting entity as far as his cognitive performance is concerned, whereas Islam sees God as an absolutist ruler over man helpless without him: self-determined man as Prometheus[18] against externally determined man as passive.

A world created by God as perfect and a human being who obeys the will of Allah unconditionally does not invite research; for what nature is, is no longer a question, while the concept of nature as an "object of possible experience" (Kant) virtually implies empirical research. The sciences (as an exception mathematics and medicine) have no ancestral place in Islam, because in the Koran everything is written what one must know about the nature, so that natural science would be only a tinkering into God's plan. [19]

The consequences of such a merely passive reception of nature can still be seen in Islam today. The idea of progress, which with the help of Darwinism also advances society, science and technology in an evolutionary way, is alien to Islam, because a constant God demands a constant world, so that there is

---

[18] In *Greek Myths, retold* (Vernant 2000), the role of Prometheus is interpreted as a being between gods and men. Prometheus, as he is called, is the one "who understands in advance, who considers in advance" (77); he embodies the exploratory urge of man, "a rebellious, whip-smart, and undisciplined mind" (65). In a fennel plant he hides the divine fire and brings it to the people from whom Zeus took the fire and then hid it. For this, and still for other stratagems against Zeus, he is forged on a rock. Every day Zeus' eagle comes and eats his liver, which always grows back.

[19] The anthropomorphic interpretation of the development of domestic animals seems particularly bizarre. For Darwin, the breeding of domestic animals, their domestication, is a selection process deliberately designed by humans, which he transfers to the entire biosphere. In the Koran, it becomes a teleological creation orchestrated by God for man's convenience in obtaining food. Sura (23:21) states:

"And in the cattle there is a lesson for you. We give you to drink of that which is in their bodies, and ye have many uses of them, and of them ye eat."

Here the Koran gets into great argumentation trouble, which it could escape if it would allow a historical and symbolic interpretation.

therefore no self-dynamic social, scientific[20] and technical development; Islam thus consistently demands a stagnant, static and history-less world. Like Tibi, the author believes:

> The theocentric worldview of Muslims, anchored in Islamic revelation and having survived centuries of historical change with a high degree of resilience, makes it difficult to culturally manage social change" (1991, 221).

Moreover, for the Muslim, the Koran is the highest authority in matters of knowledge, because it proclaims God's word unadulterated. Through Moses and Christ, God's message moves further and further away from its original prophet Abraham until it finds its final universal and supratemporal truth through the "seal of the prophets," so that only the study of the Koran and not the study of empirical sciences leads to the highest insight. (However, as the understanding grows even in Muslim countries that there is no economic and social change without them, adventurous constructions are devised, some of which will be referred to in the course of the discussion to prove how to make the worldview of Islam compatible with the positive sciences).

The nonetheless latent rejection of the 'Western' sciences corresponds to the rejection of fine art. Because of the prohibition "Thou shalt not make unto thee any graven image of God" (not even of nature, because subjective premises are thereby co-presented in God's work), which is nowhere documented in the Koran, there are no fine arts. Art has claimed calligraphy for its own. The wonderful ornamental variations of Quranic verses in mosques serve to glorify God's eternal Word, which also describes the natural world; the calligraphic master is unrecognizable in his work. The artist as *Deus secundus* is alien to Islam because Allah created the world perfectly.

In the Suras (6:96 - 6:100), Muhammad describes how Allah created this world to suit the needs of all living beings. He paints an almost perfect world

---

[20] Prenner (2005) takes an unclear stance on this question. According to him, there is a scientific interpretation of the Koran that "recognizes its miraculous character" (120 f.) because it (the Koran) "contains scientific facts that were unknown at the time of the Prophet and were discovered more than a thousand years later" (121). As an example, he cites Abduh (in Goldziher 1979), who claims that Darwin's basic ideas are to be taken from the Quran (an outrageous provocation), as well as that the jinns (demons) were in fact microbes, so that the Quran "[anticipates] the viewpoint of the very most modern medicine" (356). - In the former GDR, a similar linguistic regulation was common, in that discoveries and inventions had to be attributed to the Russians first.

in which means and ends fit together in such a way that man finds an earthly well-ordered living space from which everything grows for him without much effort. Allah makes the grain germinate, brings forth life from death and death from life, creates the day to work and the night to rest, creates the stars for night orientation, creates man from a lump of clay, makes it rain and then grow. "[...] We then bring forth green things, from which we make rowed grain sprout, and from the date palms, from their flower umbels (sprout) low-hanging date grapes, and gardens of grapes, and the olive and the pomegranate [...]" (6:100). The gardens and the paradise modeled on a garden are culturally anthropologically 'twisted' projections.

For the poetic praise of Allah and his creation has an obvious flaw: it is not true! The Arabian Peninsula in particular is plagued by permanent drought and thus infertility; instead of fertile olive groves, deserts hostile to man are spreading. Why do we learn nothing of all this? Allah is a perfect being, and such a being cannot produce a nature hostile to life. The prophet projects the perfection of God onto a perfect world created by him, almost to be called paradisiacal, which provides empirically certain circumstantial evidence for the existence of God.

We find here a very pronounced ideologically deficient circle: a perfectly created world points to its perfect creator, the perfect creator to his perfect creation: an ontologically closed world, which insists on absolute truth claim against other designs. But as the still to be discussed, according to Kant untenable teleological proof of God shows, a non-teleological structure of the world (see quantum theory and Darwinism) means at the same time an impossibility of the logical proof of an existence of God as creator of such a world.

Such critical questions are inadmissible in Islam and are answered with the formula 'Allah willed it so in his unfathomable plans', so that with it everything, even contradictory things, can be 'explained', consequently the uncritical contemporary can actually be convinced of the absolute truth of Islam. Thus, even the dominance of the West in the 19th and 20th centuries can be justified by the fact that Allah only apparently abandoned the Muslims so that they could return to the original power of Islam.

Thus, an independent anthropology does not exist in Islam for well-known reasons, because man is not an autonomous being there whose cognitive and practical competences could be described, so there is no need to research his being, because it is fixed for all time as a supra-individual type. He is a being who is completely determined by the dogmatic value background of Islam as a religion, social order and politics and cannot show his own face to God and his own abilities because they have also been given to him by God; he is only a tiny grain in the collective of believers.

In contrast to Christianity, which in the Middle Ages founded itself theologically and conceptually through the adoption of Platonism and then through the Enlightenment had to allow for historical-critical and hermeneutical-scientific Bible commentaries, Islam lacks such theologization and philosophical character because it did not make use of the ideas of the individual philosophers of the Golden Age. Because biblical hermeneutics assumes a hidden meaning of the text that is not identical with the traditional form of language, a distinction can be made between metaphysical beliefs and time-bound conditions of the origin of the text.

Islam forbids a contemporary interpretation of scripture, since it assumes an unchanging, eternally identical sense of the text. This is connected with the fact that, although Muhammad knows the basic features of Judaism and Christianity and 'processes' them and other contemporary currents in the Koran, the fiction of a text not only inspired by God but also formulated by God can be represented. Consequently, the Koran (with the exception of the Golden Age) has remained free of philosophical and theological speculation. It is written popularly in the sense that every Muslim can understand this text even without interposed 'professional hermeneutics', because it may only be understood literally.

Therefore, his position on the "last things" such as soul, resurrection, paradise, last day and judgment, hell, predestination cannot be described with philosophically theory-heavy terms.[21] This becomes especially clear with the concept of resurrection.

The life principle of man is his soul. This is given to him by God and can be compared with the conception of a psychic vitalism. It has a share in the physical properties, thus possesses e.g. a space. It lives on at the death of a human being without him, so to speak as a "sleeping potency". At the end of the times it unites again with its body. With the death of a human being his life cycle closes; with his resurrection he is a new creation of God, which gains a radically new existence in the hereafter. This hereafter is the paradise, an ideal

---

[21] The following remarks are based on Khoury, A. T., Hagemann, L., Heine, P.: *Islam-Lexikon,* Freiburg 1991.

garden, in which everything, what he needs, grows to the human being without own efforts. The paradise narratives of the Koran are similar to our fairy-tale descriptions of a land of milk and honey.

The projection character of this idea of the hereafter becomes clear when one compares the hard life of the desert dwellers with the pleasant one of the oasis dwellers. It, the unrelenting and barren nature appears as a cultivated place in the sense of a garden, where nature, tamed and peaceful without much effort, produces the whole abundance of crops in abundance. In it, beauty reigns instead of untamed force of nature: streams irrigate the land, ripe fruits lure the blessed, wine sparkles in beautifully shaped goblets, virgins and boys as servants gladden the heart of the Muslim who used to walk piously on earth, conversations among friends in casual company provide spiritual exchange. However, it is clearly noticeable that the feminine does not find its own form of expression in paradise at the beginning. The woman is a servant and an ever-ready sexual object. (It is difficult for me to understand that many Islamic women living in the West, after their demise in paradise basically entrusted with the same tasks as they had to perform on earth, react with demonstrative religiosity to their 'heavenly' disadvantage. Horovitz (1975) qualifies, however, because in later suras Muhammad also grants wives an independent residence permit in paradise:

> Gradually, the colors began to fade somewhat, and the youthful comrades of heavenly delights receded into the background. With the entry of the spouses and children into paradise, the traces of former unboundedness fade away, although the sensual pleasures remain, jewelry and precious garments, delicious fruits and fragrant wine (73).

But to what extent Islam itself has practically comprehended the transformation of the concept of paradise in the sense of spiritualization is unknown to me. Islamism demands only a literal acceptance.

There are no limits to the imagination to imagine the horror of hell as a contrast to the eternal joys in a paradisiacal garden. But the believed idea of hell as a place of eternal human torment is certainly a main motive for keeping the commandments, so that with the principle of "carrot and stick" the believers are rationally and realistically left only with practicing Islam. "Every Muslim will one day be freed from the torments of hell" (364), even if he has transgressed grievously against God, while the unbelievers must 'burn' eternally in hell.

Between resurrection and eternal bliss stands Judgment Day, when an account is to be given before the Last Judgment. For everyone there is a book in which life is balanced, whereby the good deeds are set off against the evil ones. For this purpose, a "heavenly scale" (423) makes it clear which way the decision leans. The "bodily souls" now set out on the "road to hell" (424). They step onto a bridge "thinner than a hair, sharper than a sword" (424), while hell opens up beneath them. The bad fall from the bridge directly into the mouth of hell, while the good can save themselves by jumping to the saving shore, paradise. The definition of guilt remains problematic here, because its attribution is also due to Allah, who is the Lord of heaven and earth, so that it would be in his power to prevent guilt. The relationship between predestination and determinism and freedom on the other hand is varied by the Koran in many versions, but not resolved. Here, too, this question is to remain open.

What concept of truth underlies the Qur'an? We will only briefly hear the coherence and correspondence models on this question. **Coherence** is understood to mean that the "truth of a statement exists in its compatibility with other statements in a systematic context" (Schnädelbach 2002, 180). Already the emergence of the Koran through explosive prophetic illuminations of Muhammad point to a not always coherent text, which is supported by the often contradictory textual contents, which is why the statements of the Koran are best received through repeated reading, which in my view leads to "Zwiedenken" (Orwell), the thinking of the simultaneity of mutually exclusive statements or ambivalence. In this way, its incoherencies, which can often be observed, are to be overplayed and all statements are to assume the same truth value, so that, from the point of view of the whole, a system results which, with great benevolence, embeds the individual verses and suras in a higher context.

The correspondence **model** is most appropriate to the Qur'an, which starts from the *adaequatio rei et intellectus*, the correspondence of consciousness and object, or the linguistically determined over agreement of sentence and thing as fact. Schnädelbach (2002) criticizes this definition because it requires agreement between two different spheres of being, between the mental or semantic and the extra-subjective reality and objectivity, and no one can say how this is possible. This "metatheoretical agreement" dominates the Koran's conception of truth as the metaphysical agreement of God's word with the world.

Values, knowledge and word form a unity there. What God wants, his metaphysical will laid down in the Koran, corresponds exactly to the reality of the world, because he himself created it from nothing. God's word as potency fits exactly to the reality created by it. One can call the truth concept of Islam, concerning the Koran, as already said an illocutionary act, i.e., with the formulation as a speech act a speech action is connected at the same time, so that between text and action developing from it a close connection exists. So similarly, the word of God in the Koran means at the same time its direct transformation and realization into an act of creation. "The Creator of the heavens and the earths! When He decides a thing, He only speaks to it, 'Be!' and it is" (2:118). Thus, there is strict isomerism or congruence between word and deed. This establishes the absolute truth claim, which cannot be shaken at this level. One can call this conception of truth "absolute realism," the seamless transposition of God's word in the Koran into reality, to which the intellectual abilities of man must conform.

Man occupies a mediating position between nature and God in that God has granted him an "official power" (Djassemi 2002, 22) vis-à-vis nature that allows him to enjoy the fruits of nature. However, this "feudal relationship" also implies subjection, submission to God's will. This **"contract of submission"** (26) is at the same time a model for the practical power structures in Islam, because it also applies to the "shadows of Allah" (Tibi), the caliphs, so that slavish obedience is also shown to the authorities. It is, so to speak, the social consequence of the Islamic way of life.

It follows from this that also for the individual, because "ultimately God makes history" (26), there is also no evolution and no individual human development, not the maturing, individualizing, moralizing, self-shaping, outgrowing. Man is the sum of his good and bad deeds. But this theological anthropology, which is entirely occupied by Islam, is supposed to apply universally to the (weak) human being, a claim that can release an unforeseeable potential for conflict with the naturalistic-cultural anthropology of the human being as a cultural subject. Both anthropologies can be summarized in the image **"anvil or hammer"**.

A cultural anthropological phenomenon still needs to be addressed. As can be easily proven, in the Koran men are placed one rank higher than women. This has major social implications, because Islamic society has historically formed a male society, a patriarchy, for this reason, so that women have disappeared more and more from public perception by means of some obscure masking commandments, ostensibly to protect them from eager (Muslim) male gaze. What kind of man's world is this, in which the essence of women must be hidden behind some flowing garments? It thus presents itself with a deplorable indictment of sexual unrestraint.

Among such Muslim families who have recently immigrated to Germany, but not only among them, but also among many in the third generation, the authoritarian behavior of the fathers toward the mothers and daughters is copied by the male youths as macho behavior and therefore the rights of women are trampled underfoot. This divides our society into an authoritarian and a democratic one, which are like fire and water to each other. Since the state authorities also reckon with self-determined people, contrary to their name, German institutions are openly mocked by many Muslim youths.

3. From Islam to Islamism

Already the religious Islam contains principles which promote an ideologization, so it is claimed here. We had already pointed out the mutual legitimization of a perfect God by a perfectly teleological creation. As a unity of political form of organization and religious practice, the task of Islam - its spiritual effect will not be presented here - is to legitimize the respective form of rule as being in accordance with Allah's will, because the rulers are seen as the "shadows of Allah" (Tibi). Since Muhammad, religious and political life have formed a unity.

Religion is responsible for the theological safeguarding of secular structures of rule. Today, it can be identified as the pool of an inexhaustible supply of arguments for the legitimization of dominant Islamic forms of government. The principle of "Islam" is about to assume global domination as the only legitimate form of rule morally justified by God. The implicit universalism of Islam is preparing to shape the world according to its specifications through the ideologically deficient explication of its value system. It, it is argued here, already contains many ideologically vulnerable structures that favor its actualization into political designs of Islamism.

3.1 The Beginning of Both Religions (Christianity & Islam)

Indeed, every beginning also has precauses, nevertheless, one can say, with such a one forces of a new-formed strong causality appear which are more effective than the sum of the partial causes absorbed in it. The formula *principiis obsta* "Resist the beginnings"![22], expresses something similar, because in the phase of reorientation the chance of an influence is big. It is the case here that not one cause splits itself into many partial causes and weakens with

---

[22] In *1984* (Orwell 1978), the problem of the beginning of a totalitarian ideology literarily synthesized from communism and Nazism is addressed. During a bombing raid, the Wilson family comes into contact with a down-and-out representative of the bourgeoisie who still remembers the transformation of "English socialism" into "Engsoz", the dictatorship of "Big Brother". He gives vent to his heart in alcohol:
"We shouldn't have trusted them. Didn't I always say that, Mom? That's what you get for trusting them. I always said it. We shouldn't have trusted those ragamuffins" (33).

it, but many partial causes bundle themselves in a main cause with big thrust, the Islam, a monotheistic religion, which unites Christianity and Judaism in that it lets both merge in the Islam, so that from the many polytheistic Arab local religions with just as many different forms of rule of Mohammed a prophet rule with supra-regional goals becomes.

Together with the belief that Islam sees itself as a natural religion, because it traces itself back to Adam, the main goal is already visible at the beginning, the universality of the claim to validity and rule. However, because Abraham is named as the first important prophet, God's revelation begins with him, which, however, is falsified by Jews and Christians until Mohammed, as the last prophet of Allah, can proclaim the true doctrine for all time. We must take the time of Muhammad's work as the main date of the beginning of Islam, because only through it can the before and after of the history of Islam be determined. Once this initial potency is awakened and triggers further movements, its own development can hardly be stopped. The religio-political dynamic of Islam is thus already contained in its conception as the only true and world-spanning natural religion. Thus, the religious essence of the Koran in the sense of **ideology(-) is** already ready to be realized when suitably 'ignited'. Therefore, it is claimed that already in Muhammad's time the change of Islam towards a global Islamism and imperialism has already begun, so that it can be described cognitively. The intention here is to influence and defuse it from knowledge of this development. If, in our recent history, racism had been examined and criticized more critically in terms of ideology earlier, when there was still time, there might not have been Hitler's fascism.

What do the two founders of religion, Jesus and Mohammed, leave behind? Jesus is the great loser who ended ignominiously on the cross because he pretended to be the son of God. His promise to lead humanity to eternal life in an afterlife is made *absurd* by his death on the cross. He has no political ambitions such as the establishment of a secular state of God ("My kingdom is not of this world"). He leaves behind a frightened congregation of followers, disciples and apostles, and it takes a very long time for these early congregations to be able to communicate a doctrine of salvation through texts that are considered authoritative.[23] In 391 A.D., after the edict of tolerance of the Roman Emperor Constantine of 313 A.D., Christianity becomes the state religion,

---

[23] A canonization of the biblical texts of the New Testament reaches its conclusion around 200 AD; the Gospels were written between 70 and 100 AD (see Helferich 2001, 70-75).

now contending with secular powers, especially the papacy and the emperors, for supremacy in the Holy Roman Empire. An unspeakable entanglement of state power and fundamentalist religion begins, which is only partially unraveled by Luther. Anyone who takes Christianity seriously must orient himself and his life to the concepts of "original sin," "love of neighbor," "forgiveness and pardon," "redemption," "faith," "hell," "Last Judgment," "resurrection from the dead and eternal life," "sacrificial death," to name most of them. The *imitatio Dei*, to shape one's life as a follower of Christ if possible, gives Christianity a humanistic ethos, because even opponents of Christianity cannot fail to acknowledge the exemplary morality of Jesus the man. This is connected with an elevation of the intrinsic value of man as "*Deus secundus*," namely to be endowed with a similar creative power as God, which is to be exercised responsibly. However, the many references to the OT also ensure a potential militancy of Christianity due to the claimed monopoly of truth, so that in the Middle Ages all other religious confessions are brutally suppressed.

Muhammad begins proclaiming his divine inspirations in 613 A.D.; however, few are persuaded, even members from his own tribe of *Kuraishites,* because the prophet attacks their gods and social order, so he must flee. This flight (*hejira*) leads him to Medina, where he is welcomed as a mediator of many disputes between the tribes. His recipe for success is the renunciation of the tribal principle and the introduction of a general religious socialization, the *umma*. Muhammad is thus the founder of religion and the promulgator of a new idea of the state, which are inextricably linked. This state idea is further ontologized by establishing God as the sole but invisible ruler over the *umma*, the community. This addresses the problem center of Islam, the inseparability of religion and politics, i.e., its implicit **ideology(-)**.

In Medina, Muhammad's idea of a divine state, of which he is the executor, gains contours by subjugating the surrounding territories. In order to weaken the Meccans who had forced him to perform the *Hajj,* he resorts to the "use of raiding at that time" (Barth 2003, 23). Even in *Ramadan,* he raids a Meccan caravan. The Jews of Medina, because they are said to be in secret communication with the enemy, are besieged in Medina in the deepest peace, and many of them are killed. This also changes the relationship with the book religions. Sura (5:52) reads:

> You believers! Do not take the Jews and the Christians as your friends! They are friends with each other, but not with you. If one of you joins them, he belongs to them

and no longer to the community of believers. God does not guide the people of the wicked rightly."

He intensifies the fight against renegades (apostates) and has them killed in secret operations.[24] Many moral commandments originate from this 'founding era'.

On the ladder of truth, Muhammad's sayings (hadiths), collected in the Sunnah, are second highest. Since the prophet is believed to teach and act on God's instructions, the Sunna is also binding for Muslims. As a blessed person of God, he is mentioned in the creed, so in terms of his conduct of life, he is a model to aspire to. If one reinterprets all contemporary influences with the potential for violence to which Muhammad is exposed in his cultural sphere as 'extenuating circumstances,' a progressive religious foundation can be read out of this.

But Muhammad's role model function by today's Islamism is not so much focused on his role as prophet, messenger of God, role model for the faithful, chosen one of God (Khoury 1990), but the sector "violence in state-political and religious terms during the 'founding era' " is hugely over interpreted and

---

[24] Both in the book by Khoury *Who was Muhammad?* (Freiburg 1990) as well as in that of Serauky *Geschichte des Islam.* (Berlin 1991), the opinion is expressed that Muhammad, as far as the use of violence is concerned, did not go beyond the measure of his time. Serauky embeds this in the context of religiosity, politics and violence of the time and shows the dialogical relationship between the world and the founder of the religion. Primacy is given to the proclamation of the new faith, which meets with great rejection until a new inspiration shows a way out of the crisis. Violence to enforce political and religious goals serves only as an extreme means. The Qur'an can therefore be seen as a handbook of political maxims and religious convictions, resulting in a mix of the two that inextricably links time-bound historicity and supra-temporal faith.
The *Islam lexikon* (Freiburg 1996, 547) summarizes:
"He could not content himself with preaching a doctrine inspired by asceticism and directed toward the hereafter; he had to concern himself with the everyday life of Muslims, to set up a social order, to lay the foundations of the solidary Islamic community, whose solidarity was no longer based on blood relationship but on common faith. Finally, Muhammad had to lead the political struggle against the enemies of Islam externally and within the community."

transferred to the present time. It determines "the collective and individual consciousness of Muslims whenever "major political, social and religious crises" (Barth 2003, 26) occur. Especially today's Islamism in its terrorist variety invokes the 'true' Islam under Muhammad. Islamists are those "who orient themselves to its roots or foundations" (25). Thus, as under Mohammed, an irregular war against the infidels is to be repeated, of course with more effective modern weapons. Thus, Islamism is to blame for Muhammad's negative image in the Western world, which also sees him as a terrorist because Islamists focus Muhammad's actions on this relatively marginal fact.

Here religion is degraded to the advocate of terrorism. The rigor of Muhammad's implementation of Islam, which is to be explained, is being revived today - reinforced by modern means of destruction - as the justification for a terrorism that despises humanity. The absolute truth claim, which Mohammed represents for his new religion, justifies today the liquidation of political and religious dissenters, as far as they do not voluntarily bow to his dictate. I would like to push the cynicism even further, in that through the political and religious murders, the murdered have been deterred from insubordination to Allah, so that they might still win paradise, which might otherwise have been lost to them.

The hypothesis that Islam, because of its indistinguishability between religion and political calculation, is already particularly susceptible to ideology from its very conception can already be considered proven here, especially for its beginning. If one follows the maxims of both religions, "*imitatio Dei,*" *following* Christ, and "living a life pleasing to God like the Prophet Mohammed," then the grave consequences become clear. Even if the Christian ethic, which was exemplified by Jesus, has often, very often, been broken by servitude for political and personal calculations, this break has also been perceived, branded as a sin against God and remedied by reforms.

The striving for a 'godly' life in the sense of Muhammad especially today by the Islamists, who believe to find themselves in a similarly distressed situation as their prophet at that time, leads to the militant basic attitude known and lamented on all sides. And this only by cultivating a misunderstanding in that Muhammad's deeds must not be seen in the historical context that could justify then what cannot be justified today. Insofar as all Koranic claims, even those that must be understood as reactions to daily events, are indiscriminately accorded the status of eternally valid truth, the Koran opens the door to Islamism's manipulative interpretation. This is where the term **ideology(-) comes in**, whose most important criterion is the claim to be in possession of absolute truth, but which cannot be redeemed. The way out of this, to find a "second message" in the Koran that can claim a second supra-temporal truth status in comparison to the first historical one, earns the scholar Taha the death penalty.

But there is another argument that has determined the history of this political religion since the founding of Islam. As a prophet, Muhammad proclaimed God's word. At the same time, however, this makes him the political leader of the converts by making him the representative of a state religion. He is thus subject to two genuinely different claims, that of the religion "Islam" and that of the political leadership of a community that is surrounded by enemies. Consequently, religious and political premises become confused, in that punitive expeditions are justified religiously or religious premises imply political actions. This "mutual legitimization" (Kalikov 1984) continues to this day.

The "cartoon controversy"[25] is an example of the political instrumentalization of Islam. It is also undeniable that already at the beginning of Islam there are "fire and sword" to go to war for Allah, which often enough in history have served as instruments of armed jihad, but mostly in a conventional but not in a totalitarian sense.

The chief ideologue of Islamic fundamentalism, Qutb, recognizes four stages of jihad inherent in Islam, which merge into one another and extend to the present:

---

[25] The antipathies of the Muslim world toward the West were focused in this "insult to the religious feelings of all Muslims. Now a reason had been found to stage 'popular anger'. Incited by mullahs and coordinated by networking and clandestine support of many governments, such emotionalization was brought about that Western embassies were vandalized in 'retaliation'. This 'righteous' popular anger curiously never discharges when hostages are taken by Islamists to extort ransom or enforce political demands with their threatened killing. 'Destroy my sanctuary, and I will destroy your sanctuary' is common everyday practice in the civil war between Shiites and Sunnis in Iraq - or so we see almost daily on television. Such 'desecrations' are strangely only marginally noticed by world Islam. If the West, in its function as a 'red rag', believes that it must react to such repressions by restricting the freedom of the press in order to signal good behavior, we will be amazed at all the things that Western culture is capable of insulting the religious feelings of Muslims and that are withdrawn from any criticism with the "desecration argument" as sacrosanct.

1. Stage: Restraint in battle, establishment of the religious foundation of Islam by Muhammad, i.e., self-discovery, Meccan period.
2. Stage: Hejira, permission to fight the Meccans, Medinan period.
3. Stage: Activation of the fight against aggressors, 2nd Meccan period.
4. Stage: Fight against all polytheists, whereby this term is interpreted very generously, a period that is still ongoing now (after Prenner 2005, 138).[26]

It is easy to see that the jihad after Qutb is becoming more and more universalized in concentric circles. Today's 4th stage means quasi the permanent historically necessary fight against all non-Islamic world views. Only the intellectually 'blind' can continue to assume that Islam is oh so tolerant. Parallels can be drawn with Hitler's *"Mein Kampf,"* where a great many intellectuals dismissed this work as the product of a political crackpot. Thus, Islamism from Qutb's pen wants to realize a totalitarian rule of God on earth; and anyone who becomes a fighter for God is acting on his holy behalf. In this context, it should not be forgotten that Bin Laden was a zealous disciple of Qutb.[27] Thus, the Koran provides good reasons for Islamism today.

3.2 Islam's Threefold Claim to Universality

---

[26] Missionary Islamism, politically supported in Europe by Turkey, is proceeding according to this pattern today. While until now the Swedish Muslims led an inconspicuous existence, phases 3 and 4 are now beginning, the forcible introduction of Islam, because a Muslim should only live in a Muslim state. The bloodless struggle of the "march through the legal institutions" is suitable for this. Under the heading "Sweden: Islam-State within the State?" the RP of 18.05.2006, A5, describes the following list of demands:
Exemption from work for Friday prayers and for important Islamic holidays, instruction of Muslim children by imams in religion and in the local language, no swimming lessons for girls and boys together, introduction of special women's days in swimming pools, granting of interest-free loans for the construction of mosques.
Muslim immigrants are welcomed with a brochure praising male patriarchy and female inferiority and denouncing immorality through sex education. The special Islamic laws are supposed to correspond to those of a minority worthy of protection (such as the Danes in northern Germany).
[27] See: "The 911 Commission Report," page 68, Chair: Thomas H. Kean, 2004. https://avalon.law.yale.edu/sept11/911Report.pdf

From its internal religious self-image, Islam demands a threefold universalization, a claim to absoluteness, a claim to totality and a claim to globalization, and this already with its foundation; it is thus wide open to an explicit ideologization.

3.2.1 Absolute claim

This is based on a thought model of the more and more condensing truth. From the bottom to the top, the following stages result as a reminder:

The *fatwa*: It is a religious legal opinion that is obtained in response to inquiries about disputed matters of faith and is written by *muftis*, highly respected Islamic scholars. It provides certainty of faith, but not of law, because it has only the status of a recommendation. However, the case of "Rushdi" shows what such 'expert opinions' can be used for.[28] (Does God really promise paradise to such murderers?).

The others, the analogy, the consensus, the *Sunnah* with its *hadiths,* and the Quran have already been presented.

In the colloquial language two truth terms are predominantly in use: absolute and relative truth. Here, too, working with the pair of opposites "absolute/relative" is of some advantage. "Absoluteness" means detachment from all determining conditions, object in itself, subject only to its own laws, argumentatively unassailable, true and objective. "Relativity" means dependence on other objects, object for other objects, subjected to foreign laws, argumentatively provisional, true and objective only insofar as there is a participation in

---

[28] The High Islamic *Imam* and *Ayatollah Khomeini* [It is important to know here that an Imam is a "divinely inspired leader" similar to Mohammed. See Koran introduction by Schwer, T., (ed.): *Der Koran.* Munich 2003, 11] disseminated the fatwa on February 14, 1989:
"That the blood of the author of this book [...], which was written, printed and published in contradiction to Islam, the Prophet and the Qur'an, and of all those who participated in the publication of the book and knew its contents, is hereby declared forfeited. I call upon all proud Muslims to quickly send them to the hereafter, wherever they may be, so that no one may ever dare to insult Islamic shrines again. Those who lose their own lives in this endeavor will be considered martyrs" (after Barth 2003, 69). With this, the head of the Iranian Shiites justifies political murder, and lets the murderers, if they are killed in the process, enter paradise. The West should not forget that its value system is turned upside down by this fatwa. And such a 'light figure', buried in a pompous mausoleum, demands public veneration where we speak of incitement to murder.

the absolute. Relative therefore means shortened: second-hand truth, which always remains directly related to the absolute truth.

Now Islam claims to be "the ultimate figure of religion" (Khoury 2001, 112). The relevant sources are found in (3:68-69), (33:41), (33:19-20). Abraham as a "gentile", posthumously deprived of his tribal affiliation by Mohammed for ideological reasons, so the Koran knows to report, was actually the great prophet of Allah; but the Jews had falsified this pure doctrine through their many prophets; but even Christ as the messenger of Allah had stained the pure doctrine with false teachings, so that only through Mohammed the true doctrine had returned to its roots and had been finally pronounced and also sealed.

Basically, then, it is God's message that has been distorted by the Jews and Christians, so that it is a good work to free them from their errors, even if by force. Basically, then, revealed Islam begins with Abraham; and since Judaism must not be at the beginning of theological Islam, Judaism is denied *post mortem to the* progenitor of Israel. Thus, first the Jews, but then also the Christians can be criminalized as falsifiers of Islam. Consequently, Islam elevates itself to the only true and natural religion, because all others represent religious aberrations, so that Christianity and Judaism form only a mutilated form of Islam. These two exist only in relation to Islam, do not possess truth on their own, but only relative truth in relation to the absoluteness of Islam, indeed, they can be seen negatively as different versions of apostasy from God.

It is precisely this claim to absoluteness, combined with the relativization of the claims of other religions and the annulment of the truth claims of non-religious or animistic worldviews that has had a twofold effect in history. In the Islamic Middle Ages, Islam's view of the two book religions was positive because its many similarities with the other two religions promoted active tolerance; in the present time, Islam's view is more focused on the antagonism and believed inferiority of the other two book religions, so that wherever it forms the majority, it systematically suppresses religious minorities[29] , while

---

[29] In the RP of 10.07.2006, the creeping 'religious cleansing' by the Islam is proven by figures. Within 30 years the number of Christians in Syria decreased from 2.8 to 1.9%, in Iraq from 2.6 to 1%, in Israel and Palestine from 1.9 to 1%, in Iran from 0.1 to 0.01%. Christians have emigrated there because they no longer saw any possibility of living in an intolerant Islam. Conversely, the number of Muslims in Western Europe is growing. Why is that?

A revealing historical experiment is taking place here. Wherever Muslims form the majority, a **"silent expulsion"** of Christians is taking place. Why do the gullible think, Europe is so

in Europe, which it scolds, it is steadily increasing. Here, too, we can observe the phenomenon of ambivalence to enter by any means the 'realm of evil' that is so bitterly fought against. This ambivalence is one reason why Muslims generally find it difficult to integrate into a Western society. As long as Islam regards itself as the natural and absolute religion of all people and disqualifies other religions as aberrations from the true faith, dialogue is impossible. Here, too, the image of ever-expanding concentric circles applies.

The concept of the "sacred," which originates in the realm of myth, is a great help in absolutizing a claim to truth. Overall, a strengthening of symbolic messages can be observed for Islam, an "upsurge in the significance of external signs and symbols" (Galter 2005, 171). Special clothing, a beard, martial presentation of the Kalashnikov as a display of masculinity, kneeling hostages, coffins with green pall, open Koran, flags, and chanting of anti-Western slogans are supposed to symbolize the Muslims' new awareness of power.

For rationalists the "sacred" is only an irrational or metaphysical concept, for the religious and mythical man it is an extremely significant concept.[30] But even for a rationalist the "sacred" should not be a pitiable regressive concept, but he should meet it not with veneration, but with respect. Yet the "sacred" must remain open to taboo questioning, so that it can be rationally conceived as a metaphysical entity or as a projection of value.

With the words "holy scripture", "holy book" not so much a literary text is meant, but a presence of God in the scripture, removed from the profane. So whoever disregards the Koran blasphemes God. The Quran is a sacred text, and sacred texts are of a different quality than profane ones, so they must not be treated as such. It has a high ritual significance, is therefore kept in a special

---

attractive to Muslims and what will happen if, as projections suggest, they form the majority of the population by the end of 2100?

[30] The sacred has its origin in mythical thinking. This is concentrated in the conception of the numinous, a being that is neither a pure object of nature nor a disembodied phantom. Spirit or matter, inside or outside is omnipresent in the sacred time; it is simultaneously present in many places, which thereby gain the status of a sanctuary. Man encounters this numinous, which is also worshipped as a deity, with fear, awe and respect, but also with a shudder, because he feels both attracted and repelled by this being. But what appears in the myth as a being that has always been, is in reality a human projection of something significant for life into the rapt dimension of what is now absolutely to be followed; it acquires an eternity value and is thus withdrawn from any everydayness.

place and has a mythical aura in the sense of being close to God. With its veneration, God and Islam are venerated; with its desecration, God and Islam are directly desecrated. "If a copy can no longer be used due to age, it must not be burned under any circumstances. The unusable texts are usually kept in mosques. Any form of disrespect for the Koran is at the same time passed off as an insult to God, Islam and Muslims." (Heine 2003, 61 f.).

The reason for this high regard for sacred writings may be the belief that they contain a transcendent textual meaning that transcends human comprehension and can be deciphered only by chosen people, but this is not the case with the Koran. The sacred is simply God's word. The concept of the sacred, because it embodies the highest but transcendent value of a religion or state, lends itself like no other to the hypostasis of many profane abstracts such as people, absolute truth of God, fatherland, party, state borders, persons, which means their rapture into a sphere of uncritical veneration. Now they are unassailable presence of the sacred, which can only be 'desecrated' by rational argumentation. Islam and Islamism, by expanding the concept of the sacred, very effectively suppress any form of criticism.

Although Muhammad may not be revered as holy like God and his scripture, the Koran, "sacred feelings of Muslims" are hurt by caricatures of the prophet, as the recent case in the cartoon controversy makes clear. Even living Islamic dignitaries are sacred, as Rudi Carrell's bra affair teaches us. Thus, if this is accepted by the West, what the Enlightenment interprets as superstition, what mythology interprets as projection, must be returned to its mythical function, which may then be found in our constitution as incompatible with the Basic Law and human rights. If what a religious community regards as a sacred incomprehensible is addressed with due tact and not in the sense of vilification and denigration, it has to accept that. We let Islamism, through the inflationary use of the term 'holy'; bargain away the enlightenment against the myth of the holy as if in a bazaar. Just politically 'canonizations' have a significant function, as we recognize by the refusal of the Prime Minister Erdogan to the EU to delete the article for the "insult of Turkishness" from the penal code (RP of 31.10.2006, A5). Thus the 'holy' Turkish state can criminalize all critical questions to it, which has also effects on our domestic policy. Even worse is the mental terror that is exercised with such a law; because if the citizen is deliberately restricted in his freedom of opinion by such a 'rubber paragraph', so that he no longer knows what is allowed, he soon says nothing. One can only strongly disapprove of the legalization of opinion terror. In any case, we can see that Islam and especially nationalist Turkey is very often 'offended' at Western measures.

Religious texts prejudge an absolute claim to truth, which is transfigured as holy, thus made resistant to criticism and essentialized as absolutely valid, an ideologically-metaphysically constructed premise, with which an absolutely set truth approach authenticates itself. From this an argumentatively useless, but practically very effective illusory syllogism can be gained[31] . Such a one works, since it formally satisfies the logic, plausibly and does not permit any contradiction, so that such ones are very popular in world-descriptive arguments.

Philosophically, they are analytical judgments masquerading as synthetic ones, tautologies, trivialities. Doubts and criticism of the contents of religious dogmas must not be indexed and stifled as blasphemy, as is unfortunately the case in many Muslim countries dominated by Islamist thought, so that intellectual dialogue becomes impossible. According to the Koran, we are once "*Djimmi*", protectors, immature beings who can only find their true salvation in Islam or infidels to be eradicated.

The Koran itself supports its claim to absolute truth by proclaiming itself to be in possession of absolute truth and indexing any criticism with severe sanctions. Thus, critical questions can be rejected and questioning can be punished as profanation, as blasphemy, so that it immunizes itself with an almost unbreakable ideological wall. So the member of such a coherent ontology has no reason at all to engage in a dialog. He has internalized the "form of thinking fundamentalism" (Tepe 2000, Internet), which from now on prescribes to him what has to be thought how and what alone is forbidden to think.

There is another, politically very virulent instance of truth in Shiite Islam, "the special caliphate of the imams" (Djassemi 2002, 44). This means that an intermediate authority has been established between human official power and the absolute power of God, the "imamate" (45). This imamate applies to specially chosen Muslims, called the "special caliphate" (44). An imam has a relationship with Allah similar to that of Muhammad with God, thus realizing

---

[31] Top sentence: The Qur'an as a holy text is true.
Sub-sentence: In sura x, y is asserted.
Conclusion: What is asserted for y is true.

God's counsels on earth in the exercise of spatial, temporal and salvific power, i.e., an imam can interfere in all matters of state and religion and proclaim this interference as God's will. Imams are not subject to any controlling authority, but for their part they have an absolute monopoly of control over state and religion. The example of the Iranian Ayatollahs makes it clear that this "dictatorship of the background" favors an extremely dangerous political model of a state of God. The thesis, often proclaimed by spokesmen for Islam, that the terrorists are criminals indexed by Islam is often only lip service; for those behind the scenes, who promise heaven for carrying out murder (Khomeini), enjoy high veneration.

Islam in the form of Shiism divides the faithful into two groups, "spiritually immature" (57) and "chosen saints" (57). The religiously basically immature mass of believers is crying out, so to speak, for an elite to lead them[32] , which claims to be divinely inspired. This claim to leadership is justified[33] with the sura (4:59):

> You believers! Obey God and the Messenger and those among you who have to command [...].

After all, it directly invites the imams, who are, after all, the best experts on the Koran, to place themselves in the succession of God and Mohammed, so that they, like the latter, are "unsinable" (58), which, fortunately, is rejected by other Muslim faiths. But the Shiites continue to insist on the monopoly of truth held by the elite Ayatollahs and Imams, so that, according to Goldziher (1963), Shiism still has a sixth pillar of faith: "the divine authority of the Imams" (61). This variant of Islam is particularly rich in ideology.

Sometimes the claim to absoluteness produces strange blossoms. The fundamentalist Al-Gundi claims (after Tibi 1991 228 ff.) that because the Koran is the all-encompassing source also of the sciences, that Bacon, who is regarded as the father of the natural sciences, in reality says in the *Novum Organum* "nothing new" (quoted after Tibi 1991, 238), because "the Arab-Islamic scientists, however, had long since practiced this [empirical - the author] method in all fields" (238). This means that Islam would have possessed the

---

[32] This form of religious official and functionary type resembles that of Catholicism.

[33] In order to justify the elitist exceptional position of the imams in Shiism, a sentence of Imam Baqir was used: "Faith means: to love us, unbelief means: to hate us" (after Djassemi 2002, 60).

key to the sciences with its Koran, which it would have sent to the West after the Golden Age, which thereupon would have developed them further. Now Islam could take back by "re-appropriation" (230) what had actually always belonged to it. Al-Gundi has remained completely hidden that these mathematical-scientific sciences are quite predominantly based on positivistic positions, which represent everything else than divine points of view. We always encounter such appropriative errors with built-in self-contradiction where the Koran and science are to be brought to a common denominator in the sense of Islam and Islamism.

The all-encompassing divinity of the Koran with its absolute supra-temporal claim to truth and its knowledge of salvation, which is represented in all seriousness by Islam, prevents any substantial dialogue with this religion, because the other dialogue partner is downgraded from the same rank to the level of a supplicant or "protector", *Djimmi. It is* a scandal of Islam that, with its absolute concept of truth, it divides people a priori by nature into the good (Muslims) and the bad (non-Muslims) and predicts eternal torments of hell for the latter after death. The representatives of the book religions, Jews and Christians, should actually enjoy a high level of acceptance; however, under the rubric of "Western crusaders," they are demonized today as enemies.

Apostates, Muslims who convert to Christianity, fare even worse. They are not human beings but subhumans, whose killing in Islam goes unpunished, indeed is praised as an act pleasing to God, while conversion to Islam is celebrated as an event pleasing to God - a particularly perfidious kind of ambivalence. Hitler's genetic racism becomes Islam's similarly inhumane religious selectionism. Not only Islamism demands the killing of the apostate from Islam, but already Islam. It refuses to concede an unconditional value to man as such, independent of denominations: it measures the value of man a priori according to his religion.

51

In the sense of social science, "totality" is a descriptive term. According to Lieber, it is two-dimensional: on the one hand, as a system of meaning that overarches and supersedes the particularities in the state, which on the one hand vertically dominates all intellectual spheres, and on the other hand is to be seen horizontally as infecting all spheres of life with this system of meaning. "In this sense, then, the term totalitarian means both the exclusivity of the claim to rule and the unlimitedness of the sphere of rule" (1985, 108). The "exclusivity of the claim to rule," the vertically absolute claim to truth, has already been discussed under the concept of the absoluteness of its validity and its hierarchical structure. Both dimensions apply to profane as well as religious systems. However, insofar as a religion performs a state-bearing or state-forming justificatory and real function, what has been said above also applies to religions to a special degree. Here, "horizontal totality" means "enforcing God's law in all areas of life" (Khoury 2002, 112). Let us let Khoury continue:

> Thus, Islam knows no separation of religion and state, of faith community and political society. The Islamic community, as well as all communities living in the Islamic-governed state, are under God's law and must act according to its provisions. God's law serves as a guide for the government's political decisions, as a principle of state institutions, and as a measure of the state's authority [...] (112).

Insofar as Islam appears as a religion or an idea of the state, or both, in an unresolvable combination, its claim to rule is not only total, but totalitarian, at least as far as its relationship to non-Islamic groups is concerned. This is directed at all horizontal sectors of human life. Islam totally determines, i.e., without room for maneuver, the horizontal everyday life of the faithful, which is governed by the sharia or similar clerical orders in all areas of life.

Executive, legislative, judicial: they all follow God's law, if possible, in a holistic theocratic form of government. Religious crimes are state crimes and vice versa. Science, art, everyday life, clothing, food, religiosity, intimacy are subject to the control of religious officials in extreme cases[34] . Thus, according to sura (3:110), God's will is fulfilled that Islam would produce the best community among people. The horizontal appropriation of man in Islam, which

---

[34] There is even a religious police force in Saudi Arabia. So Orwell is not far away there either.

strives for totality and collectivization, finds its legitimation and limit in the Koran; but by means of a fatwa, a conclusion by analogy, etc., a further dissolution of boundaries is possible. What then still cannot be appropriated gets the stigma "un-Islamic" branded on it.

Islam's claim to totality, to determine the life of man in all areas of life from the 'cradle to the grave', may also be called a constant source of **ideology(-)**, especially when other groups are forced to subordinate to the Sharia. Who can be against such a perfect divine order on earth? [35]

3.2.3 Claim to globality

It can thus be seen that in Islam the structures are pre-formed which, in the Western sense, lead to a hypostasizing of religion; from Islam is derived a state of God which is binding on all and which can declare all other forms of rule to be inferior and therefore has a right to destroy them. Thus Islam implies a constant readiness to expand; for "Islam rules, it is not ruled." The consciousness of being on the right side of world history and the consciousness of being God's instrument form the legitimizing framework of a constant expansive readiness, at least where Islam comes into contact with Western views. The often quoted saying "Islam is a tolerant religion" is only valid if the other book religions submit to it. These brief remarks show that Islam has a large inventory of arguments ready to be called up for the ideological justification of universal rule.

How does Islam come to the imperialist claim to a world-dominating role in history? Abraham, the progenitor of Israel in our eyes, is claimed as the first monotheist by Mohammed for Islam as a prophet. "Abraham was neither a Jew nor a Christian; yet he was always inclined (to God) and obedient (to Him), and he was not the idolater of any" (3:68). However, the Jews would have perverted the pious traditions of the Torah (3:79): "And verily, among them is a portion who pervert with their tongues the Scripture (Torah), that ye may suppose it from the Scripture, whereas it is not from the Scripture." Be-

---

[35] This is meant ironically!

cause the 'true' revelation had been falsified by the "appropriating interpretation"[36] of the Jews, Yahweh had sent Jesus as a prophet to revise the errors of the Jewish "holy scriptures" that had been interpreted into it. But also Jesus' teachings, to whom only the role of a prophet of Allah is conceded, have opened themselves by 'appropriating projection' of the Christians to polytheistic influences (trinity doctrine) and have become a false doctrine, particularly since also still the God-likeness of the son of God is assumed. That is why Allah sent the Prophet Muhammad to mankind: as the final herald of God's will, not as an intermediary between God and man, and it says: "It is He who has sent His messenger with guidance and the true faith, that He may make it prevail over all (other) creeds, even though it may be repugnant to the idolaters" (9:33). The Quran thus advocates a permanent imperialism that is covered, even naturalized, by divine statute. [37]

---

[36] In *Myth & Literature* (Tepe 2001) this concept is specified. It states "that the meaning content of the art phenomenon is adapted to the interpreter's belief system in a projective-appropriative way" (125). This statement also applies to the case of a scientific theory or a hermeneutic interpretation of texts. Muhammad also accuses the Jews of a projective interpretation of the Abraham figure, because they had adapted his conception of God to theirs and thus falsified it.

[37] In the RP of 16.09.2006, the member of the Bundestag Griese expresses herself "that the very essence of Islam is peace-loving and humane" (A1). There were two eras where Islam was generally peaceful, the Golden Age of philosophy and the times of cooperative trade with other cultures. The latter, however, was just another form of jihad in the sense of spreading Islam. It has always maintained its expansive character because of its claim to the monopoly of truth.

Elkin Deligöz can sing a long song about the peacefulness of Muslims. She (MdB) had called on Muslim women in Germany to take off their headscarves. Both Turkish media, which disparaged her as "disgrace for the people" and "Nazi" (RP of 03.11.2006) and the Turkish federations in Germany, which disqualified her call as "nonsense" like also death threats of Islamists are a strong indication for the fact that Turkey wants to extend the influence on the freedom of opinion and the German politics altogether by means of the Islam ever more strongly. These reactions demonstrate the ambivalence of Turkish politics. While in Turkey, because it wants to be a laicist state, the headscarf is forbidden to be worn as a religious symbol in public buildings, those who express themselves critically about the wearing of this symbol in the West are vilified by it. Turkey arrogates to itself the right to take care of citizens of Turkish origin who are naturalized in Germany in a 'journalistic', i.e. propagandistic and political way.

Ideologies(-) have the tendency to projectively reshape the history that precedes them in such a way that the 'now' presents itself as a necessary consequence of its history, which can now be extended towards the future, so that one can feel oneself to be the trustee of a legal development towards the future. Such a legal hypothesis of progress acts as a historical amplifier on the motivation of its adherents, so that it is used by all major ideologies.

It should be recalled here that communism, developed as a social theory by Marx and Engels in a certain phase of world history, reinterpreted human history as a scientifically describable process of progress by means of the theories of historical and dialectical materialism. Beginning with the classless primitive society, various class societies alienating man would develop, dialectically replacing each other according to historical, scientific laws, until the alienation of man would be abolished in the classless society in communism. Much more forcibly the National Socialists adapted cultural phenomena to their ideology, so that Greeks, Romans, Teutons as well as poets like the Romantics, even Goethe and Schiller were interpreted as National Socialist precursors and a historical and genetic[38] continuity of the necessary development up to the National Socialist present could be constructed.

Mohammed also uses the artifice of projective historical interpretation by declaring Abraham to be the progenitor of the proclamation of the original religion Islam and the first monotheistic prophet, whose Judaism he apodictically denies. Thus he stands at the origin of Islam, which is falsified several times until Mohammed can proclaim its completion.

Thus, there are four phases of the one and only true religion: the original Muslim Abraham proclaims the pure faith in Allah; the Jews falsify his message; Jesus, as a Jew and prophet of Allah, is supposed to correct this falsification again, but falls prey to polytheistic influences; and finally, Mohammed appears as the last prophet of Allah to finally proclaim the true faith for all time.

---

[38] Hitler (1925) commented: "It is, moreover, the task of a folkish state to see to it that a world history is finally written in which the race question is elevated to the dominant position" (II, 60). Here, too, Islamism and National Socialism resemble each other. Earlier art eras (see the Buddha figures blown up by the Taliban in Afghanistan, and the destruction of 'pagan' testimonies planned by the Muslim Brothers in Egypt) correspond to the outlawing and destruction of "degenerate art" under National Socialism. It is about the utopia of genetic or religious purity of the beginning of one's own history.

Thus Islam is the origin and completion of all religions, "the most ingenious of all religious creations"[39]. Mohammed has anticipated here Hegel's dialectic of history. There is for the Muslim only one religion, which begins with the successor of Adam, with Abraham and will spread avalanche-like over the whole world.

The sequence of steps of a deficient historical utopia, namely idealized initial state (Abraham), fall into sin, (Jewish prophets and Jesus) and an ever continuing fulfillment of the promise of the initial state (Mohammed), which is still ongoing, makes that Islam can pass off its development as historically necessary by its ontology resting in itself. This 'fall from grace' (Jewish prophets and Jesus) is declared to be an 'accident', a historical aberration that delayed the expansion of Islam. The further history of Islam, then, consists in its linear continuous spread over the whole world, which is as certain as an acting law of nature. It claims to be the universal religion par excellence and to realize its message of salvation step by step in a teleological process in a world-spanning theocratic state in which only Allah's laws have unlimited validity.[40]

The proclamation of the 'true' history of salvation begins with Abraham, leads to Jesus and ends in the "Seal of the Prophet". This now final revelation of Allah in the Koran is historically continuously transferred into reality and historically continued by its representatives, the caliphs. Anticipating the literature review in the appendix, I would like to refer to Akbuluth (2002), for whom it is self-evident that Islam, on the basis of its mission in salvation history, has the right to work for 'justice' throughout the world, even by force of arms, because the Muslim is obliged to bring God's law to bear throughout the world. Here the door is opened to the arbitrariness of the interpretation of the Koran and the factual political reality with the word "justice".

The universal state of God is not a utopia that, in the sense of Kant's regulative ideas, prescribes a goal that can perhaps only be reached in paradise, but a development determined by God and history in the direction of earthly theocracy, or better: theodictatorship. This concretely understood utopianism

---

[39] In: Hurgronje (1923), quoted in Barth (2003, 20).
[40] To erase the memory of pre-Islamic advanced civilizations, the Taliban have blown up several larger-than-life Buddha figures carved in stone (a World Heritage Site); the Egyptian Muslim Brotherhood can only be prevented from destroying their Pharaonic advanced civilization under threat of brute force. This is to internalize a 'bombproof insight': Only Islam is the world culture that can redeem mankind, everything else is idolatry.

gives Islamism, which is fed by Islam, its sense of mission and justifies its obligatory missionary command, makes it, so to speak, the bailiff of a faster realization of its objectified program and therefore seduces it to a very limited perception of reality, through which politically irrational strategies out of the feeling of a deceptive security can prejudice devastating wrong decisions. Again, the principle of concentrically widening circles applies. In addition:

> Islam's claim to produce "the best community (...) among men" (3:111) and to establish God's state on earth has led to a model of life in which God's authority sanctions concrete institutions and concrete decisions and severely restricts the free initiative and creative freedom of human beings (Khoury 2002, 113 f.).

God's law breaks human law. The introduction of a separation of powers to prevent abuse of power would be an open declaration of mistrust in God. Is not the constant increase of the number of Muslims on our earth the best empirical proof for the reality of the presented historical utopia?

It is now less and less possible to dismiss the question, "*Is the being around whom this controversy revolves, for whose sake bloody wars are waged or great cultures have developed their self-awareness, God, a being present in reality who can vouch for an absolute claim to truth. Does God exist or does he not exist, or is the question undecidable?*"

This topic, which still moves philosophy today, will be discussed here only briefly[41] . According to Kant there are only three basic proofs of God: the ontological, the physico-theological (teleological) and the cosmological, which appear again and again in the history of philosophy.

1. The ontological proof of God, developed by Anselm of Canterbury (1033-1109), starts from the concept of God as *ens realissimum,* as a most real being, God. It is a concept of reason a priori. Since reason predetermines a transcendental concept of the most comprehensive being, all possible knowledge is already given in it, so that there is no object of possible experience that is not already determined as an object by it, because it contains fewer predicates compared to the concept of the most comprehensive being, i.e. it has fewer attributes. It is now the question whether this concept of reason, which is necessary for reason, of the allness of being, by which we have already anticipated and can locate every possible object of experience a priori, also exists in reality. Anselm is of this opinion because, since this concept contains by its scope also reality, this concept must also exist quasi from itself. Now there is the vulgar-empiristic objection that this thus empirically existing object must be able to be perceived, which is not the case, but is denied by mysticism.

For Kant, there is a sharp separation between the thought concept and its possible perception in reality. From a concept of the "unattainable perfection" (Kant IV, A 529)[42] , which is to be thought even if necessarily, the reality, which must be empirically given as datum, cannot be deduced synthetically. Thus, a concept cannot force its existence, which Islam vehemently denies. Between reality and linguistic conceptuality there is an ontological leap. To overcome this is, Christian or Islamic interpreted, just privilege of the divine creative power.

In the Qur'an, this argument has great probative force; for it says there:

---

[41] A detailed description and appreciation of philosophical attempts to prove God's existence as a real and effective fact deductively or inductively can be found in v. Kutschera, F.: *Vernunft und Glaube.* Berlin 1991.

[42] Kant is quoted according to Kant, I.: Werke in 12 Bänden. Ed.: Weischedel, W. Frankfurt am Main 1964, giving author, volume and page number.

Sura (2:255): Allah - there is no God but He, the Living, the Existent from Himself and the All-Sustaining. Slumber does not seize Him and sleep. His is what is in the heavens and what is on earth. Who is it that will intercede with him, except with his permission? He knows what is before them and what is behind them; and they comprehend nothing of His knowledge except what pleases Him. His knowledge encompasses the heavens and the earth; and their preservation does not weigh Him down; and He is the Exalted, the Great.

The power of the own being-forcing is called creationism, so that God brings forth Himself from Himself and from Himself also the world; because "it is He Who forms you in the womb as He wills" - Sura (3:6). The Koran rejects a flat empiricism, because Allah is the "Unseen" - Sura (16:77), which means that beyond our world there is a transcendent one, in which Allah will show himself to the people in paradise. God's language about winds the ontological rift between naturalism and metaphysics, in that God's word immediately brings forth the propositional object that was not before.

2. The physical-theological proof of God "deserves to be called with respect" (Kant IV, A 632). Especially in the biological nature there is no "for itself", everything is coordinated with each other, every living being is at the same time means and end, so that one can assume the purposeful nature of the biological nature. What is an end? According to Kant, will means: action according to ends. The latter mean "determinant of volition" (Kant VII, A 39), of the empirical will. It is "then the conception of an object, and that relation of it to the subject, by which the faculty of desire is determined for the realization of the same" (A 39). Or, in other words, the conception of a thing is the condition of the reality of the thing, insofar as the will is capable of realization. Purposeful thinking in the sense that according to a goal to be achieved the means for realization can be determined, does not prove that nature is of itself purposefully ordered. However, if one operates with the concept of purposefulness, one obtains order criteria for gaining an overview of nature. And the more a coordinated whole can be constructed, the stronger grows the belief that, since purposefulness has its cause in reason, there must be someone pulling its strings outside this whole, a reason transcending man, God, who causes the world to reveal itself as a "realm of purposes." This bears strongly anthropomorphic features, because in pre-industrial societies man experiences it daily in his manual activities and can therefore ascribe to God a similar but more formidable creative power. I would like to cite here as empirical counter-evidence the theory of evolution which can be used neither for nor against a proof of God. For a teleological proof of God speaks the (as objectively believed) purposefulness which we find. Such a fine tuning of nature cannot be a coincidence, because no matter how long some monkeys hammer away at the typewriter, a drama by Schiller does not emerge from it.[43] There must be therefore a world leader, after whose plans the world is arranged. The purposefully arranged nature proves, since it cannot bring about such a performance itself, the existence of a God planning the world. This proof has at least strong analogical probative force.

But nature itself is not determined by the *causa finalis* (final purpose), but by the *causa efficiens* (effective cause), says the principle of Darwin's theory of evolution.[44] The principle is also valid for the teleological proof of God, because:

> "this purposeful arrangement is quite alien to the things of the world, and is attached to them only by chance, i.e. the nature of different things could not of itself, by so many uniting means, concur to certain final purposes [...]". (A 626).

But even the crudest materialist must concede that there seems to be something like objective purposefulness in animate nature; one need only look at organic structures and interdependencies in a biotope.[45] It is based on mutation and selection. The former is a random chemical event that produces some heritable organic change in the genome and thus in the organism. The environment provides the criteria for whether that mutant meets those criteria. Thus a

---

[43] Similarly, W. Paley concludes: If someone finds a clock in nature, he inevitably draws the conclusion that the purposefulness of this object cannot be a coincidence, but must come from a rational being. The relation "clock-man" can be transferred to that of a purposeful nature, which was created by a world-planning being, God.

[44] Rapoport (1988) proves that there is no correspondence between a "cause pulling from the front" (causa finalis) and a "cause pushing from behind" (causa efficiens). The causa finalis is in reality a causa efficiens. Evolution, thus also the evolution of seemingly teleological actions of organismic systems can be causally explained by Darwin's evolutionary mechanisms. "Teleonomy" or "as-if-teleology" is therefore also Lorenz's term for causa efficiens, which are treated like anthropomorphic final causes for reasons of linguistic economy, e.g.: 'Gases, fluids, living beings, political systems, states have the "endeavor" to achieve this or that ...'.

[45] For example, the beaver has its webbed feet not because it moves almost constantly in water, but because hereditary mutations caused the skin between the toes to grow together, which turned out to be a great adaptive advantage. But from the appearance one can believe in purposefulness in nature.

"fit" (Lorenz), an assignment of biotope and living being is achieved. Dawkins has chosen for the interplay of mutation and selection the relational book title *The Blind Watchmaker* (1996).

Inherent in the Qur'an is the teleological proof of God, and Muhammad cannot praise Allah enough for creating the world in such a way as to provide an orderly habitat for man. See Sura (6:99):

> And it is He Who sends down water from the cloud; with it We bring forth all kinds of growth; then with it We bring forth greenery, from it We make sprout rowed grain, and from the date palm, from its umbels (sprout) drooping date clusters, and gardens of grapes, and the olive and the pomegranate - similar and dissimilar to each other. Consider their fruit when they bear fruit, and their ripening. Verily, in this are signs for people who believe.

3. The cosmological proof of God concludes from the general theorem of the conditionality of everything existing in a regress to an existing, which itself has no cause, God, the unmoved mover, as already Aristotle concluded. But such a regress is empirically never to an end, there is no possibility to come to a first cause, which must possess empirical existence, because it produces an effect, as well as belongs to transcendence as an unconditional beginning. It is an infinite regress that cannot escape by an ontological somersault from empiricism to transcendence and vice versa.

In the Quran, this proof is reversed in its direction when God's attributes are mentioned. He is "Creator of the heavens and the earth" (6:101), "gazes cannot reach Him. But He reaches the gazes" (6:103). In the author's view, this refers to Allah, the unmoved mover, through whom the world is created but which does not interact with Him dialogically. Causal chains move irreversibly from God toward the world without the possibility of counter-movement toward God. Therefore, human research can never penetrate up to him himself, because he is transcendent, therefore unseen. From him springs the causality which brings forth all being. But however far man climbs on the causal chains in the direction of the beginning: God is unreachable. Thus his presence cannot be justified. The Islamic mysticism has not strictly adhered to the principle of the inscrutability of God and has tried to approach him recognizably so far that the abrupt contrast "God-man" can be softened.

Thus, there are no logically and argumentatively compelling proofs of God, but also no logical proofs of the non-existence of God. v. Kutschera, however, finds a wealth of justifications for a deep belief in supranaturalistic entities. Similar to Tepe, he explains religiosity as a response to human suffering and existential pressure in terms of projective needs:

> There is a deep need of man to reach beyond the limits of his limited, accidental transitory existence and to have a share in the eternal. From this point of view, the transcendent not only spreads light over the empirical world, but also broadens the horizon of human life (1991, 170).

He thus addressed the shortcoming of Western rationalism and secularism: the need for religiosity as a means of emotionally coping with existence, which is not satisfied by it. The sciences, although endowed with the monopoly of truth in the West, at least in the cultural perception, cannot compensate for this deficit.

In the further course of his investigations, v. Kutschera asks about the historical relationship between immanence and transcendence. In the mythical world, they form a whole in which the numinous is "interwoven" (168) with the profane. The religious world separates the two aspects. There is now, on the one hand, the creator of the world who is out of himself, with a higher claim to reality, who is confronted by his created as a profane, inferior world. Finally, in scientism and positivism the relation "immanence - transcendence" is turned around, immanence as empirical reality claims assured knowledge, while transcendence, the desire for ultimate meaning, is granted only a shadow existence in the sense of Offenbach's *Orpheus in the Underworld*. Everything that cannot be proven rationally and conclusively is deprived of its claim to a noteworthy existence. But also realism as a consequence of rationalism is based on presuppositions, premises and positings, which for their part can no longer be investigated with the same inventory of methods with which it tries to break the ontology of religions.

To this end, v. Kutschera asks the question already posed by Kant about the perceptibility of the world itself. But behind the question there is already a belief, namely that there must be at least an external world independent of our perception and that our cognitive faculty is suitable to take cognizance of it. Only this transcendental belief in Kant's sense constitutes the experience of cognizability, i.e., that we must already be convinced of a world that is cognizable and a subject that cognizes, that is, we must presuppose experience in the sense of naive realism, that the world is as I perceive it, before we can ask the question about the cognizability of the world. To be sure, we would have to be able to take a world-elevated standpoint; but even in doing so, the problem arises, namely, that our perceptual faculty is adapted to naive realism and could fail if it had to step out of it. Also the questioning of the question about the knowability of the world always brings up the same question behind this question, so that we may assume the fact that there are "borderline questions", which are rationally reasonable, but cannot be solved rationally.

Thus, rationalism has to admit white spots of weakness in its field, so that it is not for it to look down full of malice on the weaknesses of religious ontologies. That is why v. Kutschera distinguishes descriptive from cognitive statements. The former describe the reality and objectivity of scientific facts. If religions insist on an absolute, thus also descriptive concept of truth, then they are like Christianity, which step by step had to give up this monopoly under regrettable circumstances, whereby then often the baby was thrown out with the bathwater. If Islam continues to insist on a descriptive monopoly on truth, i.e., one that can also be understood scientifically, then it faces the same fate. For fundamentalism in Islam, therefore, such an absolute monopoly on truth, which serves as an ideologically grateful instrument for enforcing its own interests, is worth defending with all means, including violence and terror, so that it becomes ever more anachronistic, but thereby also ever more dangerous.

The latter, the cognitive ones, to take up again the truth content of religious statements, do not assert what is, "they do not aim at conceptual precision and want to clarify for us what they are talking about in its meaning for our life, to bring it close to our experiencing and feeling, not only to our thinking [...]. In their parables and parables, they want to show aspects of divine or human reality, to bring them close to us, not to describe them" (81).

At this point I would like to leave this problematic, but without banishing the religions completely into the "realm of illusions", because they contribute to the human enlightenment of existence and culturalization. They contribute to the enlightenment of human existence as well as all philosophical ontologies, which cannot do without basic assumptions. Although they appear much more plausible than these, even the most plausible one does not possess truth in itself stringently in the sense of supra-temporal continuity. Even the positivist understanding of truth, which we regard as evident, swims on a bottomless lake which can swallow it. Summing up, I agree with v. Kutschera's point of view that there are "epistemological borderline questions" (194) that "cannot be decided rationally" (195). To this I also count the question about the existence of God.

But since the Islamic belief in God guarantees objectivity for the believers, there is no reason for them to doubt Allah's existence and claim to rule. Thus, two irreconcilable ontologies confront each other, the secular Western one of doubt with small islands of undecidability, to which Christianity has taken refuge, and the dogmatic-theological one of Islam, which believes to encompass the whole. Especially in the philosophy of science, the two views position themselves diametrically. Anyone who earns a diploma at an Islamic university must, in a preface[46], much like Stalin, Lenin or Marx in communism, thank Allah for the wisdom and insight with which he has only been able to complete this work. The scientist is thus only tool of God, because he fulfills his will, even if he does not know it.

The certainty of God's existence, which is not shaken by any reflection and to which Islam's absolute claim to truth is inextricably linked, explains its growing acceptance, especially today, because the brokenness of Western ways of life with their permanent crisis scenario can no longer spread any socializing warmth. But just when a worldview wants to produce such a descriptively derived social consensus by synthesizing a popular theory (think of the Ethnic concept of National Socialism and the propagation of a "socialist man" in a polity in which state, people and party merge into one), it has long since turned into a vulgar-theorizing **ideology(-).** In it, values are constructed whose validity is also commanded as descriptive, although they only spring from the ideology producers' will to power. The arguments of deficitary Islamism do not have to be invented; for they are already available pre-formulated in the Koran.

We can compare Islam to a dormant volcano whose stored potential energy discharges from time to time for lack of discipline through rationality. We can

---

[46] As is still customary in Islam today in any scholarly treatise, Al-Ghazali begins his writing *The Niche of Lights* with praise to Allah and the Prophet:
"Praise be to God who sends forth lights, who unlocks sight, who reveals secrets, and who lifts veils. Peace be upon Muhammad, Light of Lights, Lord of the pious, Beloved of the Almighty, Glad Tidings of the One who grants much pardon, Warner of the Almighty, Subduer of the disbelievers and Exposer of the wrongdoers. Peace be upon his family and comrades, the pure, the good and the elect.
Now to the subject!" (Al-Ghazali 1987, 3).

name as potential energy its absolute claim to truth, the globalization of its claim to rule, its claim to total domination of all areas of life, its distinction between religions and people who are pleasing to God and those who are deficient, its historical world mission, understood as an obligation, for the improvement of mankind through Islam, the only beatifying religion, and its immanent claim to political realization of these stored energies. Islamism with its dogmatic theory of religion and state is in the process of transforming the potential ideological energy of Islam into kinetic energy.

4. The value problem

The explosive that threatens to tear Islam and the Western world apart consists basically only of the opposition "subjectivity/objectivity and the interpretation of the two terms "value" and "truth".

The Christian Middle Ages is determined by the opposites:

"Faith - Reason,
"absolute truth of God - human limited knowledge",
"absolute God - humanity in need of redemption and powerless",
"Religion - Beginning of Sciences,
"eternal bliss in heaven - eternal damnation in hell".

The separation of faith and knowledge with the beginning of the modern era turns into the dichotomy "value/truth", which also strongly influences our thinking, but also has political consequences, in that a demarcation between the sacred and the secular takes place.

We can compare our ontology with a coin that represents reality as a whole. One side symbolizes reality as it exists cognitively as fact and is subject to general laws of nature, the other what does not exist by itself but must be produced by man, the world of culture, of artifacts to which a value can be ascribed.

A thing as an object is an object of science, which can be assigned a value as an artifact or an object useful for humans. The concept of value belongs to the area of practical philosophy, norms, preconceptions, human value-boundness, ethics and morality. In the historical excursus that now follows, the development of the philosophy of value will be traced because the concordance or dichotomy between truth and value is of far-reaching socio-political significance. Both 'worlds' are, it is claimed, of the same root, but nevertheless incompatible. Nietzsche is to be used to open the argument about the concept of value.

His philosophical analysis starts from the not further questionable phenomenon "life" when he states: " [...]. The *living* is being: further there is no being"
(1 [24]⁴⁷). It is characterized by the fact that it is in need of the other according
to principles of self-preservation and enhancement in order to be able to be
itself. It must appropriate the being outside of itself, or repel it, assimilate it.
In doing so, it has to perspective the other on its appropriateness for itself.
Now, however, the existing no longer appears as it is, but only in the light of
the scanning perspectives. The subject becomes the perspectival being of seeing, the spotlight, whose rays of light form a "light coating" on the objects,
which thus become values. What becomes visible in the light of these spot-
lights is the human being reflected in the values, estimates, "valuations" (7
[2]) set by him. Nietzsche calls the process of determining values "interpreting", even better would be "appropriating interpreting", because he imple-
ments his valuations into the object, in order to then rediscover them, transformed by the object. Nietzsche transfers the image of perspective and
projective interpreting also to the being as a whole:

> "[...]. In truth, interpretation is a means itself of becoming master of something. The
> organic process presupposes continuous *interpreting*" (2 [148]).

Thus, valuations and values are projections of our needs, indeed of all forms
of life, onto the Other, the external world, and we can actually perceive only
these in the cone of light of our needs; but by covering the object as a "film,"
we consider what these perspectives show us to be objective. They are, in
themselves, beliefs and illusions that we have ontologized. We thus confuse
value with being, which actually cannot appear as itself at all. "Reasoned
thought" (5 [22]) is also such a perspective; we "interpret according to a
scheme that we cannot discard" (5[22]). This is equally true of the "*proper*
conception of the object, which originally [is] *only a means to* the end of
grasping, grasping, and grasping *itself*" (7 [3]). Therefore, for Nietzsche, there
are no facts as such, but only interpretations. Human needs are thus projected
onto the existing and appear transformed as 'true' interpretations of the world.
The objectively existing and its condition is in reality a value projection of

---

[47] Nietzsche is quoted according to Colli and Montinari (eds.): Friedrich Nietzsche - Kritische
Studienausgabe (14 vols.). Berlin and New York 1988. The quotations here refer to vol. 12.

man, but also of life as a whole. It can be inferred from Nietzsche's thesis that, in that the concept of object has been destroyed so that there are no objects in the believed sense, there can be no objective truth either. This double negation, that objectivity is only a projective illusion, that reason is only one perspective of empowerment among many, leads to a truthless state veiled by illusions, so that, taking the latter for what they want to appear, one can lead one's life.

Tepe interprets Nietzsche's theory of illusion not so aggressively, putting the term "value" in place of illusions, so that he can make the value-bound nature of human existence intelligible (1993, 90). But there is a contradiction in Nietzsche's theory of the evaporation of the object; for the perspectival projection film cannot be grasped as a hologram-like image, but must have a substrate on and in which value can only become visible, whose special properties by 'nature' can document its suitability for the appropriating perspective. Value perspectives allow objectivity to appear only behind the scenes, but nevertheless as a constant presence. Thus, there can only be perspective if there is also an object world. From this it follows that many different perspectives can also promote the intersubjectivity and objectivity of a conception.

But Nietzsche decides in favor of values and against being in the question of whom he wants to give priority; at least if one consults his *Zarathustra*. In the second part of this work, he poses the question of "immaculate knowledge" (4, 154-159). The ironic allusion to the "immaculate conception" of Mary and its equation with the idea of "immaculate knowledge" is meant to shake the belief in pure knowledge and pleasure-free conception. The fairy tale of the "immaculate conception", dogma of Catholicism, corresponds to that of the "immaculate knowledge" of the old philosophy. The latter spread the belief in pure truth, in a subject-free, i.e. intersubjective knowledge of the full self-representation of the world. The interest-free, intersubjective cognition is a lie like the pleasure-free, thus 'pure', "immaculate cognition". Nietzsche thus harshly rejects an interest-free contemplation, a value-free philosophy and science:

> "And this means to me untainted knowledge of all things, that I want nothing from things: except that I may lie there before them like a mirror with a hundred eyes. -
>
> Oh you sensitive hypocrites, you lustful ones! You lack innocence in desire: and now you slander desire" (4, 157).

With the hypostasis of values and the dilution of being to appearance, the concept of truth also evaporates. Since this refers to the cognizing subject, what this subject speaks becomes untrue itself: the philosopher Nietzsche/Zarathustra becomes a "*Only fool*, only *poet*" (4, 371-374). If the subsuming of the concept of truth under the concept of value demands the "revaluation of all values" for him as well, then for the philosopher only the role of the fool, who speaks nonsense, or that of the poet, who falsifies appearance to being with "lying word bridges" (4, 372), with metaphors, which pretend a deep meaning.

Nietzsche's philosophy of value, thought by him consistently to the end, leads to a catastrophe, which he visualizes in the dithyramb "*Nur Narr! Nur Dichter*" (*Only Fool! Only Poet*).

4.2 Monod - a representative of the strict dualism of descriptive science and normative object references

While Nietzsche's starting point of his value philosophy is a philosophical subjectivism, Monod approaches this problem from the other, the scientific side. For this purpose, he divides world history into two phases, that of "animism"[48] (1996, 43) and that of (Platonic) objectivism. "Reality pressure" and "suffering pressure" by the omission of instinct-guided acting (instinct reduction) force the human being to face this basic fear. For this, in the sense of Nietzsche, man "invented" "values" which gave him life security by fastening in the belief in a sense of life. But in reality these values are only human projections on a level, which overpowering and determining as myth and religion value-reinforcing retroactively enable a human society. Myths and religions, because they offer a coherent ontology, can comprehensively satisfy man's need for explanation and thus provide valuable help in socialization and problem solving. But there is also the profane thinking, which offers people rational explanations for their everyday problems. The date of the final separation of the two from each other is to be fixed with Bacon's new concept of nature in the sense of its mastery as "knowledge is power" and Galileo's nature as quantity (everything can be mathematized) in the 17th century.

Is the dichotomy between objective truth and humanly set value an antinomy determining now and the future?

---

[48] With this term Monod describes both the vitalism in biology, which says that with "physical laws" the life phenomena are "not completely explicable" (41, footnote), thus within the matter still a "spiritual principle" slumbers, which appears together with the matter in living beings differently strongly, and the mythical-religious animism. This means the coincidence of the sources of the knowledge and value conceptions. "It regards them as two aspects of one reality" (152). A current prominent representative of this view of nature as both an ethical and cognitive system is Konrad Lorenz.

There are no problems for animism because it does not draw a sharp line between being and ought, so that it can be counted among the "metaphysical-metaethical naturalism"[49] (Birnbacher 2003, 360), whereas Lorenz's bioethics in his extensive book *Der Abbau des Menschlichen* can still be counted among the "empirical-metaethical naturalism" (1983, 360). Thus, even today there are Western representatives of a worldview close to animism (Hegelians, Marxists). Once the "demand of objectivity is raised as a necessary condition for any truth of knowledge, a radical separation is introduced between the realms of ethics and scientific knowledge, which is essential for the study of truth" (Monod 1996, 152). This strict separation of the two (if normative, then not objective; if objective, then not normative) has penetrated cultural memory only to a very limited extent to this day, because in everyday life this antinomy is only dimly perceived. Therefore, **ideologies(-)** can mix both categories again with the consequence of legitimizing politically very questionable intentions. Religions are also susceptible to such 'reunifications', since, like myths, they originated before the separation of the two spheres and have not yet comprehended it, or have comprehended it with difficulty. Thus, the question here is also whether Islam, as a myth-drenched religion, has overcome animistic holism, a holistic way of looking at what exists.

Thus, according to Monod, there are only truthless values, norms and moral concepts on the one hand and a value-free true science on the other hand. The realization that the scientifically unjustifiable postulate of objectivity is the condition for scientific work, that a moral precept which cannot be falsified without blocking the scientific enterprise is the condition of objective knowledge, seems to be para dox. On the one hand, this paradox attacks the belief in absolutely valid values with a similar truth status as that of natural science; on the other hand, the normative realm emancipates itself through a new reality set by humans, efficacy. Values move something.

It is therefore only too understandable that religions, if they are understood only as a value system without objectivity, defend themselves against this attack threatening their existence. Monod articulates here, however, also the heavy loss which people have to accept by the expulsion of values from the realm of truth. But on the other hand, he is now free from the paternalism of unquestionable values. Myth and religions can only take over the existential

---

[49] This concept is explicated in the chapter "Birnbacher - the naturalistic fallacy".

71

creation of meaning privately. Man becomes more and more the one who must prescribe his own maxims of action, because he has been released from the compulsion and the care of descriptive normative systems of meaning. Thus man gains a freedom of decision which he can no longer hand over to 'higher' authorities.

Monod calls man "a being that is simultaneously subject to two dominions: the realm of animate nature and the realm of ideas" (154). Both together constitute the being "human": when a process or object is evaluated, the claim to truth vanishes; whenever scientific research is conducted, no value can be extracted from it alone. But without submitting to the science-ethical postulate of objectivity, no science thrives. But like the two royal children in the fairy tale, they cannot come together. (Monod's theory of action, which reunites the two entities into a workable collaboration, will be left aside here). The times that man could rely on mythical or religious ontologies with a claim to truth and an unquestionable system of norms derived from them and justify his deeds with the claim of 'higher' existing beings are over. The world as perception of a meaningful wholeness has become impossible. Thus man becomes existentially a tragic figure, of whom Monod says:

> If he absorbs the message in its full meaning, man must finally wake up from his millennial dream and realize his total abandonment, his radical strangeness. He now knows that he has his place like a gypsy at the edge of the universe, which is deaf to his music and indifferent to his hopes, sufferings or crimes (151).

Man has philosophized himself out of the paradise of the values supporting him: they are necessary, but not true in the sense of permanence; the natural sciences have discovered the Platonic structure of matter and its objective laws, but their truth behaves indifferently towards man. The human being, however, gains with the understanding of the consequences of this dualism potentially the ab solute freedom to establish himself between transcendence into nothingness and immanence of being as a border crosser.

In our everyday realism, we are rarely aware of this logical separation of the two postulates and argue and act according to a tried and tested mixture of both; we could not live otherwise. But the moment we want to base our claims on truth criteria or normative systems with absolute truth claims are exposed, the hidden value-truth dualism breaks open again.

If the Koran testifies to the truth of its contents, then this statement must be differentiated, since there is definitely "an immanent rationality of myth"

(Tepe 1988, 32), so that first of all two equivalent rationalities must be assumed. "The truth of myth," advocated by Hübner (1984) in the book of the
same name, bases a religion on a system of experience like that of our scientific worldview. While the scientific interpretation of the world proceeds from
a background ontology directed according to certain rules, here realism, thus
also from an axiom system, according to which the objects appear and can be
hypothetically determined, the religious-mythical thinking moves in a unity of
the material and non-material world, in which, however, "comprehensibility,
justifiability, consistency, clarity and generally binding insight" (Tepe 1988,
31) prevail, thus rational conditions as in science. Also, a myth is to be judged
according to its function of conveying information, codes of behavior, and
emotional satisfaction.

But why is the mythical-religious (supranaturalistic) thinking more and more
replaced by a realistic thinking? The explanatory power of realism is, at least
for us, considerably higher; it can make natural causes responsible for the in-
trusion of the numinous. We live in a historical process in which the ontologies
have already changed several times; however, the greater explanatory power
of realism must not tempt us to endow it with a dogmatic claim to truth.

At this point the author would like to point out the close relationship of
mythical and religious thinking. The unity of *value and action model of* myth
(Schupp 1979, 63) has already been pointed out, "religion, art and science do
not yet have a clearly delimited form in myth (Cassirer, *Symbolische Formen*
II, 1969, IX). But when the axiology of myth is problematized, reflected upon,
and codified, myth becomes "a system of abstract theological and metaphysical concepts" (Schupp 1979, 69).

Religion and myth, however, reach their limit when they have to question
their own axiology; they immunize themselves by constructing the "metatheoretical concept 'revelation'" (73), which is wide open to any understanding as
well as misunderstanding. According to Cassirer, the result is that "religion
makes the cut to which myth as such is alien: by making use of sensuous images and signs, it immediately knows them as such" (Cassirer, II, 1969, 2856).
Religion, then, is reflected myth. So, a reflected mythical thinking can be compared to religious thinking. Here, no distinction is made between mythical and
religious thinking, especially since mythical texts are found in abundance in
our world religions.

Tepe takes mythical thinking as a model of "interplay with profane thinking" (1995, 168), which is such that there is an overarching profane thinking, an ontogenetic body of knowledge filtered out through evolution, without which the execution of life would be impossible. We are thereby in the sphere of the naive or everyday realism that things are as we perceive them to be. This profane knowledge corresponds to a "system-wide profane rationality" (168), the quality of which is to be set higher than the system-immanent rationality inherent in myth. We therefore assume a meta-rationality that has its object level in both profane and mythical thinking.

Within the myth both forms of thinking take the same rank, while on the meta-level a reality deficit must be attributed to the mythical concept. What is written in the mythical thinking to the gods, becomes in the profane thinking the naturally explicable cause, in the scientific thinking probability or natural law. From the meta-point of view of the overlapping rational thinking, the actually mythical area is reduced more and more and the rationality contained in it is sucked off and attributed to the profane thinking. Scientific thinking replaces the mythical (and thus the religious) more and more. However, this process, understood as a loss of meaning, can also be interpreted differently: as the "replacement of one system of meaning by another" (Tepe 1993, 191). The process of the gradual emptying of meaning from existence as a displacement reaction of myth and religion (not meant normatively) by the positive sciences is thus not only a process from myth to logos, but one of separation of values and facts. Insofar as mythologies ontologize their value-settings with the claim of rational bindingness, they produce false knowledge as illusion. This can then no longer take the status of a believed mythology or religion, but only support my value system as "as-if myth and as-if religion"[50] (192) in the sense of a "fictional myth" or fictional religion". But such "fictional religions" have historically failed.[51] Thou shalt not kill', because you thereby

---

[50] The argument that Islam is a largely myth-free religion and therefore unaffected by demythicization can be easily refuted. Beltz (1980), in his book *The Myths of the Qur'an,* examined texts containing myths. The chapter "Allah is God" alone lists the following subheadings: "Revealed in Mecca," the creation myth "Allah as Creator of Heaven and Earth," "The Weather God and Nature Conqueror," "The God of Fertility," "The Judge of the World," "The Lawgiver," "The Light of the World," "Allah and the Other Gods."

[51] "The practical need of the life of the mind and of the order of the state will sooner or later lead to giving our monistic religion [deification of nature - the author] a certain *cultus form, just as it has* been the case with all other religions of the culture peoples. It will be a beautiful

transgress God's commandment, becomes 'Thou shalt not kill', because we thereby destroy life worth living.

Transferring our problem to Islam: Insofar as rational scientific ontology prevails, this religion becomes an illusionist project when it cognitively exaggerates normative questions, so that it becomes open to illusion-critical and ideology-critical attack. The result, historically generalized, is a secularization of religions.

In order to avoid this fate, Islam has developed since industrialization, and especially in recent years, into a religion that, through its insistence on a literal interpretation of the Koran, considers itself a rock in the storm and is striving for a new boom in religiosity. Insofar as re-religionization occurs as a side effect of worldwide fundamentalism, one can speak of a renaissance of the world religions other than Islam only to a limited extent, but of their **ideologization(-).** One only has to read the Koran to see what punishments are threatened to all those who fall away from God or behave in an unbelieving or critical manner toward the existence of Allah. [52]

With the idea of a personal existence of God one can be quite sure that they are anthropomorphic projections of the idea of human perfection.[53] Man has formed an image of God on the basis of his experiences. This must be personally bound to a human-like being, because only this can express a will. Super-

---

task of the *honest theologians of the* 20th century to develop this monistic cultus and to adapt it to the manifold needs of the individual culture peoples" (Haeckel 1905, 462, note 18).

[52] Sura (2:162): "Those who disbelieve and die as disbelievers, on them the curse of Allah and the angels and men", (2: 213): "The worldly life is made beautiful to the disbelievers, and they mock the believers. But those who fear Allah will be above them on the Day of Resurrection; and Allah gives to whom He wills without reckoning," (18:30): "And say: 'The truth it is in the sight of your Lord: therefore, let him believe who will'. Behold, we have prepared for the wrong-doers a fire whose tent will enclose them. Then when they cry for help, they will be helped with water like molten lead that burns the faces. How terrible is the drink, and how bad is the (fire) as a camp!"

[53] Feuerbach's projection theory towards the Christian religions can also be applied to Islam. According to this theory, "religion subtracts the powers, the qualities, the essence of man from man and idolizes them as independent beings - regardless of whether it makes each one its own being, as in polytheism, or, as in monotheism, combines all of them into beings - [...]" (Feuerbach 1969, 41 note). By bundling his positive qualities and making them into a "highest being", only the creature in need of redemption remains for him, because he thereby misjudges his being, which can only be saved by this "highest being".

natural powers are attributed to God, which in reality bundle all positive qualities of man in his person, so that only deficient predicates remain for man, which mark him as a helpless being.

But if these projections are transformed back and purified of all anthropomorphisms, then "all metaphysical determinations of God are therefore only real determinations if they are recognized as determinations of thought, as determinations of intelligence, of understanding" (Feuerbach 1969, 85). He is convinced of the historically more and more clear dying off of religions, in that "man more and more abdicates God, more and more ascribes God to himself" (78), because then every projection into the metaphysical is omitted, and this design loses more and more of its attractiveness. For Christianity, Feuerbach's thesis has been largely successful; for Islam, it does not seem to apply, for it is in a stage of expansion, in a phase of religious rebirth.

Tepes' and Monod's argumentation schemes are similar in their historical approach like positive and negative, even if one starts from the mythical understanding of the world and the other from natural science. What one calls myth and religion, the other calls "animism" from a scientific perspective. However, despite their different approaches, both researchers arrive at the same conclusion of the dichotomy between objective existence and the subjectivity of valid values.

4.3 Lenk - constructivism and value-truth dualism

'Everything we perceive are constructs of interpretation' is the motto of constructivism. Thus Lenk reverses the assumptions of a scientific realism of an extra-subjectively existing, recognizable world and shifts its ontological primacy to the physical-psychic layer of perception, and only secondarily he allows a real external world to be valid. In a model of the gradation of cognition developed by him, which he calls "stages of interpretation"[54] (Lenk 1995, 103), the "primordial interpretation" (103) is the one closest to the object. It is a "level of pattern formation and- distinctions that are biologically unchanging or biologically laid out, insofar practically unchanging for us, which could be

---

[54] His hierarchical "stages of interpretation" in short form are:
1. productive primordial interpretations, 2. pattern interpretations, 3. conventional conceptualization, 4. classification interpretation, 5. justification interpretation, 6. meta-interpretation (103).

called the level of *primary schematizations*" (104). Consequently, according to Lenk, the notion of an external world that can somehow be recognized must be abandoned in favor of a "model," "epistemological and everyday psychological" (56).

As a supporter of the theory of evolution, which regards the evolution from the Big Bang until today as a fact, which is only possible if we assume largely constant (Platonic) conditions of a really existing and at least hypothetically recognizable external world, I would like to weaken constructivism to the effect that, even if I share the psychic general thesis[55] of being as an interpretation construct, I nevertheless assume that this must be structured in such a way that it stands in a somehow fitting relation to reality. He also moderates his "internal realism" by arriving at a theory of interaction in which both sides are interlocked:

> The world in some way contributes something to its capture by us; we secondarily structure what the world contributes, but the structuring is not arbitrary but tied to the impression of and interactions with world factors [...] (44).

Lenk thus opposes the belief that an object can be perceived in itself. Thus, a person's prior knowledge determines to a great extent the kind of perception and its classification in the hierarchical system of his levels of interpretation.

Lenk calls the term summarizing these actions "imprinting" (45), "according to which the so-called real just plays along, has to play along, in an interplay with the interpretations" (57). Thus, our cognitive apparatus does not at all deliver fact-neutral data, but "products of interpretation". What is perceived and how, is decided by the subjective pre-understanding, which depends decisively on the socio-cultural context, but mostly unconsciously. One speaks of "selective perception" when the consciousness is already controlled by concrete preconceptions. If the consciousness is dominated by a deficient ideology, then one speaks with Birnbacher of "will-determined distortions of perception ".

After the presentation of these epistemological premises of constructivism, it might be of interest to reflect also on his theory of value. First of all, he makes the already known differentiation of "cognitive and descriptive". He

---

[55] Also psychosystems are based on a material substrate, the nervous system, so that the "interpretation products" become possible only by a material-real component.

avoids dualism by introducing the already clarified notion of interpretive con-struct as superior to both here as well, speaking of "normative and descriptive use of interpretive products" (Lenk 1994, 162). It is therefore better to ask about the meaning of the term "value" than about its being; for already here a possibility of confusion between "cognitive and "descriptive" lies close at hand. According to Lenk, values have a "validity"; they are bindingly set and accepted for a certain grouping of people, which is why they are "artificial, fictitious objects, abstract artifacts" (164); their "sociofictional" function (164) consists in establishing validity through convention, tradition, institutionaliza-tion. Yet they are also real in some way because they can have great efficacy by virtue of human will. They obey the principle of causality.

Already here this discussion of values becomes extraordinarily significant, namely when the value character of norms is denied. This can lead to the fact that by raising an absolute claim to truth of a worldview, norms can also be postulated as true or false in the descriptive sense, so that there are strict pre-scriptions for action that cannot be put up for disposition. The cognification of normative statements is the main criterion of fundamentalist ideology; it produces only a semblance of objectivity, in reality a "theoretical deficit" which, however, can serve all the more effectively as a justification, justifica-tion and expansion of **ideologies(-)** because the descriptivity of fact and norm no longer requires freedom of decision. The same is true for religions and mythical conceptions when they maximize their claim to truth. In this case, we can also speak of a projection with confluence in an "ideological self-am-plification process" (Lenk 1994, 168), the first part of which Feuerbach (1956) described. The projection of the idealization of man as God, whereby for man now only his weakness remains reinforced and its repercussion as divine rev-elation, which brings man the longed-for salvation, acts like a value-system-reinforcing impulse.

Lenk, too, is a representative of Hume's law or the logical untenability of a "naturalistic fallacy," a logical extraction of an ought from being, although the term "interpretive construct," which applies to both norm and descriptive, would actually have suggested a blurring of the differences between the two. Thus, it can be generalized, the separation of being and ought also holds in the contemporary philosophy of constructivism. The fact that, on a meta-level, normative and moral behavioral attitudes can, of course, also be descriptively represented, for example, in the description of an ethical conception of a cultural area, is again a fact from which a generally binding judgment and action of the scientific or profane actor can in no way be derived.

The resulting confusion of values, which is lamented everywhere, is therefore a logical and historical consequence of the separation of both categories, which as a unity in animism guaranteed the meaningfulness of human existence, but today only resurrect as **ideology(-)** to a new holistic illusory life with the danger of the formation of totalitarian systems. But without secured values, which convey social security, human life is impossible. Can there be possibilities to stabilize again the emptiness of meaning of a knowledge society, which at the same time produces very unstable and conflict-prone social entities, by religiously based values? Can't a renaissance of religions in the Western camp put an end to the chaos of values with its general battle cry of "profit" of a global industrial society? If this question were so easy to answer, a lot of paper could be saved.

For Islam, the separation into value (life orientation) and methodological rationality (science) does not apply. But religious value premises have no place in science. But a separation of Islamic life orientation and rational thinking is forbidden (see Sharia); since the world carries the ontology of its creator Allah, it is actually enough if the Koran is studied, in which all necessary knowledge (God is omniscient) is found. As long as Islam insists on the Koranic monopoly of truth, it must make use of many ideological crutches to reconcile this monopoly of truth with the claim to truth of the rational sciences.

The code of conduct of the *scientific community does* not apply in Islamic countries. The relationship to technology and science in Islam is still tense, even ambivalent, because it is difficult to link the underlying positivist concept of thought with one's own supranaturalistic one.

Basically, the "naturalistic fallacy"[56] (Moore 1970) is an expression of the separation of value concepts from descriptive statements, i.e. a variation of the theme "faith - reason" or "value - truth". The former are under the criterion of "validity/non-validity" and thus are historically mutable, the latter under the truth criterion of "true/false" and thus are historically resistant. Between both there is no logical relation of implication. Logically no ought can be derived from a being. But it is worth remembering Monod, who names with the term "animism" the unity of scientific rationality and mythical world view, as it has shaped and lived the pre-industrial society.

Kant has shown with his critique of the proofs of God that the conception of God has only contingent quality: There is no evidence for the existence or non-existence of God. However, nothing speaks against a convinced and convincing belief in God. Many good reasons can be given for believing in God; but even an infinite plethora of these plausible arguments can force beyond doubt the being of God as a fact or logical consequence. The consequence of this fact leads to two ways of life. The one who accepts the separation of descriptive facts from normative imperatives downgrades the absolute truth claim of many religions to the concept of "validity", to which subjectively the concepts of "faith" and "conviction" correspond. He will advertise his convictions, let arguments speak, give reasons. But this means that he will not dismiss other convictions as generally wrong. However, this does not result in the uncritical acceptance of other drafts, but in a confrontation with their truth claims, so that a peaceful competition of ideas becomes possible.

Things are more difficult when starting from an object that places both sides of the coin, prescriptive and descriptive, under the primacy of description: The Qur'an. "The Qur'an is regarded by all Muslims, without exception, as the direct and divine word and as absolutely infallible" (Schwer 1992, 7). Esposito (2003, 23) speaks of the "eternal, literally valid word of God," Abdullah (2001, 27) calls it "the ultimate authority, the word of God," Barth (2003, 62) "expression of God's will," "only truth that cannot be debated." Leiner (2006, 41) relativizes the Qur'an's claim to truth by conceding that it contains "no error,"

---

[56] The term "naturalistic fallacy" must be treated as a generic term. It means not only natural processes in nature, but also facts of other areas, from whose being one believes to derive an ought, facts of anthropology, metaphysics and theology (Birnbacher 2003, 360f.).

"no falsity," "no lie," but makes no claim to exclusivity, which I vehemently deny.

For the fundamentalist Qutb, there is "no other knowledge except that which is built upon the Qur'an, which is the complete and ultimate revelation" (quoted in Barth 2003, 119). We can thus assume that for Muslims the Qur'an contains the sum of all descriptive and prescriptive knowledge: Cosmology, legal texts regulating coexistence: Food and clothing regulations, moral teachings, presentation of an objectively understood ethics of values, anthropology, theology, metaphysics. Thus the conclusion is valid: 'The Koran is absolutely true, and exactly in such a way it announces an objective value ethics, thus the Koran contains true knowledge and supratemporally valid values'. According to the Koran, there is no difference between value and truth, so that both are subject to the truth criterion 'true/false'.

The consequences of such a conclusion are enormous, in that historical resistance is attributed to values, which is partly what happened through the 'mummification' of social conditions at the time of the prophet. However, the criterion 'wrong' is not included in the calculation on its own account, but only branded onto opposing positions. By possessing the knowledge of all times according to Qutb, the Koran levels the fundamental difference between value and truth, as is usual in animism, so that Islam can represent a self-contained ontological conception of the unity of description and norms (Sharia) with all its consequences.

All areas of human life have been frozen by the descendants of Muhammad in the state in which they were codified in the Koran and preserved there until now, so that the impression of the validity of superhistorical values can actually arise. But fundamentalism claims that the values of Islam have become more and more distant from its basic statements in the course of history, so that only the recourse to Muhammad reactivated the true values that are binding for all time (return of the 'true' Islam and its assumption of world domination). However, historical flexibility and social evolution remain alien to Islam. Religion and politics form a mutually supportive system of top-down rule. A reformation of Islam remains a dream, because the entire truth is hidden in the Koran, which allows only a "renewed revelation of the stock of knowledge" (Nagel 1994, 244); "for Islam is at the same time the complete knowledge, attainable by man, of the perfectly just cosmos, the work of the Creator" (245). Thus, there is nothing new in this world that could be explored;

even the knowledge of European civilization is only part of this 'unchanging treasure of knowledge'" (Prenner 2005, 125 f.).

Religious reforms are at the same time political reforms, these at the same time religious, so that no reforms could question Islam as a whole. For even the philosophy of the Golden Age (750-1200 A.D.) is only briefly able to melt away this ice age. Until the time of Napoleon, Islam remained an exotic world ignored by Europe. When Europe, with the Enlightenment, philosophical criticism, scientific discoveries and inventions, technical achievements and its economic potential behind it, begins its colonial policy of conquest, historically embalmed Islam, because it has neither material nor ideal resources at its disposal to stop this creeping occupation, remains in historical immobility, in lethargy or in secret admiration of the West. Today it believes that the Europeans have taken over, even stolen, parts of the teachings of the Koran that reached the West with the translation of the ancients, so that these borrowings must basically be attributed to Islam: Islam thus represents something like a worldwide monopoly of knowledge, also in the positive sciences, which it simultaneously fights as positive knowledge.

This dichotomy of Islam with regard to a thing which, if it can be brought into line with the Koran even in a miraculous way, enjoys high veneration, but if it is successfully practiced by the West is branded as the devil's work, creates in the believer the danger of falling into Orwellian "Zwiedenken" (doublethink). "**Double think**" is a thinking of the simultaneity of opposites, of which, depending on the political situation, one or the other alternative can be advocated.

The Qur'an is based on an analytical claim to truth that presupposes what is inquired about as knowledge, so that it only needs to be made explicit. (The term "old man" can be used to demonstrate this fact of already presupposed knowledge. With it, among many things, the gender of a human being is definitely and a priori given). Thus, the concept of truth as a whole is attributed to the Koran and a single truth is deduced from it quasi as a new insight. Their fundamentalist systems of thought are, it is certain for Islamists, absolutely resistant to error. But the protagonists believe that they can make synthetic judgments, i.e., that they can extend the claim to absolute truth even further by means of logical conclusions. [57]

---

[57] May a Muslim have a Christian as a friend? The Qur'an says, "O you who believe! Do not take Christians and Jews for friends. [...]" Sura (5:51). Your friend Achmed is a Christian. So

But the claim to the possession of the sole truth, if it can be subsumed under the concept of the naturalistic fallacy, is logically questioned. It says, briefly repeated: No ought can be derived from being This fact can be explained by the historical example of Social Darwinism. This is based on Darwinism, whose theory of selection leads to the fact that only the best-adapted living beings survive, which has led to an evolution of life up to the human being. Through self-domestication, man has evaded this natural selection, so that the human population has been led into genetic degeneration. How is this to be reversed? 'Nature' with its laws is our teacher here by providing a natural law, the law of selection of the weak, to enable biological progress. The law of the selection of the weak implies thereafter with logical necessity its application to the living being man, if he is not to degenerate further, but to develop further.

This higher development is a fact to be observed everywhere in the living nature. So it is wanted by nature - here nature is personified and provided with a will - if 'worthless people' are selected, nature does it every day with all living beings. Hitler, for example, had people killed by the millions according to his biological ideas of "racial mixtures" and inferior races in the feeling of being the executor of a morality governed by natural law.

Birnbacher (2003), whose ethics this paper follows, makes the following conceptual distinction: "Ethical naturalism" (362) means that "the natural [is] a *criterion* for the morally right" (362). Thus, the nature of a thing can provide good reasons for a moral decision, but not logically compelling arguments. Social Darwinism can be subsumed under the term "metaethical naturalism" (361), which means that this form of objective ethics tries to "derive moral consequences from descriptive laws [...] in a logically compelling way" (361). Thereby, it does not only need to be about laws of nature, but about formal-logically required moral consequences from a certain state of affairs of anthropology, psychology, sociology, metaphysics, theology and so on.

What happens when religions claim to possess both descriptively scientific and normatively moral truth, that is, when they make an absolute claim to truth? Is there a metanaturalistic fallacy when fundamentalism "strives for a unity of politics and religion in which religious laws and rules are the immediate basis of the political constitution and public life" (Schmidt 1990, 31)?

Achmed must not be your friend'. In this way, an infinite number of statements can be 'made true' so that the future is also under the Quranic truth.

Can "the Koran be called the constitution of the [...] Islamic state?" (Wielandt 1990, 51). Is "Islam a perfect system that regulates all concerns of human life exhaustively and unrepeatable well" (51)?

The Islamists answer all three questions affirmatively because the Koran also demands comprehensive political consequences, logically implying the constitution, so to speak, to lead every individual into the best of all communities. However, all of this only applies if there is factual or logical evidence for the existence of God, because "the persuasiveness of metaphysical moral justifications stands and falls with the credibility of their assumptions of existence [...]" (Birnbacher 2003, 373). According to Kant, such assertions-see proofs of God-are contingent, that is, neither provable nor unprovable. To deduce from such a questionable construct - Birnbacher speaks here of a "distinctively anthropomorphic image of God" (373) - an absolute claim to truth with morally commanding judgments and actions is logically wrong and morally questionable. Even if God exists, it does not yet follow that one should reflexively do what he wills; for then God's will makes man his puppet by predestination. But the human freedom to decide also against God, which the Koran expressly affirms, points to the Koran's deep contradiction between predestination and human freedom of action. But the latter premise, to act according to God's will, is normative, so I am free to follow it. And it is precisely the neglected criterion of the metaethical fallacy, namely that of individual freedom, that has no great significance in collectivist Islam.

There is only a slight linguistic difference between metaethical and ethical naturalism, so that confusion is likely. If Qur'anic arguments are used only as reasons for plausibility, we have ethical naturalism, which pursues only a hypothetical claim to truth, but for this very reason shows itself capable of dialogue; if, however, one believes in a logical implication, one stands on the uncertain ground of metaethical naturalism. The former makes a moral argument plausible, but must therefore renounce an absolute truth claim, the latter proclaims an absolute truth claim against logic, an epistemological absurdity.

The unconditional attribution of truth to the Koran as God's authentic word has a particularly devastating effect. The Koran is thus removed from profane thinking and elevated to a sacred, untouchable transcendence that demands veneration, submission, uncritical acceptance and worship. Even an explanation of the content would change the meaning of the text, so that the Muslim tries to "understand his holy book in another way, namely in recitations recited aloud. He makes the Koran his own in this way. Consequently, he also uses Quranic formulations in profane life and appropriates a Quranic way of thinking that shapes his worldview" (Abdullah 2001, 28)[58], but with what consequences? (Even critical questioning of the Koran is like blasphemy).

Imagine the children in a Koran school, how they rattle off the suras and are thus guided in their vocabulary in such a way that they can no longer think in any other way than Koranic and are then released into life as "Koran templates". In this way, we are led to believe, the students learn what they need in life, because the Koran is also the sum of all science. In reality, the graduates of these schools are completely incapable of orienting themselves in an urban life. A report by Arab intellectuals commissioned by the United Nations in 2003 came to a similar conclusion:

> Religion does not make people stupid, but its political instrumentalization has a long-term negative effect on a country's education system. Where unconditional obedience is a must and the creative self-affirmation of the individual is not desired, the thirst for knowledge and the urge to explore slacken." [59]

In this form of recitation, the belief in Islam's absolute possession of truth can be handed down. Rational argumentation would only disturb the prescribed reception of the Koran. Instead of rudimentary rationality, emotionality, which suppresses cognitive processes, is overdeveloped. Everything that the religious functionaries are convinced of is handed over to the people to cheer as Allah's will; everything that somehow has to do with the West is re-

---

[58] The Koran proceeds purely intuitively from the hypothesis formulated by Weisgerber, Sapir-Whorf and v. Humboldt, "that the individual can only recognize environment - and from there: - only think in the categories offered to him by the language community in which he grows up" (Pelz 1996, 36) If the student is supposed to learn the Koran by heart, then also for the reason that he cannot think and speak in any other way than in the categories of the Koran. This is also why the Quran is authentic only in the 'language of God', Arabic. Here, too, Orwell's *1984* offers itself:
"The New Language was the official language introduced in Oceania and was invented to meet the ideological needs of the *Engsoz. Its* purpose was not only to be a means of expression for the worldview and mental attitude appropriate to the followers of *Engsoz* alone, but also to eliminate any kind of other thinking. Once the New language had been adopted once and for all and the Old language forgotten [...], unorthodox thought - i.e., thought that deviated from the principles of *Engsoz* - should literally no longer be possible to think, at least insofar as thinking is a function of language" (Zurich 1976, 74).
[59] *Arab, Poor, Disconnected.* In: SZ, 27.10.2003, 11.

functionalized as the work of Satan for the accumulation of hatred in order to demonstrate stability internally and readiness to fight externally.

Orwell's book *1984* shows literarily how the education to hate is organized and how the medial, synthetic generation of feelings of hate is calculated. Metaethical naturalism likes to hide behind enemy images. The absolute evil they embody quasi logically forces the corresponding liquidation reaction.

After this excursion the author wants to come back to the naturalistic fallacy and to the antinomy "being/value". The summary of both in an ontology claiming truth cannot be justified - as shown here. Islam now has two options; either it withdraws its absolute truth claim in favor of an ethical or religious naturalism based on plausibility by sifting the Qur'an historically-critically, or it takes every opportunity to protect this absolute claim from intellectual attack. In the first case, he has to change his strategy: instead of the imperative "You, man, as God's creature, must absolutely fulfill his will!" there can only be convictions whose explanatory power can find approval. Thus, there are many plausible arguments that can support religious Islam, but no logical implication. Neither sciences nor religions can justify an absolute claim to truth, because they are both based on ontological assumptions which themselves can no longer be questioned. There is a tightrope walk between metaethical and ethical naturalism. No matter how many normatively plausible arguments make a necessary being out of an ought; logically no ought can be derived from a being. If one projectively makes a being out of an ought or an ought out of a fact, the ideologically questionable **naturalistic fallacy is** present, which makes a universal claim to truth.

Because the two are mixed together in everyday life, fundamentalist ideologies have an easy time recruiting followers, as history proves. We need only recall the beginning of Islam, when there was great opposition to Muhammad's prophecies. Even the extinguishing of life was justified then for the sake of asserting God's rule before and by God; and this is exactly how militant Islamism presents itself today, because it has evaded current solutions to problems.

The premises for a metaethical fallacy are provided by Islam, which is prone to fundamentalism. Its consistent advocacy of an inseparability of political rule and religious convictions, its ignoring of the "value/truth" dichotomy, its claim to triple universality, its belief in proclaiming the only true religion and its knowledge, believed to be true, of its world-historical missionary mandate are the breeding ground on which modern Islamism builds its political argumentation. Instead of comforting people in borderline situations, the Islam afflicted by Islamism is not only indifferent to individual suffering through politicization, but deliberately brings it about by legitimizing violence.

God created the first human being as a Muslim, from whom all other humans are descended. The temporary disobedience to Allah's autocracy is countered by the promise that sometime in the near future humanity will return to its original Muslim state. But before this utopia has become reality, the high end also sanctifies lower means.

Specifically, these means, considered criminal and therefore reprehensible in themselves, lose their despicability when they are used for the sake of a noble ideal. A crime is thus transformed into a good deed.

5. Ideology criteria that characterize Islamism as a deficient ideology.

Already in the previous chapter, in which I tried to justify the high potential ideological character of Islam, which at the same time means its high susceptibility to ideology, the discussion has been conducted on the basis of ideology criteria; but the focus was on content implications. Now there is an extension in that the psychological ideological criteria, which have not yet been discussed, take over the leadership of the argumentation. The ideology criteria discussed may be mentioned again: Absoluteness of the claim to truth, totality claim, globalization claim, in addition an eschatological utopianism, the unity of religion and state and ignoring the naturalistic fallacy. Now the remaining criteria of "knowledge deficit," "knowledge monopoly," "dichotomous interpretation schemes," "demonized enemy stereotypes," "empty formulas," ambivalence, "asymmetry," and "selective perception" will be presented as characteristics of a deficient ideology, which - as much has already become clear - also includes Islamism.

But before that, I would like to present the **"ideological circle"** that leads ideological thinking around in circles. It consists of the interaction of the "reverse naturalistic fallacy" (Bayertz 1987, 157-185) and the "naturalistic fallacy". Both are logically untenable. The first, as a production process, infers from the subjective ought to an objective being; it is a projection mechanism, "will, drive, and need drive interpretations of reality-especially each one's own reality-again and again beyond the limits of reality into the realm of illusion, fiction, and self-deception" (Birnbacher 1996, 46): they objectify human desires and longings for certainty. The second starts from an ideology-infused concept postulated as fact and infers a normative ought from this object believed to exist objectively: being thus implies at the same time not only a being, but additionally a maxim of belief or behavior. Terms such as God, nature, history, justice, world, people, freedom are rarely used descriptively; ideological connotations resonate in them to varying degrees[60] . Many of the following ideological criteria can be seen as psychological reflections of these false conclusions and empty phrases, as "will-determined distortions of perception" (47).

---

[60] The concept of "border violation", which resides in the political sphere, turns the abstract idea of a state whose laws can only claim validity in a delimited area into a being with a very

First of all, it has to be asked whether the scientific criteria, because they can separate evaluative from descriptive statements, are not at the same time suitable to exclude ideologically shaped parts of theories. Vollmer's "Evaluation of Theories" (1998) serves as a catalog of criteria.[61] Geiger is of this opinion when he states:

> The logician and epistemologist decides between right and wrong statements. The ideology critic searches for the legalities that govern behind some false statements. (1968, 181).

He invokes the traditional concept of truth of adequation. According to this, ideology determines itself from the standpoint of rational objective thinking as "false thinking" (1984, 185), but explains this "false thinking" as being based "on the theorization and objectification of a primary emotional relation" (186). Just as for Tepe, the criterion "wrong" is not sufficient for him. Behind the statement of falseness there are projections or "legalities"; the cause of a theory deficit thus means here at the same time projectivity as the cause of the source of error.

Like a Kantian apriori, our way of life is only conceivable according to certain premises, they are "value attitudes as such" (Tepe 1988, 9). They cannot be explained away, but "we can change our 'value system'" (9).

How does man come to be at the mercy of such apriories? There must be a reason for their existence, and cultural anthropology finds it in the nature of man as an instinct-reduced being in the sense of Gehlen and also Lorenz, who has to compensate this reduction culturally (internalization of one's own culture). These culture-anticipating background assumptions do not spring from nothingness, they are "illusion-genealogically" (7) attributed to the subject (his habits of thought, his socio-cultural value system, his character, his conscious and unconscious will efforts and feelings), which he cannot reduce to zero. The question of the nature of these background premises can then lead

---

sensitive skin that is injured by an illegal border crossing and therefore has the right to prevent such "violations" with all due force.

[61] There, the latter names "internal consistency", "external consistency", "testability", "explanatory value" as scientific criteria (107-111).

further to the question of their origin, so that biographical and psychological elements can still be consulted.

If the subjective and quasi-objective value premises remain in the background, then they can do no 'harm'. Not infrequently, however, they are projected outward - consciously or unconsciously - and change the producer's relation to reality and his perception of the object. This then confirms in a cognitively inadmissible way one's own decision of will, one's own wishful thinking, one's own value premises. The workshop "Wishing, Wanting, Values" now works at full speed and produces rationalized utopias, illusions, theories, i.e. seemingly descriptive products. Functions and intentions of **ideologies(-)** 'eat' the object, so to speak, and excrete it again assimilated to both.

The "pressure of reality" already described forces man to invent compensating projections in order to escape the meaning-rejecting reality, his frailty and mortality. They are such that they can often depict exactly the opposite of what is, so that the ideal illusory world appears as true, the real world as illusory. In myths, religions and philosophies such behavioral patterns tending to collective projections have set themselves a monument.

There are now four ways to come to terms with the pressure of suffering. As a nihilist, one can turn to cynicism, which adds ridicule to the motto 'There is nothing worth living for' or 'Being is always already being to death'. As a normal citizen, one can seek protection and help in constructions that not only reduce the pressure of suffering, but also lead people into a world of values that they can defend with all their strength and in which they can find peace. Topitsch and Tepe show the third way in their analyses *"Erkenntnis und Illusion" and "Theorie der Illusionen"*, respectively. They see in their critiques an approximate method of "purposefully reducing the self-deception components [...]" (1988, 13) or "facing the harshness of reality, doing what is humanly possible and bearing the inevitable with composure" (1979, 228), a state of mind close to existentialism. However, it is difficult to convey to the normal person. The fourth way is shown by myths and religions, which promise a meaningful life through the belief in a higher being, which in truth guides the destiny and history of man by following its precepts.

Two different strategies of ideology critique correspond to the two ideology terms. The term "**ideology(-)**" (knowledge deficit) is assigned, as a basic theory, an epistemological approach; to the term "ideology (value attitude), insofar as it threatens to be overturned by cognitive claims in the sense of a normatively solely binding and absolute model of action, corresponds a socio-critical approach. A "true state of God," a "only true religion," the "best of all communities," the "seal of the prophet," "Allah as the only true God," the "true human rights" are vocabulary in which the absolute sociopolitical claim of Islam, today still instrumentalized and strikingly simplified by Islamism, manifests itself.

The social-critical method analyzes the value structure of social systems for its internal contradictions in order to avoid them. The projection theory can explain when a false theoretical and when an ideologically deficient argumentation is present. Both are untrue: the former, however, is subject to a correctable error (see the fallibilism[62] of Popper), the latter is a projection of will onto being, which is now voluntaristically impregnated by desires, but want to appear as being and secure this claim by an absolute truth claim. If this truth claim can be shaken, great social upheavals are to be expected. Metaphysical truths, however, are not falsifiable, not to be shaken, because they explain all processes as working of a supernatural force. However, they are also not empirically verifiable. Thus, the Muslim thanks Allah when his life proceeds in happy circumstances; but he also accepts calmly when great catastrophes befall him, since God will already know why.

5.2 Monopolies of knowledge

What is a "monopoly of knowledge"? Can such a 'monopolization' also be demonstrated in Islam? Monopolization of knowledge, which always implies a claim to absolute truth, is evident where access to knowledge is no longer generally guaranteed, where elites seek to legitimize their claim to power by making people believe that they are in possession of a higher truth. Such elitist institutions can be: God, priests, world-historical personalities, classes, races, religions, parties, scientists, doctors, gurus, and so on.

---

[62] Theories are not closed entities, they always contain parts that can be falsified, so that truth is reached step by step in terms of a scientific progress process. The falsification requirement also applies to social theories. Totalitarian worldview theories cannot be falsified because of the insistence on absolute truth possession; for if one breaks a piece out of this theory, the entire theory is called into question. Non-falsifiability as an imperative is thus a criterion for total systems of domination; but what has been said also applies to metaphysical theories.

"Justification instrument" is what Salamun (1975, 30) calls this kind of uncontrollable charismatic knowledge. Knowledge monopolization means justification and thus domination monopolization (shepherd - flock), which 'by nature' forces the excluded to submit to the will of the elite[63] , so that someone who denies this monopoly violates an order given by nature. The very questionable claim to rule on the basis of an even more questionable attribution of a 'higher' knowledge can thus refer to a naturally guaranteed order in the broadest sense, against which there is no appeal. We still know, after all, the "providence" by which the pronouncements of the 'leader', however nonsensical, could be passed off for higher insight. The claim to truth grew with the hierarchical position in the party. Lenin, Stalin and Mao are also prime examples of an elitist monopoly of knowledge by one person and one party, the terrible consequences of which still reverberate today.

Islam sees itself as a natural religion and world order that has built its monopolization of knowledge - already described in detail here - hierarchically. "The entire design of the Islamic religion is an expression of strong theocentrism, of unrestricted devotion to God and unconditional submission to his will," is how Khoury (2001, 49) assesses the "conception of God in Islam" (59). All other religions can only claim a temporary possession of truth, since Muhammad "abrogated" the historical errors of Judaism and Christianity in Islam. The Prophet's pronouncements, the hadiths, are also of divine origin according to the Islamic conception and are likewise regarded as non-deniable guidelines of faith and life. Muhammad's life's work also remains uncriticized because it is regarded as pleasing to God. Although he does not claim divinity or godlikeness like Jesus, he is revered as godlike, which has exacerbated the cartoon controversy.

---

[63] In *1984*, Orwell vividly described a social construct that is determined by monopolization of knowledge. There are the "proles" who are excluded from any rule and live under reduced conditions, the representatives of the "outer party," small functionaries who are fobbed off with only crumbs, the representatives of the "inner party," who can be compared with the rule of the Soviet "*nomenklatura*," and the "GB," whose pronouncements immediately congeal into "iron laws" that must be followed absolutely. This has emerged from a real party leader, but in the meantime (see Lenin) has been transfigured into a fictitious being. This transfigured "nothing", this "superman", whose immortality is guarded by the "inner party", stands for the irrefutable truth. It is valid because the "GB" has said it so. He is a 'truth instance' which legitimizes itself.

Between the people of faith and the highest metaphysical authority (God), a religious functionary class has established itself, which in Shiite Islam enjoys not only high esteem but also, in some cases, the privilege of being "second in the universe to the omnipotence of God" (Djassemi 2002, 71). Why in Shiite Islam the imams are allowed to occupy a god-like position is explained by Djassemi (2002), who has already been quoted several times, in his book *Power and the State in Islam*. Here, the genesis, facts and consequences of such a privileged position, which has not occurred until now, will be presented only very briefly.

The original conception of a Muslim state as founded by Muhammad envisions a "theo-absolutism" (28) that provides for an identity of religious pervasiveness of the body politic with the official power of a caliph. By enlarging the Islamic territory of rule, a particularism develops through which several parallel ruling sultans embody power, so that the personal unity prophet-umma, caliph-umma in the sense of a theo-absolutism can no longer be maintained. The "twin theory" (28) of state and religion now applies and becomes constitutive for Shiism. As God's governor, every Muslim holds the "general caliphate" (44) of being Allah's governor on earth in certain areas; on the other hand, only a select few hold the "special caliphate of the imams" (44). But many people are not capable of satisfying even the general caliphate. The "spiritual immaturity of the masses" (57) is justified, how could it be otherwise, with a Koran verse, Sura (6:116):

> "And if you obey the majority of those on earth, they will lead you away from the way of Allah. They follow only a delusion, and they merely presume."

(This verse can also be interpreted anti-democratically.) In contrast, there are the divinely inspired imams, whose elite status, "based on the divine habitus of reason" (57), is established by the following Quranic verse:

> We offered the perfect pledge of trust to the heavens and the earth and the mountains, but they refused to bear it and shrank from it. But man took it upon himself. Verily, he is very unjust, ignorant" (33:72).

Together with the next verse, according to the interpretation of the Imams, the following meaning results: Man, as a weakly created being, can only have been afflicted with hubris when he accepts the difficult office of becoming God's confidant, while all other forms of being reject this request. Therefore, first of all, he is arrogant and stupid. This is generally true; however, there are also people who are worthy of spiritually representing God's concern in the world, the Imams, so that they are "in possession of the entrusted knowledge of salvation" (58). They possess the *wilaya*, the divine perfection of power. Together with unsinfulness, the "temporal right to rule" (59), and participation in "the divine substance of light" (61), they form the new class, "divinely ordained, aristocratic authorities" (61). The separation of the faithful into the caste of imams with divine authority and that of the immature people of faith has political consequences, namely a 'natural' relationship of domination and a 'natural' relationship of dependence.

How can a democracy be advocated under these conditions, since one cannot leave the shaping of a divine state to the immature people of God? Political and religious rule are therefore exercised in personal union.

Particularly among the Iranian Shiites, a monopolization of religious-political life is taking place. On the one hand, there is the incapacitated, sinful people with little intellectual wealth; on the other hand, there are the incapacitated, divinely inspired mullahs and imams who exercise God's power on earth. Djassemi sees in this already practiced form of rule the ideal of bringing a state under a "total domination of divine ideology" (92). The monopoly of God-knowledge reserved for the elite becomes an unassailable monopoly of total, even totalitarian rule. The lowest in this pyramid of truth are we, the possible *djimmi, who,* because according to God's will they possess only a share of knowledge afflicted with deficiencies, are in need of Muslim guidance and direction in the most favorable case.

5.3 Dichotomous interpretation scheme

What do "dichotomous interpretive schemes" mean? Does the Qur'an make use of such schemes? The term "schematizing" does not describe an extrasubjective reality, but a mental procedure according to which a very differentiated fact is brought into a clear but factually reduced form (see Lenk chapter). Thus, in schematizing, reality is swallowed, which, however, is negligible on the basis of pragmatic considerations. This art product fulfills the task of rapid orientation without taking every detail into account. A dichotomous interpretive scheme or pattern thus represents a perspective for evaluating reality for the purpose of better cognitive receptivity. In the examples cited, however, it is not so much a matter of cognitive receptivity as of appellative influence.

Our reality is so differentiated that it cannot be adequately judged at a glance, which is often necessary in everyday life, so that nuances are neglected in favor of bipolar judgment systems. Harsh dichotomies, namely black and white painting, friend - foe, beautiful - ugly, pro - con simplify everyday thinking, but also reduce it alarmingly. The dichotomies essentialize where one's own projective thinking intervenes. Although they are only subjective categories of a preliminary and simplified assessment of an issue, they are often objectified. Before that, the negative or positive tint of the schemata is connoted accordingly. One's own conception then gets the predicates good and right, that of the opponent those of evil and wrong. Thus one and the same process can be judged completely differently depending on the point of view. (The 2nd Gulf War is evaluated by the USA as a war of liberation from a bloody dictatorship, by the fundamentalists as a "crusade against Islam").

Dichotomies can degenerate, i.e., by becoming increasingly charged, one's own point of view becomes the point of view par excellence, and the other is defamed as completely unacceptable. Dichotomous thinking is, as will be shown, a typical method of debate in the Koran, which can very quickly turn into a friend-foe image according to the motto "Whoever is not for me is against me. The many shadings of the real are lost in the dichotomization.

The social function of dichotomies: Those who think alike and similarly form a community, find a center of identification, exclude other interpretations of other groups, polarize relations between opponents, gain a 'fixed' point of view, give the world an a priori interpretation. In the Koran, the dichotomy "heaven - hell" occurs in many variations. In Sura (5:2), whoever denies faith is a loser in the hereafter, whoever believes gets eternal reward (5:10), the disbelievers are "inmates of hell" (5:11), "Allah loves those who do good" (5:14,), "Allah has power over all things" (5:20), "That would be a disgrace to them, and in the hereafter they will have severe punishment" (5:34), Whoever follows Allah succeeds (5:36). The disbelievers "will have a painful punishment" (5:37), "Their chastisement will be everlasting" (5:38), "He punishes whom He wills and He forgives whom He wills" (5:41), "Whoever does not judge by what Allah has sent down - these are the unjust" (5:46), (...) - these are the outrageous" (5:48), "Verily Allah does not show the way to the people of the unjust [Jews and Christians - the author]" (5:52), "Evil indeed is what they do" (5:63), the unbelievers incur "a painful punishment" (5:108), those who "disbelieve [.... are inmates of hell" (5:87), "For the truthful are gardens through which rivers flow, therein they shall abide forever and ever" (5:120).

The believing part of the followers should thereby gain reinforcement and fortification of their value system, the opponents should be unsettled or deterred from harming the followers of this faith, and the undecided should be convinced of the truth of the message. The proclamation is secured by the appearance of a higher being and a human herald who delivers the divine message to the religious community without any additions of his own. In doing so, the prophet, in order to elevate his and his message, uses the rhetorical form of the dichotomous interpretive scheme; for psychologically differentiated, the message has no socializing power. He himself, the prophet, is not aware that he is operating a propaganda tool in epistemological terms; he is deeply gripped by the truth of his message, which is why he insists on it and its authorization by Allah. A function of order and orientation takes on a life of its own, is objectified and essentialized by means of truth-pathetic rhetoric, and is projectively secured by a higher being.

The following dichotomies of content are played out in the cited examples in the Qur'an:

Believers	Infidel
Sky	Hell
Winner	Loser
Reward	Punishment
Just	Unfair
Muslims	Atheists, Animists, Jews, Christians
Life Orientation	Disorientation
everlasting joy	everlasting torment
Believers do good	Unbelievers do evil
Believers tell the truth	Infidels lie

The dichotomies incorporated in the Koran are actually only variations of the "good-evil" dichotomy. The Koran proclaims a priori a Manichaean world in which there is no place for intermediate tones: only the either-or applies. God or Satan - both principles form the world of a relentless dispute, in which, however, good always remains the victor in the end. The West, we are on the sloping road of losers. The dichotomizations, if relied upon alone, degrade the power of judgment and thereby make the one who believes them to be true the victim of political and religious strategies, especially since the dichotomizations can easily be emotionalized as love or hate. An instrumentalization of these dichotomies lends itself, as it were, to ontologizing the divine prophecies in such a way that, in the name of God, leniency is shown to one's own co-religionists, but relentless persecution to those of a different faith is practiced. Thus they turn into a "friend-enemy stereotyping", into a highly exaggerated image of the enemy. Dichotomies negate all intermediate values between good and evil, so that the multi-layered reality cannot be perceived at all, which we witness every day. The world is divided into friend/foe, into the "house of Islam" and the "house of war," into believers and "crusaders," into martyrs and "human garbage" (if one follows the language of the Islamists) and is also perceived in this way.

5.4 Demonization of the Enemy Image, Glorification of One's Own Role

In Frisch's Andorra and Orwell's *1984,* the emergence and work of such enemy images is shown in literary terms. They are projections that misunderstand each other, they are alienated and distorted self-images. By stylizing the opponent as the enemy, the enemy as a demonic grimace, totalitarian regimes in particular fulfill the goals of "integration of [their own - the author's] social groups," reduction of "internal conflicts" (Salamun 1975, 25), total emotionalization of the masses up to their collective suicide, destruction of the opponent made into an inhuman as a morally imperative act. They follow an inner logic which, especially in the case of warlike conflict, brings the projection machine to ever higher speeds.

In reality, soldiers face each other who are sorry family men, good work-mates, helpful[64] comrades, in other words, men involved in a rich life. If they shoot their counterpart, then it is exactly as if they would kill their own comrade. A random generator could play fate here. But in reality, behind every soldier of his own and the other side there is a political, religious or ethnic or multi-base value system that instigates killing as a motivation; for, as I said, one would hardly kill a friendly neighbor even on orders. Soldiers who see the humane neighbor in their enemy are extremely unsuited to their task. So the state brings out prejudices, reawakens historical enmities, recalls victorious battles, creates atrocity tales about the enemy, surrounds its own heroic figures with a transcendent aura, labels opponents as horrible brutes, in short: a figure of light now fights against absolute evil.

Since the other side is then forced to start the projection machine as well, their opponent also becomes a monster deserving hatred and death, their own position, on the other hand, is thus idealized into a just, necessary, justified fight against evil. It comes to an all-out war, because there are no opponents to neutralize, but monsters to destroy. The bad thing is that an invaded people, if it does not want to perish, cannot help but strengthen its will to resist with **ideology(-)**-soaked enemy images.

The emergence and use of enemy images is vividly described in Orwell's novel *1984*. They have the aforementioned function of assigning everything positive to their producers, everything negative to their opponents.[65] The figure of light, the *Big Brother*, "is infallible and omnipotent. Every success, every achievement, every victory, every scientific discovery, all wisdom, all happiness, all virtues are directly attributed to his leadership [...]" (191). His despicable counterpart, Goldstein, "was the first traitor, the earliest defiler of

---

[64] The 2nd World War has shown that the anti-Hitler coalition, in order to mobilize the masses (when no concentration camps had yet been liberated), according to this inner logic itself promoted this ideologization, so that this coalition resorted to similar war atrocities as National Socialism. Therefore, whoever starts a war must not be surprised, on the basis of this almost natural law process of parallel ideological self-stimulation, that these mechanisms have an effect on himself.

[65] As high school students in the former GDR, we went to see the film "Ernst Thälmann" in class. Thälmann and his fighting colleagues, although they should have appeared emaciated and ragged as exploited people, had well-fed, sympathetically healthy faces, while the 'exploiters' appeared repulsive with their ugly, gray appearance.

the purity of the party. All crimes later directed against the party, all treacheries, acts of sabotage, heresies [...] went directly back to his heresies" (14). Compared to the shining aura of the "GB", his negative counter-image is ugly, his appearance "resembles a sheep's face" (14).

Both manifestations perform quasirational functions:

- Demonization of an opponent as the worst enemy and glorification of one's own role as the absolute good,
- Stabilization of one's own power and personification of the demonized enemy image for the purpose of destroying reality by means of bogus argumentation,
- Emotionalization that leads to permanent activation of commitment to the "GB" and against its antagonist Goldstein, a repulsive-looking monstrosity,
- Standardization and control of all human life expressions into pro "GB" (good) and contra "GB" (bad and evil),
- Prohibiting rational counterarguments, reinforcing irrational arguments such as faith and trust (falsification prohibition),
- Justification of political repression and murder,
- Mobilization of accomplices for whom it provides an alibi,
- Solidarization of the underprivileged with the privileged in the face of their own fictitious impending doom or coming great political and economic successes.

With their "special official power," the Shiite ayatollahs already partially embody the figure of the "GB. Images of the enemy can be constructed like dummies on the drawing board; skillful propaganda only needs to instill them with 'lifelikeness'.

Orwell describes a scene in which a propagandist is in the middle of enumerating the atrocities of Eurasia, then, when he learns that Eastasia is the enemy, sings praises of the enemy he has just reviled (Zwiedenken). Behind the production of demonizations is the will to annihilation of the producers. Demonized enemy images can completely neglect reality and have their own logic of incorrigibility. A negative projection is present in an enemy image, but also a self-recognition, because one's own negative characteristics are exaggerated there to the grotesque, so that they appear as alien characteristics of the enemy. When you look your enemy image in the eye, you see yourself, but so far away from your own ego ideal that you do not recognize yourself. In addition, there are many reinforcing illusion mechanisms, so that enemy images have a long life and are resistant to concrete experiences of a different kind. Orwell's novel has a clear political goal, namely to expose such constructs as instruments of power politics. He chooses the medium of "film" here and has Wilson, his hero, take notes in "neo-speak," a very reduced English:

> "The little boy screamed in fear and hid his head between her breasts as if he wanted to crawl into them, and the woman put her arms around him and comforted him. Although she herself was beside herself with fear, she covered him as well as she could, as if she thought her arms could keep the bullets away from him. Then the helicopter dropped a 20 kg bomb between them [...] then there was a wonderful shot of a child's arm flying high, high and higher and higher into the air [...] there was much applause from the party voices" (11).

The physical destruction of the hated enemy is supposed to be accompanied by voluptuous pleasure and deep satisfaction in order to emotionally satisfy and strengthen the feeling of hatred. Decapitations or dragging the dead enemy through the streets are delivered to us free of charge by the media and provide proof of Orwell's negative utopia of the rule of a deficient ideology.

The Koran does not know any demonization of enemy images; Satan is more the evil principle than a concrete figure, so that for several centuries a relatively peaceful coexistence with Islam was possible. But the dichotomy "good/evil", "God/Satan" is always in danger of being transformed into the demonization of the stereotypes "true believers/subhuman infidels".

At the moment we are witnessing a demonization of Christianity and the Western world, which is leading to an ever-growing confrontation with the Islamic world.[66] Unbearable is the statement that the killing of Americans is a

---

[66] The newspaper Al-Quds Al Arabi writes on 23.2.1998 in London in a "Manifesto of the International Islamic Front for a Jihad against the Jews and Crusaders:
"In the name of God, we call on every Muslim who believes in God and asks for forgiveness to obey God's command to kill and steal from Americans wherever he encounters them and is able to do so. Moreover, we call upon the Islamic scholars and leaders and youths and soldiers to launch attacks against the armies of the American devils and against their allies among the devil's helpers" (quoted in Barth 2003, 152 f.). The mass murder planned by English Muslims - in August 2006 - shows that the constant hate preaching against the West has been successful because, legitimized by ideologized religious justification, they pass off the killing of people as God's will. Again, I was hoping for a clarifying word from the Muslim clergy; but they show understanding for the potential assassins by referring to England's foreign policy. For me, it is a matter of spiritual complicity, because the Koran is deliberately

divine command. Everything that can be seen negatively in this world is attributed to the enemy image of "Israel," "America" or the "West in general." The entity that creates enemy images is Islamism, which can invoke many Koranic dichotomies. But that Allah should have issued a kill order against Americans is a perfidious instrumentation of God by Islamism. If anyone (figuratively speaking) should be punished by death, it is only propagandists who, by synthesizing and demonizing enemy images, incite religions, peoples, races and individuals against each other.

5.5 Blank formulas

Salamun divides them into three groups: "pseudo-empirical," "pseudo-normative," "and pseudo-essential" (1975, 32-36). The pseudo-essential ones he calls "illusions of true entities" after Weldon.[67] What they have in common is that their content is considered sacrosanct and that it is a sacrilege to inquire into or even criticize their content. They are "holy words" and represent truncated **ideologies(-)**.

Pseudo-empirical empty formulas are terms that only pretend to have an empirical content, but are in fact compatible with many interpretations, so that they cannot be falsified. They are politically versatile products of interpretation. The term "salvation event" can serve as an example, which believes to describe the actual action of a supra-naturalistic force, which is not possible. Pseudo-normative empty formulas are terms that are intended to influence behavior, but for which "no operational definitions" (32) can be given: they elude clear criteria of their scope of application. They have the property,

> that certain linguistic formulas have been recognized through the centuries as relevant insights or even as fundamental principles of being, knowing, and valuing, and still are today - not although, but precisely because and insofar as they have no or no further specifiable factual and normative content (Topitsch 1960, 236).

Their content is vague, diffuse, so that as catchwords they can fill in the problem areas of an ideology and at the same time as 'battle cries' of groups,

---

misused to appropriate Allah for crimes against humanity. Thus, the true godless are the Islamists.

[67] Quoted from Salamun (1975, 34).

parties and states they can consolidate and legitimize their own position, defame the opponent, motivate for the 'final battle', liquidate the 'enemy' and strengthen national consciousness. These empty words conceal two pragmatic aspects, not only:

> give the appearance of higher justification to any ideology, but they can also pretend a constancy of the highest moral-political principles by their always constant wording, while they are compatible with any possible normative order [...] (264).

Every **ideology(-)** immediately takes possession of such empty words and interprets them according to its theory. Pseudo-essential empty formulas appear with the claim to contain relevant knowledge, i.e. already a concept analysis should bring to light their significant contents, the 'true' meaning which this concept has. This is an illusion, because concepts must refer to a content. If we assume any kind of assignment of concepts to an external world, then the concept must have a meaning that is empirically or logically demonstrable.

This is not the case with pseudo-essential empty formulas, so that for them there is no "true meaning of words" (34). They are, as Lenk says, similar to values in a special way "constructs of interpretation" (1994, 164). In them, positions are reflected "sociofically" (164) "through social convention and safeguarding, precisely through institutionalization or ideal obligation or normative expectation [...]" (164). What Lenk defines here for the concept of 'value' is especially true for ideologically synthesized word-shells. This makes it clear that there cannot be a 'true' interpretation of pseudo-essential empty formulas that applies to everyone. Because of their vagueness, they are capable of absorbing projections of a community's ideals, which are then analytically reinterpreted as entities into cognitive facts.

It is worth recalling the times of the Cold War, when the terms "peace," "democracy," "'true' justice," "just and unjust war" had completely opposite meanings depending on the political system.[68] Islamism is beginning to embrace these 'ambiguous' vocabularies. These terms have their justification when criteria of their use are given, because then they can be criticized.

They have a genesis. In the age of "animism" in the sense of Monod, such concepts and ideas were held to be true until then the "process of rationaliza-

---

[68] To be read in *East Good - West Bad. On double standards and divided consciousness in politics.* (Dittmar 1977).

tion leading from mythology to philosophy" (1996, 236) diluted their cognitive content so that they had to seek a new refuge, namely in the realm of worldviews. As long as the practice of Islam was entrenched in mythic and religious thought, that is, until the European Enlightenment, it knew no empty formulas because it represented a mythic-religious ontology. With secularization, the unambiguous semantic content of these terms also disappeared. In the context of the Islamization of Islam, they then became buzzwords, empty words that also resemble secular Western thinking. If someone believes in God, mind you, is personally convinced of him and his work, then this concept contains a constitutive content that can be stated. If, however, God is set as an absolute quantity, if it is claimed of him that he is in the possession of the absolute truth, which he communicates to chosen ones, then all proofs, scientific as well as empirical-practical, are missing for it; because there are several religions, which make this claim, but cannot redeem it, except with threat of violence against doubters. God has unfortunately become a political catchword in Islam (see quote Al-Quds Al Arabi), which, depending on the intention of the activists, can be tolerance, jihad, terrorism, persecution and murder of dissenters, object of highest worship, calculus of domination, unlimited power. Through Islamism, God has become a worn-out coin with which arbitrary, inhumane, political murder can be exchanged. The use of the ambiguous term "justice" is similarly problematic.

5.6 Ambivalence

The following three ideology criteria: Ambivalence, Asymmetry, and Selective Perception, which drive the projection machine toward **ideology(-)**, are intended to make understandable the irritations that unsettle Western observers in their assessment of Muslims. They are a sign of the successful overlaying of Islam by Islamism that has taken place. All three mechanisms can be well seen in the 'political' pronouncements of Iranian President Ahmadinejad, so that Western politicians are subject to a fallacy when they confront Islamist regimes with their political categories, which they consider to have international consensus. Tepes' book *"Fundamentalism as a Form of Thought,"* provides compelling evidence that all fundamentalist systems are based on a view of the world dominated by **ideology(-).** To the western-profane thinking with its constant revising and falsifying of "site-bound thinking" (Mannheim) in order to come closer to the ideal of objectivity and intersubjectivity, corresponds a completely different conception of reality of the thinking of Islamism, so that misunderstandings between both camps are the order of the day.

Predictability in politics and life serves one's own orientation, but almost more so the orientation of partners in these two areas. One's own actions are oriented according to the assessment of the other's predictability; likewise, the other can make preliminary decisions because he can assess my own trading premises. We can speak of "reciprocal trust building" here. But if one leaves several options open, the contracting party becomes uncertain. If, on the other hand, one has to assume that one's partner is unpredictable, mutual distrust arises because actions and reactions are no longer predictable. The nuclear poker game of Iranian President Ahmadinejad is a good example of this. The unpredictability of the other often manifests itself in his rejection because he is not expected to do only good.

The authors who have published articles in *"Christen und Muslime"* (2006), an edited volume of the Protestant Academies in Germany, serve here as the basis for the presentation of this problem. Alboga (2006) speaks of a "fundamental sense of justice in Islam" (67). As a result, he argues, "the Muslim community, and thus each individual Muslim, [is] called to establish justice on earth [...]" (67). This means nothing other than that Islam by 'nature' believes it has leased the concept of "justice," a very common empty formula, from which the monopoly on justice for the world then follows. Emphasis on sovereignty and simultaneous permitted and required intervention in the legal order of other states, i.e. contradictions, generate ambivalence and therefore rejection.

This is an unreasonable imperial claim that can be used to justify any military or political intervention and invasion. Such a term can only be used if very precise criteria of its use can be specified. The belief in peaceful coexistence with Muslims falters because at any time any measure taken by the Western world must pass a 'justice test' (according to what criteria, actually?) before the self-appointed 'high Islamic councils' so that the religious feelings of Muslims are not 'offended'.

On the one hand, Islam is moderate in this text with regard to its claim to absolute truth, in that the author admits that there are two layers in the Koran that are to be evaluated differently, the historical layer, i.e., the one that is strongly limited in time, and the ahistorical, unchanging layer. But this is not the doctrinal view of Islam. In this regard, I would like to cite Abdullah (2001, 27) once again:

> "For the Muslim, the Koran [...] is the image of an eternal, supra-historical original of revelation, which is kept with God. [...]. So the Muslim tries to understand his holy book in a different way, namely in recitations recited aloud. In this way he makes the Koran inwardly his own. Consequently, he also uses Quranic formulations in profane life and appropriates a Quranic way of thinking that shapes his worldview."

Which is true now: double-layeredness or eternal original? On the other hand, the term "justice" creeps in again under the cloak of supra-temporal world justice. It now appears as a global claim of Islam to install a just world. The term "justice" turns out to be a useful empty formula and meaningful-sounding catchword that can be used for all kinds of operations.[69] Any state can easily get into the crosshairs of 'justice-loving' Islamism by using this formula. But the author's 'justice debate' is about Islamization of Europe. This distant goal moves closer if his demand is met:

> Turkey's accession to the EU would be the most innovative contribution of a secular state with a Muslim population to the further development of contemporary modernity and modern societies (Alboga 2006, 68).

The many Islamic ghettos in Europe unfortunately do not confirm the "further development as a contribution to contemporary modernity towards a modern society".

That Turkey, in contrast to the goals of its founder Kemal Atatürk, has meanwhile become an Islamic, even Islamist state, i.e., that it follows principles of Islam or Islamism and increasingly dismantles secular positions, Pflüger asserts in the elevated language of "yes, but" diplomacy (2004, 274-283).

---

[69] What the skillful use of this word template can achieve was demonstrated in the 2005 Bundestag election campaign. Without any criterion of the content of the term, so that one could not be held accountable, a party claimed and celebrated the ownership of this term with holy seriousness by adding the positively connoted term "social" to it. This was successful, so that in the sense of dichotomizing the opponent, the latter was quickly demonized as the fiend of a policy of social coldness and inhumanity, which brought the 'opponent' of 'social justice' high losses of votes, but gave its own clientele such a high increase (compared to the polls) that it was almost enough to retain power. At the time (2006), both parties, which had previously accused each other of cutting social welfare and deceiving voters, were working together more or less cooperatively in a coalition.

What is to be made of the Islamist Erdogan, who said: **"Our bayonets are our minarets"** (quoted in Pflüger 2004, 275)? Foreign Minister Gül's demand in 2003 that "the Islamist organization Milli Görus in Germany must be supported" (275), of course by the German state, by whom else, is also alarming. One increasingly gets the impression that Ankara is using Turks living in Germany to exert domestic and foreign policy pressure on Germany by relying on nationalist and Islamist effects, i.e. using them as a **"fifth column.**

The lack of truthfulness of many Islamic and especially Turkish institutions, behind which political interests are to be suspected, is expressed in an article of the RP of 19.10.06, A7. Under the headline "How Christianity is portrayed in the Middle East" it says:

"According to a study, the image of Christianity in textbooks of the Middle East is often incomplete and one-sided. Researchers from the University of Rostock and Erlangen/Nuremberg had examined almost all textbooks of Egypt, Palestine, Turkey and Iran from 2000 to 2005. According to Reiss, the project was intended to find out what image of Christianity is conveyed to schoolchildren in the respective countries. According to the study, most textbooks portray Islamic culture as superior and tolerant, and Christian culture as inferior and aggressive."

One can no longer hear the assertion and affirmation of do-gooders and the Turkish public that this country belongs to Europe because it represents a similar value system. The psychological mechanisms of Islamic fundamentalism are on display here in their purest form. But even worse is the fact that Turkey, which has applied for EU membership, is deliberately educating its youth to be anti-Europeans, because it is only about our 'monetary values', not about our values. A picture is coming together here that should fill us with a great deal of distance from Turkey's entry into the EU. Neither the Cyprus problem, nor the coming to terms with the genocide of the Armenian people (they were only 'worthless Christians'), nor religious freedom, nor the liberation of women, nor the end of the defamation of the West have been redeemed as basic demands of civilization. The fundamental rejection of our Western value system generally leads to a rejection of our educational system, our language, our culture and our social structures.

The problem lies in the use of the term "culture" as a normative empty formula. As a descriptive term, it demands the fulfillment of generally accepted criteria that can describe the essence of any culture. These are downgraded to plausibility arguments when it comes to evaluating it as a normative term (high culture, low differentiated culture). In this case, subjective premises play into the assessment, so that it becomes subject to discussion. If textbooks assume the unquestioning and uncritical superiority of one's own culture and the inferior other cultures, they evade a discussion about the descriptively describing and normatively evaluating concept of culture and occupy it with propaganda and projections.

Ambivalence thus also means the gaping of a large gap between word and deed, which unsettles the perceiver. The credibility of Islam is not increased by this contribution, because here political globalism, Islamism, Turkish national interests and Islamic religiosity form a community of interests that is difficult to see through.

The author Affoldenbach (2006) analyzes the "Islamic Charter" (72); this is a critique and appreciation of this charter by a Western church official. In principle, this charter, which is published shortly after 9/11/2001 in February 2002, is to be welcomed, because "on the factual level" it "made a number of clarifications" (72).

But there are also a lot of irritating formulations that trigger the aforementioned feeling of ambivalence in the reader because they are contradictory.

Thesis: Islam is a religion of peace.

Antithesis: The religiously motivated and legitimized terrorist activities show the opposite.

Thesis: Islam affirms the "pluralism recognized by the Koran" (76).

Antithesis: Other religions have the inferior status of "protectors" in Islam, which pluralism is meant?

Thesis: Everyone has the right "to change religion, to have a different religion or no religion at all" (76).

Antithesis: This right explicitly does not apply to many Islamic states, see the treatment of apostates in Afghanistan.

Thesis: The Charter is binding for German Muslims.

Antithesis: The Central Council of Muslims has no credentials to decide on this issue with official authority, since it represents only a small portion of Muslims in Germany.

Thesis: The "local legal order" (75) in the sense of the Basic Law is affirmed and a clerical "theocracy" (75) is not sought.

Antithesis: This legal position applies only in the diaspora as a "temporary exception, behind which the rule continues to be effective" (75). The term "clerical" distracts from the topic.

What does the qualification "local legislation" mean for the Basic Law? There is still a general legislation, the Islamic one, which stands above this legislation, which, if there is a possibility for its introduction, is enforced as the final world and value order. I would like to agree with the assessment of this charter as "ambivalent" (77), which leads to the fact that "confidence building does not really succeed" (77).

In the article *"Integration and Dialogue,"* Elyas defends the Islamic Charter against the accusation of "two-facedness" (83). Here I will only deal with thesis 15, which calls for "a contemporary understanding of the Islamic sources, which takes into account the background of modern life problems and the formation of an own Muslim identity. According to Elyas, this contemporary interpretation of the Quran, tailored to Europe, does not mean "detachment from the unambiguous undisputed precepts of Islam, but rather the application of the possibilities available in Islam for interpreting the authentic sources in a way that is appropriate to the time and place" (85), which means that the historical 'now' filters out the suras that are somehow compatible with modernity. According to this, there should be two layers of the Koran, the historically obsolete and the superhistorically innovative. But Elyas is very loudly silent about which ones they are. So which suras are compatible with modernity? Or which are controversial beliefs and no longer "appropriate for the time and place"? Which ones are always contemporary? According to this sophistry, Islam is first offered to us as a contemporary religion, which then presents the 'small print' later.

It is trivial to point out that Islam has been resistant to history since its inception and therefore has not reformed. We know neither the passages of the text that can be modernized nor those that are designed for eternity. What does Elyas think about the content of sura (3:7)?[70] Its text is similar to Thesis 15. This sura also seems to allow for flexible interpretation of parts of the Qur'an. In it, the reasonable interpretation of the ambiguous and possibly historical formulations is supported by a firm belief in Allah. However, the space created by different interpretations is immediately filled in by referring to the authority of Allah and knowledgeable Qur'anic scholars. The 'free zone' sought through a contemporary interpretation of the Koran immediately becomes religiously occupied through its undefinedness and thus becomes a useless argument.

The same can be taken from the argument that with full acceptance of the German legal system, "in family life [there remain] areas in which different treatment of men and women is unchangeable for Muslims" (85). Unfortunately, this difference is not specified. The protection of privacy, of the personality, of the family, is guaranteed by the Basic Law; why this restriction? Here, too, one cannot shake off the feeling that this backdoor is intended to legitimize the well-known repressions against women, now, however, even secured by law as German law.

Two passages in the Quran make the reader wonder, Sura (4:101): "And when you pass through the land, it shall not be a sin for you if you shorten the prayer, if you fear that the disbelievers will afflict you" and Sura (2:175): "Forbidding you only that which perishes of itself and blood and swine's flesh and that over which a name other than Allah has been invoked. But whoever is driven by necessity - not disobeying and exceeding the measure - for him it shall not be a sin. Allah is Oft-Forgiving, Most Merciful."

We are experiencing just the opposite today, with Islam in Europe insisting on its food, clothing and cultural regulations. These verses can be understood as a protective provision for Muslim traders, of whom Mohammed himself

---

[70] "It is he who sent down the book to you; in it there are verses of decisive importance - they are the basis of the book - and others capable of different interpretations. But those in whose hearts dwell corruption seek out those very verses that are capable of different interpretations, in the pursuit of discord and in the pursuit of interpretation. But none knows their interpretation but Allah and those who are firmly established in knowledge, who say: 'We believe in it; the whole is from our Lord' - and none heeds it except those endowed with understanding."

was one, but also as a method of proselytizing, which the prophet already practiced. Only when enough Muslims have immigrated inconspicuously into a country and have attained a secure status as apparently adapted fellow citizens, does Islam, led by Islamist activists, suddenly begin to play a dominant role that is visible everywhere. I interpret this form of mimicry as little trust-building ambivalence.

The most significant example of ambivalence, already reminiscent of deception and hypocrisy, is the relationship between publicly religiously prescribed sexuality culture and real sexual desire. Broder (2006, 154) quotes here a Google evaluation of how often sexual pages are clicked on from individual countries. The result[71] is perplexing. Islam projects its sexual frustrations as chastity in marriage, virginity before marriage and sexual abstinence in celibacy as a strict behavioral pattern onto society and wants to enforce them in the West as well.

But the secret, very sultry real-life desires find their outlet on the Internet. And these are of the kind that in the West are publicly left to the discretion of the individual. So an indictment of the 'immoral West' is really a self-accusation. Ambivalent behavior is one of the basic features of mission-oriented thinking and action in Islamic political 'culture'.

---

[71] "There were as many as seven Muslim countries among the top ten nations: Pakistan ranked first, Egypt second, Iran fourth, Morocco sixth, Indonesia seventh, Turkey eighth and Saudi Arabia ninth. Vietnam ranked third, India fifth and Poland tenth."

Asymmetry occurs in objects and, figuratively, in arguments. Asymmetrical arguments are "one-sided", overweighting either the pro or the con; asymmetrical objects are perceived as not well-formed because no axis of symmetry divides them into equal parts, they are heavily biased towards one direction: one is now perceived as too weak, the other as too strong. Symmetrical objects or arguments are thus characterized by a state of equilibrium, asymmetrical objects and arguments by a state of disequilibrium. The vernacular has coined the slogan "Making a mountain out of a molehill" for the fact that our perception not infrequently dramatizes harmless processes. The cause of this can be seen in the projection mechanism, which gives greater consideration to ideas of wanting and desiring that are agreeable to me than to those that are contrary to me. Commitment and ambition are often difficult to separate here.

Here the author Beyaz (2006) should have his say. He advocates an open dialogue between Muslims and Christians; however, "under the guise of inter-religious dialogue" (31) no proselytizing should be carried out. Quite astonished we can hear:

> Thus, my country, Turkey, has been facing an onslaught of Christian missionaries for some time. Jehovah's Witnesses as well as Protestant missionaries and Orthodox missionaries working for Greece [the old enemy - the author] are trying to corrupt and Christianize the faith of Muslim Turks at great expense. [...]. By trying to make the Turks who find their interest to be hostile to the state, flag, nation and generally against our state values, they suggest harmful things to them" (34).

To go into this nationalistic argumentation, which has been ideologically mutilated almost beyond recognition, would be too much for the honor. Here it is shown very memorably how one can exchange the role of the perpetrator with that of the victim. If one reverses this statement, then the real distribution of roles of the two religions in both countries becomes clear. Therefore, the author studiously avoids using examples and figures to support his claim. And who can blame a victim for resisting? (We Germans are familiar with this asymmetrical role reversal, which is so easy to accomplish. World War 2 'began' because the Poles attacked us and we had to shoot back). For years Christians have not been allowed to train priests, church property has been confiscated, they are suppressed by the state and defamed as spies. How can this author explain why there are thousands of mosques in Christian Germany and almost no Christian churches in Muslim Turkey, why there are Turkish organizations in Europe that want to abolish the secular constitutional state? This asymmetry of argumentation is reinforced by selective perception. This author does not perceive the Islamization of Europe at all or considers it to be natural, the ever-increasing de-Christianization of Turkey is reinterpreted as a wave of Christianization, the religiously motivated genocide of the Armenians is completely ignored, its mention is already under threat of punishment. This role reversal justifies the suppression of Christians because of alleged constant espionage and missionary work in Turkey and the special care of the German state for Islamic interests.[72] The golden rule that what one wants oneself must also be granted to the other is criminally neglected by our state to the disadvantage of Christians living in Muslim countries.

You can tell whether an argument is asymmetrical by looking at it in the mirror. Let us assume that hundreds of thousands of Europeans immigrate to Turkey, insist on their cultural identity, want to build churches everywhere and form a closed parallel society. The Turkish state would have to behave towards the Europeans in the same way as the Europeans behave towards the Turks. One should put this question in this way once to the Turkish state, then more asymmetrical abysses than symmetrical reasons for the own position would be found.

Elyas (2002) makes subtle but all the more important distinctions between the members of the book religions and those who prefer other value systems. The members of Christianity and Judaism are "other believers" (33), with whom Islam tries to "practice peace [...]" (33). "We are not speaking here of infidels, not of pagans, but of other-believers," he continues. Again, the mirroring does not work because Western states are largely neutral to worldviews unless they were planning a violent change in the democratic order. What does it mean when "unbelievers" and "pagans" are not under the protection of the peace obligation? Atheists, materialists, representatives of positivism, scientists in their scientific work are explicitly stigmatized and fought against. The term "pagan", probably the followers of religions which are not based on a

---

[72] I would like to refer here to a circulating anecdote on this subject, the fact of which has not been verified. The former rector of Heinrich Heine University, Prof. Kaiser, is said to have told Muslim students when they asked for a prayer room to be set up: 'If you see to it that such a facility is also set up for Christian students at the University of Istanbul, you will of course get a prayer room here'. To this day, to my knowledge, neither exists.

revelation according to the book, extends the range of the faith communities to be fought.

In Germany, if the 'heathens' were removed, no university could operate as it does now. The "duplicity" under the guise of peacefulness creates a distrust in the credibility of such 'proclamations' which is justified in my eyes. Not the human being as a value in itself, but religion from the point of view of political appropriation is here quite naturally applied as a human value standard.

This asymmetry can best be shown by the religious claim of Islam to practice religious tolerance towards other religions (the "owners of the scriptures"), to grant religious freedom.[73] "There is no compulsion in religion" according to Sura (2:257). In addition, there is the historical argument of tolerance[74] of Islam, which is fervently prayed after by many politicians, scientists and 'do-gooders' of the West, so that it enjoys sacred veneration as a fact and primordial premise of the assessment of Islam in general. (However, pointing out such tolerant historical periods of Islam cannot, for logical and factual reasons, be used as proof of today's tolerance or intolerance). It is true that "scripture owners," Jews and Christians, may not be forced to convert; but converts are welcome in Islamic communities. For reasons of symmetry and balance, this process of successful proselytization would also have to be reversible: Muslims would have to be able to convert to Christianity, for example. But here the principle of reversibility fails: It is forbidden for Muslims in many Islamic countries to adopt another religion on pain of death.[75] The justification for apostasy makes one sit up and take notice:

---

[73] See again sura (18:30) "Behold, we have prepared a fire for the wicked..." and sura (109:6) "You have your religion, and I have my religion."

[74] It is once quite useful to measure the 'love of peace' of the Muslims in Germany by the personalities to whom the mosques are dedicated. One is astonished to find that the philosophers of the Golden Age are left empty-handed. Instead, conquerors such as Mehmet II or Sultan Selim are honored with mosques (Tibi 2004, 100), especially Mehmet II, the conqueror of Constantinople, from where the campaigns against Christian Europe were then led. Such a name in a still Christian-oriented country is the program of a political Islam. I call on those responsible to put an end to this scandal of Islam, which is already so 'peace-loving' in its choice of symbols. Here, too, the popular wisdom applies: "Only the dumbest calves choose their own slaughterer". According to historical tradition, after the three-day sack of Constantinople, Mehmet II went to St. Sophia's Church, which he transformed into a mosque by praying (Serauky 1991, 358). In Germany, we allow mosques to be built whose namesakes proclaim victory over Christianity (East Rome).

[75] Müller (1996, 142-146) presents this issue and its background in great detail.

"This must not be confused with the problem of punishing the apostate, that is, punishing the Muslim who leaves his religion. For this is one thing and what we have said about freedom of religion is another. The Muslim, by submitting to God, has committed himself to abide by the rules of Islam and his creed. And if he apostatizes, he violates his obligation, harms the state and rebels against it. This requires punishment [...]" (quoted in Müller 1996, 144f).

The author would like to describe this justification as an ideology-soaked pattern of an asymmetrical orientalist dialectic, so that a commitment of Islam to religious freedom in the Western world would have to be acknowledged with great amusement.[76] The death penalty is justified with the *hadith*: "If someone drops his religion, kill him" (cited in Müller 1996, 145). It has been adopted as an alleged statement by Mohammed in the *sharia*, which knows no difference between state and religion, so that an offense against Islam is tantamount to an offense against the state. One is reminded of the Inquisition. This view relativizes the idea of the existence of universal human rights, whose validity extends only as far as they do not contradict Islamic law. Many Western 'intellectuals' do not embed the term "human rights" in this socio-cultural context, but simply translate it into the Western version and are very taken with the progressiveness of the human rights debate in Islam. [77]

But the even stronger thesis "The dignity and with it also the human rights, however, Islam has given to man", with him the human rights "have already been declared 14 centuries ago, in the "most complete way and with the widest limits", "comprehensively and profoundly determined" (quoted after Müller 1996, 125f.) underlines the universal claim of Islam to sole interpretational world sovereignty. While by the West human rights are regarded as common

---

[76] Under a different aspect, this conceptual problem has arisen before, namely with the pseudo-essential empty forms as they were often in use in the diction of communism. Dittmar (1977) works on the problem that such empty formulas could mean something completely different in the case of linguistic sameness, e.g. peace, so that in the case of apparent sameness completely different interpretations, East or West, dominated the political and economic language. In *Erkenntnis und Illusion,* Topitsch (1979) analyzed such empty formulas *and* relegated them to the realm of ideology.

[77] Islam knows two feuding partial worlds, the "house of Islam" and the "house of war". If the Muslim wishes "Salam" (related to the term "Islam"), then this greeting of peace is only valid in the "house of Islam", this is supposed to encompass the whole world one day. With those, who live in the "house of war", we, there cannot be such a peace from the totalitarian claims mentioned, peace is for this part of mankind a useful, appeasing vocabulary, because this is basically not capable of peace at all.

property by the act of self-determination, as a humanistic superstructure to which it subordinates itself, Islam constructs with the dichotomy "Western human rights/Islamic human rights" a competitive relationship on an unequal level, which only one can win, the 'superior' Islamically founded human rights, which now make universal claims. What could be more obvious than that in an Islamic world state to be created, Islamic human rights should also enjoy top priority.

In the language of Islamism, therefore, totalitarian power structures have already essentialized themselves, interpreting human rights in their own way. Increasingly, distrust of Islam's verbal professions is spreading in the Western world, especially since here, too, reality is perceived in a distorted way through selective perception. More and more, Islamism is occupying the key terms of the social level, which as empty formulas permit arbitrary interpretations, with its contents, which now only feign content uniformity through compatibility of their linguistic form with Western terms. The test for symmetry is able to discover and criticize ideologically deficient implications.

Another blatant example of asymmetry should be used here. Al-Qaeda reacts to a quote of the Pope, which refers to an event 600 years ago, with the outrageous words "We say to the servant of the cross: Wait for the defeat [...]. We will smash the cross" (RP of 19.09.2006, A5). The Pope's Islam-critical quote is meant to call for outlawing all use of violence by religions. Al-Qaida's answer is the proclamation of an all-out war to destroy Christianity. Had not the Byzantine emperor spoken the truth in this quote when he challenged an Islamic scholar, "Show me what new thing Mohammed brought, and there you will find only bad and inhumane things like this, that he prescribed to spread the faith he preached by the sword" (RP, Sept. 16, 2006, A2)? Al-Qaeda's reactions expose them because they deny and at the same time preach exactly what Muhammad is accused of, in the sense of an irregular total war. Here, any argument from reason loses its force.

5.8 Selective perception

The philosophy of perception is an infinite field. A large part of it are psychological-empirical findings, which cannot be dealt with here. Nevertheless, with the help of examples a sufficient explanation of the phenomenon shall be tried, because here only the ideologically explainable aspects of the facts shall be explained.

But first some short preliminary remarks. Although the term "perceiving" wants to make believe that our cognitive apparatus can grasp the external world objectively, there can be no question of it. Sense data are taken in and bundled by the mind into concepts, so that an image of reality results - this simple formula does not work out, not even in the case of the supposedly passive and therefore particularly objective data recording, as optical illusions prove. "We are," according to Lenk," constructing beings even already on the subconscious layer of our perceptual experiences (...)" (1994, 93). Weighty objections to the "camera model" (Lenk) are also raised by sensory physiology. For physical forces emanate from an object, which are picked up by the sense organs and conducted as electrical potentials to the brain. There, in a way that has not yet been clarified, a mental image is created in the brain from a physical information. Thus, an "ontological leap" takes place, so that there can be no adequation between perceived stimulus and its pictorial reconstruction. Lenk calls the pictorial reconstruction - better perhaps construction - "interpretation product" (1995, 95), which is assigned to a hierarchically constructed subjectively acquired schematism.

I would like to refer to the "Lenk chapter" where the stages of interpretation are mentioned in ascending abstractness in order to show which processing steps an "original interpretation" (103) is subject to. Perception thus consists of two interactive processes, the object part and the subject part, through which the object [is] an *'interpretive product' in* the sense of an *'imprinting'* (96). We export our schematism, without which we would remain without cognition, to the 'object' in such a way that it is perceived altered by it. The sciences demand a certain 'scientific ethos' for all faculties, so that their scheme of interpretation is intersubjectively binding, consequently their perceptions must be traceable to the same basic assumptions, which instruments can also adopt.

But in everyday life everybody has 'made his own experiences' that quite different schemata are directed to the same object, so that it is perceived differently according to the preconceptions.[78] And this imprinting affects the

---

[78] The death of a person is perceived by his relatives with inner sympathy, while the death of a stranger leaves them quite cold.

schematisms in such a way that they interpretatively strengthen or weaken the same 'object' in the next act of perception, depending on the degree of expectation. This has a selective effect, blocking out the distracting background noise.

We see and read about Islamist-style terrorist attacks in the media on an almost daily basis. Our schematization apparatus only too readily generalizes these examples in the sense of economizing a perception and assembles these individual images into a rule that becomes stricter with each new case. What is shown and described are not deep-seated causes such as social tensions, meaninglessness of Western value systems, historical mistakes of Westernization, ulterior manipulation of Iranians shouting anti-American slogans, mistakes in integration, the peaceful life of the vast majority of Muslims, but a sensationalized surface of indescribable brutality, cynical calls for murder, rejection of Western values in the West through demonstrative wearing of headscarves, rioting Islamic youth in Europe's suburbs, hostages in fear of death. These perceptions confirm and reinforce the rule: the West feels exposed to Islamism and terrorism that are effective everywhere, that have set their sights on its destruction and trample all humanity underfoot. Positive signs of peaceful coexistence and unspectacular normality are not registered at all. Islam is perceived by us only through the distorted lens of Islamism.

The daily peaceful[79] interaction with Muslims in schools, workplaces and in everyday life, the everyday life of Muslims in their countries is swallowed in terms of perceptual economics, so that we increasingly 'see' Muslims only as gun-wielding terrorists and murderers.[80] Muslims feel similarly when they

---

[79] The events in Berlin's secondary schools, for example, (described by Sarrazin) and not only there, where predominantly girls and boys with an "immigration background" terrorize German students and teachers, must be cause for a rethinking of German policy on foreigners. It cannot be acceptable that, for whatever reasons, a minority can ignore our social order with impunity. Here, too, a reflection is useful. What would happen if, at German schools with about 20% foreigners, the foreign students were treated by the Germans in the same way as they treat the Germans in the opposite case? What do Islamic students think when they call Western women 'sluts', 'whores', 'pork eaters'? Instead of drawing clear boundaries with harsh sanctions here, an army of social workers and social psychologists is supposed to work up the "migration background" with the students, through which the aggressive reactions against the country of migration are supposedly understandable. Perpetrators thus become all too willing victims. Try arguing in a similar way with right-wing extremist youths.

[80] The Balkan wars in the last century have shown how quickly a centuries-old consensus between religions can be shattered by religiously motivated political claims.

watch the bombing Israeli air force and American violence against Iraqi civilians on television. However, those who have the eradication of Israel as their banner should not be surprised when sharp bombs fall instead of bars of chocolate. This shows a general Islamist syndrome, the hiding of the perpetrators behind a victim role.

So, as one would expect, a grotesque distortion of perception awaits us in the Muslim world. It culminates in the reanimation of the "holy war" during the time of the "crusades". The war to be waged against the West today is a response to the "holy war" of the Crusaders, which then as now will lead to their destruction. This template is filled with current images of the Iraq war, the Intifada against Israel, the vows of revenge of the activists who carry killed 'martyrs' to burial, the immoral and shameless behavior of the 'Christians' in public in the eyes of Islam, and so on. Their wastefulness, their sexism, their egomania of "after me the deluge", their unrestrained consumerism would turn 'God's creatures' into immoderate creatures, whose disappearance from the world would not be a pity. Because it is not about people in the real sense here, actually every means for their destruction is allowed.[81] The memory of the crusades serves as an amplifier; for just as the brutal and murderous Christians were finally defeated by the Arabs, they will soon be again. Western technology, Western social systems, the high level of education cannot differentiate this picture. They fall as insignificant connotations into the cultural memory hole of the Islamic world.

The aforementioned ideological strategies projectively change the facts and circumstances in such a way that they impregnate the object as desires, wills, and values, as a result of which this patina appears as an objectively given property of the object and can be cognitively endowed with a claim to truth. This object, changed by the aforementioned psychic mechanisms, is now an object in itself. A "reinterpretation or disguise of a feeling relation of the thinker to real factors takes place. - [...]. His feeling-relationship to an object enters into the statement as supposedly objective" (Geiger 84, 187). Such self-

---

[81] The behavior of Hezbollah ('God's warriors') must be described as particularly condemnable. In order to denounce Israel and the USA internationally as a disgusting enemy image, the 'warriors of God' use the population as a 'human shield' for their rocket firings on Israel, so that the population has to bear the sufferings of the war, although it does not want it, which must evoke the 'righteous anger' of every Muslim. What kind of God is this who allows 'godly' warriors to serve him by driving the civilian population to the slaughter?

confirming theories, coherent in and with themselves, can then be used to justify and ground political actions, but also to argumentatively combat critical objections. Once such an **ideology(-) is** established, it conveys coherence to its adherents, intellectual security to doubters, and invincibility to opponents.

Twice in recent history, a major ideology with an attractive axiology has been formed, which, according to the criterion "enemy image", has purely 'scientifically' labeled a part of humanity as racially inferior or class enemies. The third one has just started to endow unbelievers as pariahs in its sense with the 'license to be killed'. The latter can still be prevented if one learns to see through the ideologization mechanism that is effective behind it. In doing so, a problem arises because the ideological actors themselves are basically mostly aware of the construct character of their production, because they have designed it themselves in order to be able to rely on a closed political concept. By threatening or exercising violence, this credibility gap is closed and naturalized - in the name of God. Therefore, it is not the West but Islamism that is the greatest enemy of authentic Islam.

If we once assume that there is an intersubjectively uniformly perceivable object, then the changing effect of **ideology(-)** can be shown by the fact that between its cognitive being and its projective modification a deficient gap of knowledge has opened up. If the projective part is abstracted, then this gap or difference disappears again. Then the cognitive object becomes visible again.

Ideology critique is a form of epistemological critique through which the false appearance of an ideologized theory can be exposed so that the object can be grasped in its objectivity with the known limitations.

People who do not notice the facts deficiently altered by ideology resemble wearers of sunglasses who consider what they perceive through this darkly tinted glass to be an objectively darkened world.

6. Islamic fundamentalism

Islamism, as the preceding investigation proves, has developed as a religiously triggered fundamentalism into the "thought form fundamentalism", an **ideology(-)** which, according to the discussed ideology criteria, anticipates reality in its specific way epistemologically deficient. But it is unfortunately no other than the one in Muhammad's time, when it can be called **ideology(+),** because it created a new world; but today it appears as 'old wine in new bottles'. It is preparing to level the plurality of competing epistemologies of the Old World according to the claimed monopoly of truth. The "form of thought Islamic fundamentalism" has been sufficiently confronted with the presented criteria of ideology; too many criteria speak for its thoroughly ideology-infested constitution.

A variant compatible with the theory that Islamism builds on the already immanent ideological implications of the Koran and uses them for its own legitimization has been presented essayistically by Broder (2006). It claims [...] "that Islamism could not abuse Islam but take it literally" (54). Already in the Golden Age of Islamic philosophy, philosophical introspection has called for the symbolic interpretation of the Qur'an because a literal interpretation has led to unmanageable inconsistencies. The dogmatic insistence on absolute authenticity of the Koran today has changed Islam in such a way that it has to make use of modern theorizing constructs in order to declare its reversion to the outlived thought patterns of its founding era as progressive and modern because it wants to reanimate them. Thus, Islam and Islamism work so closely together in operating the ideologization machinery that it is no longer possible to distinguish 'bad' Islamism from 'good' Islam; their boundaries are becoming increasingly blurred, visible in the emotional outbursts of hatred toward the West, although the cause of the outburst is unknown to most Muslims.

Sloterdijk's thesis, cited by Broder, "What is on the long-term agenda is the Europeanization of Islam, not the Islamization of Europe" (29) springs from the philosophical wishful thinking of anticipatory obedience, which seems to have clearly clouded the ability to perceive, but not the facts. Euro-Islam is becoming more and more silent even abroad, i.e. in our country, while the Islamization of Europe is progressing. These 'perceptual clouds' have been collected and commented on by the essayist Broder in *"Hurra, wir kapitulieren!"*

Tepe traces religious fundamentalism, which also implies a will to shape politics, back to the basic pattern: "absolute truth, unquestionable dogmas, uncompromising enforcement" (Internet 2000, 5). This is filled with concrete content, so that in reality we have to reckon with several forms of fundamentalism.

The previous chapters have already pointed out that Islamic fundamentalism has replaced communism as a major ideology. The generally predicted end of the major ideologies with their global conflict potential did not occur, because Islamic fundamentalism immediately filled the gap left by communism and developed a new Manichaeism.

In the article *Is the decline of major ideologies also the end of ideology criticism?* Salamun (1992) examines the discipline of "ideology criticism," which is actually now superfluous, should the theory of decline be true. But Salamun advises caution, even though, when he writes the essay, Islamic fundamentalism has not yet formed in the Western consciousness. He sums up:

> that such a set of instruments for ideology critique, developed within the framework
> of the previous ideology critique, can still be useful when one thinks that the end of
> the classical major ideologies has come. Then it is fruitful for gaining insights into
> questionable structural peculiarities of thought structures [...]. I am thinking especially
> of religious fundamentalists with political mission claims, nationalist ideologies, eco-
> ideologies, modernization and progress ideologies [...]. Ideologies always emerge
> anew, and therefore it is also necessary to keep the findings of the previous ideology
> critique present [...] (31).

To this end, he explicates the ideology criteria already known here, but additionally names "immunization strategies," "messianism," and mixing "political-ideological value concepts with well-confirmed hypotheses and factual findings" (40-48), which Islamism leaves to religion in the last case, because it claims the monopoly on truth and the sciences are received ambivalently. But - how reassuring - ideology research does not run out of material, because ideology in the broadest sense of the word represents a cultural system of meaning that has emerged with man and sustains him (as a substitute for instinct), so that the changeover from culturally constructive value premises and the forms of thought closed in them to **ideology(-)** can take place at any time, which now presents itself as a rallying point of the ideology criteria in the sense of a deficient cognition theory or social utopia with claim to exclusivity and thus can be scientifically unambiguously qualified.

Islamism's Manichean conception of God and Satan, heaven and hell, good and evil, immediately finds an enemy in the Western world; but the latter pays back in kind, at least in the United States by reinforcing a latently already existing Christian fundamentalism.[82] Two very heterogeneous worlds confront each other: the ideologized Islam, which cleverly disguises the differences in the individual regions, at least externally, and the West, whose colorful and plural value background can hardly be described: Christianity, atheism, positivism, faith in technology, individualism, neurotic egomania, general secularization, rejection of transcendence, democracy, plurality, materialism [....] form a contradictory mixture, which also in a simplified form determines the daily practice of life. What generally determines the West is economic expansionism, securing raw materials to ensure its prosperity, and universalizing its materialistic value systems. Its superior economic form can be derived from its analytical methodology by breaking down a holistic production process into sub-steps that can be mastered very efficiently, from which the whole can then be easily synthesized. The basis of this rational mode of production is provided by the sciences.

From Islam and Islamism, the value conglomerate of Western civilization is greatly simplified, dichotomized, and then demonized, which can be described with the terms "decadent West" and "Christian crusaders." At the moment, however, the West is still very helpless in the face of the increasingly militant **ideology(-)** "Islamism" because it has only perceived Islam in a blurred way: as an exotic, otherwise not very significant, somewhat dusty worldview and religion. The unfortunate actions of the U.S. administration[83] , which hoped that democracy would spread from Iraq to the other Islamic countries according to the domino theory, only reinforced the emerging estrangement between

---

[82] The theory and practice of Christian fundamentalism in the United States has been comprehensively addressed by Barr (1981).

[83] Because of Saddam Hussein's bloody dictatorship, this naively started from the idea of a longing for democracy on the part of the Iraqi mixture of peoples. But no one there consulted the philosophy that could have provided information about the diametrically opposed value systems of "Islam" and "democracy. As an Islamic country that dreams of a reign of God, it cannot accept a value system of autonomous subjectivity. The Iraqis feel their own bloody tyranny of despots almost as a liberation, if they could choose between it and an American protectorate.

Islamic and Christian liberal countries, so that today both perceive each other as a mutual threat.

We have already had this bloc thinking with its ever-increasing military potential to strengthen one's own claim to supremacy. We have to expect the worst, since in world history conflicts reinterpreted as religious conflicts have so far been fought out with extreme brutality. The worldview that prides itself on being the "sword of Allah," "our bayonets," to storm the Western world has a history.

6.1 History of Islamism

The history of Islamism is to be tied to three names: Maududi (1903-1979), Hassan al Banna (1906-1949) and Qutb (1906-1966). I would also like to start here from a conglomerate of political ideas of Islam, which always sees itself as a political force, during this period: Anti-colonialism, feeling of inferiority to the technologized West, low prestige of the religion of Islam, which was perceived as outdated, uncritical adoption of Western ideas and culture, rising self-esteem due to increasing power because of the possession of oil, rejection and advocacy of communism, Pan-Arabism. In addition, the defeat in the Six-Day War in 1967, which was perceived as a disgrace, put Pan-Arabism to rest for the time being, because the military solidarity of the Arab world failed to materialize. An analysis of this defeat on the part of the Islamists brought to light two causes that were considered correct: the firm religious faith of the Jews, which made them strong in contrast to Islam, whose power of faith had dwindled (quoted in Tibi 2001, 51). Although this is not true, because the Holocaust is the decisive reason for the Israelis' will to fight, it is a clever ideological explanation of their own failure, but also of the reinterpretation of Islamism as a coming victory march through a renaissance of Islam. Therefore, the slogan can only be: Back to a 'true' Islam. Islam, now reformed from backwards, could awaken similar resources as the Jewish religion, through whose moral backing the Six-Day War was decided anew. The reformation of Islam is indeed taking place, but not through self-analysis, but 'from above', from Islamism, so that henceforth the primacy of politics over religion, which is **ideologically(-)** exploited. Islam becomes more and more the compliant stooge of Islamism and thus loses its independent religious meaning and its moral authority. It becomes the justification function of the fight against the 'degenerated West'.

The Pakistani Maududi sorts out from the conglomerate of worldviews just mentioned those that strengthen the latent anti-Western sentiment argumentatively. For him, democracy is a "work of Satan" (after Barth, 104). The fall of the first man to be autonomous like God would repeat itself in the Western democracies:

> He [the West - the author] tells people: It is not necessary for you to obey the divine law; you can make your own human laws by counting how many agree with your plans. This is a deadly danger that Islam must fight, not only in its own territory, but in the whole world" (104 f.). [84]

Hereby the western democracies have become an object of demonization, just "Satan's work", Islam gets the political instruction to fight the godlessness all over the world with violence[85] , i.e. it does not even veil its worldwide mission anymore. Allah is supposed to rule as the sovereign lawgiver in a global state of God. The Islamists presume to be able to establish this state, even if they pretend to be God's henchmen from. From Maududi's point of view, submitting to God's will is not a slave service, but a salvation and liberation of the missing human being. Armstrong (2000, 278) comments on this:

---

[84] But Ayyub Axel Köhler, chairman of the Islamic Council in Germany, continues to count on the stupidity of the Germans, claiming. "If you look at history, Islam has never been spread by violence" (RP, Sept. 23, 2006, A5). On the main problem, terrorism, he does admit: "Islamist terror defiles our religion" (A5); but I am not aware where a demonstration of Muslims against these 'defilers' has taken place, unlike the hate speech against the Pope. Of course, Islam has no real problems with the equal rights of women either, since they are capable of doing business without the man since Mohammed. But there is the "relapse into pre-Islamic customs, which we of course also fight" (A5). Thus it is clear that there are no problems of Islam with the habits of the secular West; there are only problems with the critical and one-sided view of Islam by the Germans.

[85] In *Mohammed und die Gewalt - Die Sprache des Schwert* (Kocsis, Munich 2001) the author lists eleven verses in which violence is mentioned, which I ask those to read who always talk about the principled peacefulness of Islam. Sura (9:29) in particular makes "clear that Islam, when it came to power, did not consider polite and reasonable discussion with dissenters necessary - the language of future conversation was that of the sword" (Ali Dashti in Kocsis (Munich 2001, 48)). All those who assume the exclusively peaceful message of Islam have either not read the Koran, are fundamentalists and propagandists with a very partial perceptive capacity or followers of system-stabilizing anticipatory obedience to the absolute goodness of 'multi-culti', so that the idyll of prejudice can only be disturbed by critical statements.

> Because God alone is the supreme ruler, no one can be forced to obey the commands of other people. A ruler who refuses to rule according to God's will does not deserve the obedience of his subjects. In this case, there would not only be a right to revolution, but downright a duty.

But who knows what the will of God is when the Koran offers so many different variants? Here, the idea of the resurrection of the world revolution, but now under an Islamist-jihadist banner, is celebrating a joyous revival. Islamism poses as the force that, after the violent elimination of all secular systems of rule, can realize humanity's dream of eternal peace and eternal justice, which are guaranteed by God and promise the participation of all in the goods of the earth.

These utopians cannot be called to account because, if this ideal state is not reached yet, it is always the 'evil West', since it has not yet been defeated, that may be held responsible for the still prevailing grievances, since it cannot help but fight the good in the form of an absolute reign of God.

Lest anyone be under any illusions about the intentions of this politicized Islam, a final quote from Maududi, whose writings enjoy a reputation like *Das Kapital* in the West, should be cited:

> I say it to you Muslims in all frankness that secular democracy is in every respect contrary to your religion and to your faith. [...]. Islam, which you believe in and according to which you call yourselves Muslims, is totally different from this ugly system. [...]. Even in trivial matters, there can be no agreement between Islam and democracy because they are diametrically opposed. Where the political system of democracy and the secular nation-state dominates, there is no Islam. Where Islam dominates, that system must not exist" (Maududi without year, 41 f.).

Islamism in Maududi's sense openly expresses its anti-democratic sentiments here. When Islamists speak of democracy, they do so only in the sense that the essence of man can develop unhindered only where God rules, in that the "general and special official power" is oriented toward God's laws.

Qutb's writings enjoy a similar status among fundamentalists as the 'Mao Bible' used to enjoy among the Chinese. His image of the West was formed during a study visit to the USA. The materialism, the thinking in cash, the sexism which dominates the daily life, the sham religiosity which is only supposed to cover up the greed for profit, the practical atheism which has lost any reverence for God, drive mankind to its downfall from which only one way promises salvation: the belief in God. God possesses the fullness of all being, in which he can let the believing human being participate according to his power perfection. "Islam therefore harmonizes with our nature; for Qutb it is an image of the universal order" (2001, 110), Barth holds. Here, too, the reference to a global state of God is not missing. This is appropriate to human nature alone; the divine state is thus a necessity of nature, an entity that exists by itself, from which the people of the West have turned away through their secularism.

Thus, in the eyes of the Islamists, Western man leads an unnatural and godless life from which the world must be redeemed. More or less all states, including Islamic ones, would violate this universal natural order. Here Qutb is at a crossroads: either to seek the religious renewal of Islam (from below) or to seek its politicization in order to renew it (from above). He chooses the path of politicizing this religion as it is today. For Qutb, Islam together with Sharia embodies the natural order of the world, which is disregarded by the West. He thus represents a form of metaethical naturalism that is not far removed from Social Darwinism. He sees a similar disordered world outside Islam in that which prevailed at the time of Muhammad. Therefore, like Mohammed, he preaches *jihad*, the fight against the infidels in one's own ranks, and even more the fight against the infidel West. So he does not want to reform Islam as a religion, but uses it only for his political struggle. Islam is hypostatized as a comprehensive order that supposedly corresponds to the rules of nature, the laws of existence and God. Parallels to National Socialism emerge here, which demanded the selection of non-Aryans for 'natural reasons', while the former knows the 'true' nature of man and derives from it the right to have to liquidate the unnatural in the form of the West.

Hassan al Banna compensates for the exclusively intellectualistic and naturalistic trait of this thinking by, as a member of the Muslim Brotherhood, making Islamism palatable to the people through social institutions, i.e., by anchoring it in the people. Theoretically, the contours of an Islamist world order are emerging more and more clearly, which is allowed to displace the Western world, which is dying of itself, even with the use of violence, as historically and salvation-historically outdated. Islamism sees itself more and more as the only progressive world-historical force that also promises to alleviate the material hardships of its coreligionists through its socialist-like social concept. Instead of the anthropocentric one, he propagates a theocentric world view; Allah should rule, not the individual; this implies that humans are not allowed to rule over humans either, but humans are allowed to rule over 'subhumans'.

He calls for merciless jihad "to endow his 'Islamic world revolution' and the use of violence in the form of irregular war with religious legitimacy" (Tibi 2001, 140). Here Tibi brings to a common denominator what is happening in one part of the Islamic world.

Hassan al Banna thus embodies the social aspect of Islamism (from below). His Muslim Brotherhood, now legally active in many Islamic countries, aims to inspire the people to embrace Islamism. Since authoritarian regimes are blind to the political and social needs of their subjects, who often live in misery, the Brotherhood has taken on the support of the needy, the construction of hospitals and schools, the care of uprooted people, i.e., tasks of the state, but not out of love for human beings as a value in themselves, but as a political instrument of its own power grab. In addition, this brotherhood is pushing for religious renewal, so that Islamism can offer itself to the people as a threefold alternative: pragmatically as social welfare, intellectually as the vision of an Islamic world state that is certain to come, and religiously as the liberator of Islam from its lethargy.

Barth (2003, 118 f.) lists four common features of Islamism:

1. Criticism of colonialism, but reinterpreted as a crusade against Islam.
2. Revival of theocentrism, thus "de-westernization of knowledge," enthronement of the Koran as the sole source of knowledge.
3. Forecasting the disintegration of the Western world through permanent crises.
4. Defamation of democracy as "prostitution", soon realization of "world leadership by Islam".

Two alternatives must be discussed here: Is fundamentalism an ideological child of modernity or a historical phenomenon that can be encountered in all ages as a basic anthropological condition of human existence? Barth leans toward the first. For him, American fundamentalism is not to be compared with Islamic fundamentalism, the latter is thus a singular movement of our time, although this term has inflated to a defamatory empty formula for all kinds of isms. Barth calls it "a modern anti-modernism" (99) that meets the following criteria:

1. Retreat to "pre-modern traditions."
2. Possession of a closed ontology that can be used to clarify all problems that arise.
3. Fight against the evil that has set out to corrode the good. The good are the religious roots of a true relationship with God, which call for missionary work, since most people are God-fearing beings. With this, the claim to absoluteness of one's own faith community can be asserted against the unbelievers.
4. Classification of history in an eschatological context, which comprises three phases: a religious beginning, then turning away from the true faith through a fall from grace, to be registered in the 19th and 20th centuries as Westernization, finally overcoming this transgression and expecting a transfigured world of salvation.

As "anti-modernism," Islamic fundamentalism, because it needs modernity for its constitution, partly fulfills the condition of being a modern phenomenon. Nor is it in any way hostile to technology, but it strictly rejects the Western value system behind it. If there is no other way, the implications of modernity are sophistically appropriated as implications of Islam. That is why the authors Losurdo (see literary criticism), Tibi, Salamun and Tepe, among others, contradict this historical attribution to modernity, which I would like to endorse. For Tepe, historically resistant fundamentalism results from the anthropological fact of man's lapse into ideology. Schmidt (Düsseldorf 1990, 11) also states, "Obviously, fundamentalism is an ideological structure whose essential features largely escape historical change." The author would like to base this on Tepe's theory of fundamentalism (2000), which he published in *Fundamentalism as a Form of Thought*. According to this theory, there are three levels of fundamentalism:

1. the superhistorical fundamentalism in its general structure,
2. the already more concrete religious and profane forms,
3. the historically concrete religious and profane fundamentalism, each of which can appear in moderate or militant form.

He classifies Islamism as a religious fundamentalism with a pronounced "comprehensive will to shape politics" (20), i.e., as a militant form. The term "thought form" coined by Tepe receives its authentication from cultural anthropology. The starting point of this theory is the culture-bound nature of human existence, which means that human thought and action are "worldview-bound" (72). Pure thinking as the production of truth in itself does not exist. The worldview-boundness of human thinking can be analytically shown in individual worldviews; but through such analyses an immense abundance of worldviews would have to be dealt with. Tepe wants to reduce this abundance to "general worldview types" or "general forms of thought" (2), so that the concrete worldviews can be reduced to a few basic types. This reduction method leads to two types of worldviews: the religious and the profane, ontologically and epistemologically of quite different quality. The religious ones are based on a metaphysical, the profane ones on a naturalistic ontology. Mixed forms are the rule. Both types are preceded by the "general fundamentalist form of thinking" (2), which, like a pair of glasses, changes the view of what exists, so that one can compare fundamentalism with a filter sifting through what exists; different filters cause different views and forms of cognition of the object taken into consideration.

When it comes to the question of objective knowledge, the ideological criteria presented show, in the case of the militant form of fundamentalism, under which violent change the object has to suffer, so that it can and should therefore only be perceived in a distorted way.

Since the **ideology(-)** commands and enforces intersubjectively the same maxims of thought and action among all adherents, a pseudo-objectivity of ontologically 'one cast' emerges. Militant Islamic fundamentalism can be described by means of four criteria:

1. The basic religious assumptions from the 'sacred tradition' lay claim to ultimate or absolute truth.
2. These assumptions have the status of unquestionable dogmas.
3. The great truth must be followed without compromise.
4. The addition of a comprehensive political will to shape policy (3). Point 4 may also be missing (Tepe 2001, 3).

If we omit the word "religious" from point one and allow party programs and the pronouncements of their leaders to count as "sacred tradition," we obtain the general criteria for fundamentalism. It is easy to see that, despite historically unique realities, fundamentalisms are similar in basic principles. They appear in two forms, closed (militant) and open modifications. An open (liberal) religious fundamentalism, like an open (liberal) profane fundamentalism, starts from "fundamental assumptions" (104) that cannot be questioned further. This implies, however, that there may well be other more accurate assumptions, so that no absolute claim to truth is made.

Through this methodological approach, the concept of fundamentalism is embedded in a supra-historical context; it is a constructivist template that can be updated in each case with concrete historical facts. This value-neutral concept of fundamentalism is contrasted with the ambivalent concrete one, whose historical, political and religious facts can be described as such on the one hand, but also criticized on the other. In accordance with this conception of the work, a mixed working method is proposed, which proceeds in one work step both factually descriptive, and critically and evaluatively. The terms "fundamentalism," "religious fundamentalism," "Islamic fundamentalism," and "Islamism" are used semantically as largely synonymous forms of language.

As the ontological consideration of Islam will reveal, when it has mutated into Islamism, the result is an altered form of thinking, perception and action, the causes of which describe the ideology criteria and the consequences of which lead us to expect a frequent theory deficit in the reception of cognition. This has projective, not intellectual causes, because a voluntative premise has crept into the intellectual functions to perceive the object as one wants it to be perceived. And, oh wonder: Now the internal subjective projections appear as external objective properties of the object.

Pope Benedict's Regensburg lecture provides an instructive example of this.[86] There, the pope uses an excerpt from a dialogue between the Christian emperor Manuel II and a Persian Koran scholar as a quotation to demonstrate the different concepts of God of the two religions. While in Christianity only rational action can be assumed from God, the Muslim conception of God is characterized by a transcendent understanding that does not bind God's reason to any human categories, not even to those of reason. The religious scholar Khoury reinforces this view by speaking of a "sea-wide stream of Islamic scriptures" (A2) in which the transcendence of the divine will does not tie it back to reason. The quotation used by the Pope is directed at the danger of operating with an absolute claim to truth. This admittedly difficult theological interpretation was not followed by Islamic scholars and was 'bazaarized', i.e. made 'understandable to the people', in order to be able to trigger the well-known protests.

We know now already to the sufficiency the reactions by from Islamic clergy still hyped-up masses: Insulting Islam, insulting the Prophet, insulting the sacred feelings of every righteous Muslim. All registers of emotionality are pulled out. Deprived of any reasonable argument, these reactions confirm exactly the image of irrationally uncontrollable actions and reactions of the incited Islam. So the pope is compared with Hitler and Mussolini (RP of 16.09.2006, A1). In the RP of 19.09.2006 an Ayatollah speaks of "the last link of a plot for a crusade" (A5), the Al-Qaida becomes even clearer by announcing death by the sword to the survivors after the surely coming victory of the Jihad, if they do not convert to Islam (A5), the Turks want to cancel the Pope's visit in November (A5), a Turkish lawyers' association even wants to sue the Pope and have him arrested on his possible entry into Turkey (A5).

This can be explained by the hysterical perception of a West demonized beyond recognition with its superior economic and social achievements, whose dominance is to be compensated for by giving an outlet to one's own feeling of inferiority, which takes advantage of every opportunity by reinterpreting the facts, by fanning feelings of hatred, thereby deluding oneself with the illusion of one's own world-historical superiority. (One believes to humiliate the nation itself by burning national flags).

---

[86] Pope Benedict's lecture of 12.09.2006 was printed in the Rheinische Post (RP) of 16.09.2006.

There are now two worlds: one that is open to rational arguments but also impregnated with worldviews, which it knows so that it can strive for objectivity and is subject to the criteria of truth, and an Islamist one that considers its projections to be objective. And since this worldview pretends to be the true one and is difficult to shake from the outside because the truth criterion "false" does not apply to it, the result is a missionary claim to free even the non-Muslims from their grave moral and intellectual errors, whereby the noble goal striven for justifies almost any means; scientific truth values fall by the wayside. [87]

The characteristics of religiously militant fundamentalism will be summarized here once again in a differentiated overview:

1. Being convinced of an absolute religious truth, laid down in a "sacred text",
2. absolute claim to truth of one's own faith community, erroneous, false and dangerous views of other religions,
3. unquestionable dogmatics, which must not be criticized,
4. Mythicization of important people, to whom elite knowledge is attributed, or places, in order to remove them from the profane,
5. dismissive attitude toward secular education systems,
6. uncompromising political implementation of one's convictions in a state that takes on an eschatological function,
7. religious renaissance as a response to a value-abstinent secular state.

Religious fundamentalism in the form of Islamism is a response to fundamental crises of meaning and contains the political-religious message of salvation to free humanity from this evil. With the help of a resounding **ideology(-),** utopias of one's own superiority can be synthesized from crises of meaning. As a final step, a turn is made by reinterpreting defeat as a coming victory, when the negative factors have been eliminated and old stories of victory with historical patina dusted off and polished bright. From the fact of a

---

[87] In this regard, the Islamic scholar Lewis sums up that since 1663 (siege of Vienna) the Muslims have not only fallen behind Europe and the USA, respectively, "but almost behind the whole rest of the world" (quoted by Broder 2006, 151). "[8 ...]. It was bad that they had to get the specialists from Europe or the U.S. Now the experts come from Korea, a country that 50 years ago was far behind the Islamic world." (151 f.).

total defeat, a clever **ideologization(-)** can read out a victory, which can present the sacrifices made as meaningful and pass off the coming turnaround as tangibly near, so that people can reconcile themselves with fate and gain motivation for the new (backward-looking) goals (distraction from the pressure of reality and suffering). Similarly, Marxism constructs a world-historical ideology of victory that declares the impoverished proletariat to be the engine of a new historical epoch. In line with such models, Islamism also represents a victory utopia, cleverly camouflaged with the role of victim.

Francis Bacon is driven by the question whether one should not rather trust the Aristotelian syllogism with its deductive, truth-preserving conclusions about nature than one's own uncertain observations of nature. He chooses to obtain the truth about nature through its direct interrogation, not through any theories of it. Islam has canonized with the writing down of the Koran at the same time the opinion about the nature recorded there, thus, in contrast to Bacon, has trusted a mediating instance, the Koran, more than the nature itself: with the known result.

What does "nature" mean in the Koran? For this, we consult the Quranic story of creation. In Suras (6:96 - 6:100), Muhammad describes how Allah created this world to suit the needs of all living beings. He paints an almost perfect world in which means and ends fit together in such a way that man finds an earthly well-ordered world from which everything grows to him without much effort. This praise of Allah and his creation has only one flaw: it is not true.

So the Koran does not perceive the most important problem of mankind, a not really controllable nature, in which his existence is permanently endangered. If also worst catastrophes occur - since they are wanted by God, they are to be accepted, yes, they are in reality none at all, but inscrutable expression of the will of God. To resist against the will of God is senseless, because he has the absolute power over heaven and earth, humans and nature. Thus, no matter how one argues to the contrary, Allah is always right: If a misfortune does not occur, it is Allah's will, if it occurs, likewise. Passivity is thus a characteristic of Muslim thinking and acting in the direction of God: precisely because God, who does not let man look at his cards, has willed it that way. In the direction of eliminating the 'infidels', on the other hand, Islam develops great activities. Except for the Golden Age, in which the orthodox fetters can be loosened and the recitation of suras gives way to thinking for oneself, nature study becomes possible at most as Koranic study with emphasis on "nature". Tibi sees the reason for the political weakness of Islam in the low mastery of nature.[88] The question horizon of what nature actually is, is obscured,

---

[88] In the RP of 18.09.2006, reference is made to the educational emergency of the Arab world: "Lack of education, freedom and emancipation" (A3). From 1980-2000 "the entire Arab world registered 370 patents in the USA, the dwarf state Israel 7652" (A3).

even tabooed, by creationism. In order to avoid the split between Koranic revelation and Western ontology of nature, Islamism distinguishes between Western value-free technology and Koranic ontology, through which, because adapted by the Europeans in the Middle Ages, the Koran and the observance of its precepts are also real science. Thus, one hopes to escape the secular Western natural ontology with its areligious implications. Many Islamic researchers therefore divide their lives into two areas, the scientific; which is no different from the Western understanding of science, and the practical life, which is governed by religious tradition. This questionable compromise between modernity and tradition, however, is a method of self-protection. It is not the Muslims who are incapable of scientific thinking and acting, but their creationist ontology forbids - at least interpreted orthodoxly - a questioning of the divine nature by human hypotheses.

From the holy principle to understand the Koran text not differently than literally and reality-adequately, because the world is accordingly constituted, follows a dilemma with which also Christianity had big problems with the emergence of the natural sciences: the evolution theory which assumes the self-creation and development of the living beings and strictly rejects the creationism. A similar case is also present in the Koran. There it says:

> Verily, even in the cattle you have a lesson. We give you to drink of what is in their bodies, between excrement and blood in the middle, milk, pure (and) pleasant to those who drink (16:67).

Now Darwin already took the phenomenon of domestication, especially in ruminants, as an opportunity to show that man has been taming animals for his own benefit since the Stone Age. Thereby he increased the milk production by artificial selection more and more, so that in the figurative sense man has made a gift to himself with these breedings. When interpreting the Koran literally, the paradoxical situation arises that man should thank Allah for something he himself has created. One can universalize this paradox, since here two truth claims clash: the scientific consciousness with the mythical-religious one of the Koran, the latter being supposed to be constitutive '*par Ordre de Mufti*' *for* the whole. Seen from the West, which increasingly restricts the area of myth and religion through rational, profane thinking, this development is rejected as anti-modern, as a retrograde step in the sense of the re-mythification of religion.

The essentially necessary secularization of the sciences, which is said to have been dressed up by Laplace to Napoleon in the anecdote: 'Sire, I have no need of God as a hypothesis for my cosmology', is fought by Islamism as unbelief. It argues with the catchword '*sola scriptura*', in which Islam becomes the universal force healing the world, including the Western world, from atheism, because, according to Khalil (1979, 108), it alone represents a 'holistic view encompassing all spiritual and material aspects of existence' (cited in Tibi 1991, 273), which it can glean from the 'sacred text'. God's word thus contains the mythical substance from which the command arises: 'Thus and not otherwise is it and shall it be!' The Koranic word is thus at the same time the representation of the essence of a realistic and teleological world plan. Behind a realistic conception of life of a created world, which cannot exist, however, from itself, stands the transcendence of God, by which the world is what it is.

With certain restrictions, the Islamic worldview can be called deductive, the Western modern worldview inductive. Set is the point from which all perspectives start. God is the "uncreated one" to whom there is no access, but he is at the same time the creator of everything. His direct creation is the Koran, his world plan written in Arabic language, after which the temporal being aligns itself. The word becomes world. The path of human knowledge starts from the Koran, whose words have been transformed into daily reality. The world is the image of the divine activity; God's truth is therefore present there and absolutely real. There is also the reverse way of knowledge, which Ibn-Tufail has pointed out. See chapter 8.2 Outlook. Even without any knowledge of the Qur'an, every human being has to deal with nature. Since this is God's creation, he thus learns about the world God's world plan, the sum of his will, the Koran. The inductive way is thornier, so that God with the creation of the Koran offers a help to the human being to take over the world knowledge directly from it and not to do nature research himself.

The "*sola* scriptura"[89] demands a theocentric worldview that is both the highest authority of what humans can know and of what normative principles

---

[89] There are many problems associated with the positing of Arabic as a "language of God." Fundamentally, Arabic is one language among many, a human artifact. Structure, meaning, diachronic changes in meaning, grammar, sentence forms are some criteria that apply to all languages. How is it possible that divine thoughts are expressible in a human artifact? But only by the fact that God transfers his thoughts into the language created by humans. He must

will eternally hold. With Monod we call such an order animistic; it is an onto-logical world-conception dominated by mythical-religious thinking. In it, the subject-object relation does not hold, because there are no autonomous and self-determining subjects. God is conceived as the all-controlling, creator, all-knowing, but also as an all-good being, who, if he keeps God's command-ments, gives the "weakly created man" his safe protection, so that the helpless dust grain "man" gets a lord who does not let him feel this smallness anymore. If he allies himself with this omnipotence by exactly keeping the statutes and commandments, he is, modernly expressed, all around assured: nothing can happen to him anymore. After his death, eternal life with God awaits him. Who would not want to be under the protection of such a power? This security in Allah has made Muslims strong and helped them achieve their cultural iden-tity. Even if terrible natural disasters claim life and limb, they do not lose faith in God, because God, in his all-goodness, will already know why he has made this decision. For us, the way Islam deals with major catastrophes is strange. It is very reluctant to participate in international aid efforts.

Questioning Islam means questioning its culture, its identity. The moment the believer doubts the revelation, he doubts God, the blessings bestowed upon him by Him, and must expect their withdrawal. This stake is far too high, so God's word is placed under the protection of the believer. The Quran is sur-rounded with a sacred aura that raptures it from the profane sphere, so that any misappropriation means at the same time its desecration, which arouses great emotions, as we see, among the faithful. There is even talk of desecration of Islam, against which all Muslims are allowed to act, even by militant means. I am speaking here of tastelessness and provocation, which discredit the per-petrators themselves, but insult, desecration and violation of sacred feelings are gladly spoken of by those who can harness such unnecessary provocations for their political goals by using them to make any criticism of Islam and Is-lamism taboo. Islam, like Christianity, is a spiritual entity that cannot be de-stroyed by material interference. When it comes to "violation of sacred feel-ings," "honor," "desecration," "desecration," and the like, a boom has begun

---

become man, so to speak, in order to be able to speak to people. It is precisely this incarnation of God that is strictly rejected in Islam, so that there is an insoluble contradiction between the claim of the divine message to supra-temporal truth and the historically unique, man-made and constantly changing language.

for the aforementioned empty formulas because, because their meaning is diffuse, they can be filled with seemingly relevant content that can create an ideologically highly explosive mixture whose destructive power is irrationally amplified by Islamist demagogues and can thus be steered in the desired direction.

The method of creating an inflation of desecrations, so to speak, is the 'canonization' of symbols, which has already been described here. In addition, as in the case of the "honor killings"[90] and the killings of Christians and destruction of churches, it is a matter of serious crimes that have no relation to the claimed symbolic provocations. This asymmetrical perception, which legalizes one's own crimes when there is only a degradation of symbols[91] , would, if the West were to react similarly asymmetrically, lead to the daily torching of mosques.

Tibi calls the holistic theory and practice of Islam "cosmological ethics" (1991, 223). At the top of the world is God, who constitutes two realms: the heavens, the angels, Satan, and the righteous who later dwell in these paradisiacal heavens. Opposite this transcendent world is the everyday world, which is to be created permanently by God, in which every living being and also the rocks owe their existence to Allah: "And there is no creature that creeps on the

---

[90] In the scandalous "honor killings," allegedly not endorsed by Islam, "family honor" is valued more highly than life. In Turkey, until recently, perpetrators were not prosecuted at all or only half-heartedly by the state.

[91] Solzhenitsyn (*Archipelago Gulag*) tells of a man who wraps a purchased herring in "Pravda," which is printed with a large portrait of Stalin. The saleswoman reports the incident, and the man is sent to the gulag for anti-Soviet agitation.

Similar to National Socialism, Muslims believe that the sign character of the symbols does not lie in the reference to the signified, but the signified is itself present as substance. That is why the National Socialists protected their emblems from possible reinterpretation with an "anti-kitsch law." Because, for example, the swastika on a jam jar or a cheese package could have inspired associations remote from the state. The prevailing opinion is that the image as a model shapes the mental image. This also explains the symbol fetishism of the Third Reich, which gave its symbols the character of devotional objects, and of Islamism, which surrounds its symbols with a sacred aura.

Broder (2006, 35) describes the following event, reproduced here in abbreviated form. According to it, the Savings-bank Sparkasse Mainfranken had distributed 30000 balloons with the flags of the participants of the soccer world championship. But since the Saudi Arabian flag had the Muslim creed on it, Muslims complained that their creed was being "kicked around"; and the Savings-bank apologized.

earth whose sustenance is not due to Allah. And He knows its abode and its home. All this is in a clear book" (11:6).

Elsewhere in Surah (6:59), Muhammad says:

> With Him are the keys of the hidden; none knows them but He alone. And He knows what is on the land and what is in the sea. And not a leaf falls down without Him knowing it; and there is not a grain of darkness in the earth, nor a green thing, nor a dry thing, that is not in a clear book.

The world is exactly as it is according to the plan of Allah: what is, shall be. Thus, in the world of Islam, the difference between being and ought to be is eliminated; for there is only Allah's will. God's laws are objective moral principles that are binding for a Muslim to observe. However, God's moral laws are also simultaneously cognitive statements about the world. Being and ought, metaphysical and profane, theological and practical, cognitive and transcendental form a unity interwoven by God. This system has a great community-building power, because everyone knows the morality objectively demanded by God, which may not be questioned by any critical subjectivity.

Whether it is a matter of everyday problems, religious questions or scientific and economic statements, the Koran is the binding authority for them all and offers advice and help. When disputes arise, the parties do not look for rational solutions, but for passages in the Koran that legitimize this or that solution with infallibility and a claim to absolute truth. It is thus the method of Islam, and even more so of Islamism, to very quickly leave the small realm of the mundane in matters of dispute by leaping into metaphysical ontology, thereby immunizing its statements from criticism; for "Allah has said yes, [...]." Thus Islam can be misused to exonerate politics and personal ambition and is wide open to sophistries.

This religiously determined metaphysical ontology also presupposes a certain form of thinking and acting. Mannheim's conception of the sociology of knowledge is to be recalled here. The latter draws from the premise that there is a functional connection between knowledge, science, and society the conclusion that there is no thinking, no science, no philosophy as such (see Russell), free from all social conditions, thus objective for all subjects, but dependent on a "socially location-bound consciousness" (cited in Lieber 1985, 24). According to this theory as well as cultural anthropology, one must assume a consciousness of Muslims that is different in many areas.

But also the author is integrated into a socio-cultural system that shapes his thinking, so that there is actually only "location-bound thinking", which demands reserve towards one's own thinking and restraint in judging other mental entities, except for a critique of ideology in clear language. Objectivity as detached ideational being is not possible, all mental entities can largely be traced back to socio-cultural constants. In addition, there is the theorem of concepts as "constructs of interpretation" proclaimed by constructivism, the content of which changes through higher and higher levels of schematism interpretations. And add to this the "theory impregnation" (Lenk 1995, 44) of perceptions, whereby, if we apply the ideology criteria to Islamism, they act like schemas of pre-structuring experience. It is a religious-fundamentalist genuine form of thinking with a militant basis, in which the differences with our objectivity striving thinking predominate, because the relationship to science, art, nature, society, religion is predisposed by ignorance, blind emotionality and allegiances to religious leaders. A brave and honest fundamentalist cannot perceive the West, if he perceives it, in any other way than satanic, egocentric, imperialistic, materialistic.

The dilemma between "thinking in terms of being" and objectivity has, in my opinion, been resolved rationally and conclusively by Tepe in his book *Theorie der Illusionen* (1988). His point of departure starts from the "quasi-transcendental status" (203) of value attitudes, in this case ideologically motivated Islamism and Western secularism. Both are incommensurable **ideologies(-)** if they deny their historical preference and offer themselves as truth par excellence. Both are useful designs, if they perceive their own socio-cultural conditionalities in themselves and reduce them, as far as they can; because by their own location reflection they are capable of error elimination, although always a rest of "location-boundness" remains, because even the critical subject can operate again only "bound to its location".

Tepe calls this knowledge, in contrast to relative knowledge, which presupposes absolute knowledge, "relational" (210) knowledge. It is a knowledge that, in contradiction to the absolute knowledge that Islam, Islamism, and also jihadism claim, appears modestly, because it knows about its own "connectedness to being. The practical consequence of this is that even dichotomous systems of thought, insofar as they want to see through their quasi-transcendental premises, can certainly come to a *modus vivendi*.

The ideology criteria name the elements acting as amplifiers, which can thus act as amplifiers of quasi-transcendental premises, so that they must be read in the direction of "ideology production" as their production factors, with the exception of the criterion "theory deficit", which analytically identifies the ulterior motives of ideological thinking, i.e., identifies as causes of this deficit "absolute truth assertion", "empty formulas", "dichotomous interpretation schemes", "demonization of the enemy image", "monopoly of knowledge", "ambivalence", "asymmetry", "selective perception". In a broad sense, the naturalistic fallacy, if it is known to the actors, is also to be counted among the ideology criteria, because here, despite logical prohibition, descriptive premises are made into descriptive moral conclusions, although they may function at most only as good reasons. Thus, both cognitive and moral conclusions follow from the 'authentic' interpretation of the Koran, which indiscriminately claim the same binding truth status.

The epistemological consequences from the Koranic ontology are exactly opposite to ours determined by science. There is no balance between a cognizing being and what he cognizes, but the 'right' side, the object, the Koran, describes the reality itself, it is pre-existent for a Muslim, it is potential reality, which ever and ever passes over into actual reality, created by God. The human mind is a gift of Allah insofar as it is sufficient to comprehend his world in a limited way. It can only measure itself against God's objective world. Eating from the "tree of knowledge", the human striving to be like God, is not mentioned in the Koran, although the mysticism of an Al-Ghazali considers participation in divine knowledge possible. In the Golden Age, this self-understanding changed as thinkers confronted what was handed down to them in terms of faith with human insight, with their own reason. This creates a natural opposition to the traditional interpretation of the truths of faith, to which corresponds an incipient separation of faith and knowledge. Islamic orthodoxy recognizes the danger of strengthening man's role vis-à-vis God and does what it always does. Objectivism, the alignment of the mind with the divine order and thus its and its cementation, triumphs over a subjective reason that has just set out on a voyage of discovery of its own limits and those of revelation.

Quranic Objectivism has four consequences:

1. he does not form, as already said, a subject-object differentiation,
2. does not bring about any innovations in the development of science in the scientific sense,
3. knows no human rights by self-legislation and only a low value of the earthly human existence,
4. negates evolution and historicism.

Point 2 is a fact not to be elaborated here, because it is considered indisputable also from Islam and gives the reason why the Islamic world, when it collides with the scientific-industrial Western world, first sinks into paralysis and depression. Point 1 will be elaborated in the next chapter "Islamism and Science", so that here only the questions about human rights and the value of a human life as well as the absence of historicism and biological evolutionism in Islam are left to be answered.

From the Koranic objectivity follows only a slight individuation pressure on human existence. Actually, only the collective, the *umma,* the community of believers, counts, which also strives for the world state with the goal of universal domination of the religious ideology of Islamism. The individual gains true life only in paradise; on earth, his life is more incidental because Allah determines his destiny and not so much his own performance. Man is by himself an immature being who gains a very limited selfhood only through Allah. The most important 'day' in a Muslim's life is the Last Judgment, which is determined by two symbols, the book and the scales. The book has recorded all good and evil deeds, the scales balance them and pronounce the judgment according to the preponderance of one side. For this reason, Islam has already been pejoratively called the "bookkeeper's religion" (Heine 2003, 41).

Therefore, there can be no legal order in Islam in which sovereign people give laws to themselves; for the legal order is from God and a gift to mankind. That the Islamic world nevertheless derives its conception of human rights from the Koran can only be welcomed; but the never missing hint that the laws must actually come from God diminishes their significance, because only the Koran as the authentic word of God always guarantees their validity and constantly determines the context with its moral premises, not the striving and lacking human being who himself deals with the world. "Religion without subjective risk" - this is what Islam could be called. In reality, however, when controversial issues have to be decided, the model of a universal God-state becomes very questionable; for the interpretation of the law is incumbent on an immense army of mullahs and ayatollahs who speak with one voice only when it comes to discrimination against the West, so that humanity is not well advised to uncritically adopt the human rights that are thought to be universal but meant to be Islamic.

With the philosophically little developed conception of the human subjectivity and its autonomous being also its low human appreciation is connected. The positively connoted motto "Man is the measure of all things" (Protagoras), which at the same time criticizes his hubris, corresponds to a high esteem of the subject. In return, Islam has the guiding concept of God as an absolute sovereign who exercises his rule by virtue of his own perfection. While man as a value in himself represents with Kant and today in the general understanding the goal of his self-formation, so that he must never be regarded only as a means (like a nature thing), but also as a being of freedom, which demands respect from God, he is in Islam subject of a power which rules him absolutely and therefore of low self-worth. Respect for God is also projected onto dictatorial regimes as submission to authoritarian secular forms of rule, because these derive their form of rule from the Koran. They are Allah's gift, for which the Muslim must be grateful. He owes nothing to himself. The low self-worth corresponds to a low self-esteem, which can only be compensated by anti-Western mass events; only the *umma,* the collective, grants the believer security, so that it and not the individual is the bearer of self-worth. Where the individual is nothing, but the community is everything, the former becomes an indifferent case by being only an edgeless example of the objectified norms and traditions.

Now it becomes also explicable that the low esteem of the personality can take even more clear forms if it is only about members of the scriptural religions, of animistic religions and atheists. The apostate is finally outlawed and can be killed with general approval of the *Sharia* and the *Umma*!

Islamism relentlessly exploits the low intrinsic value of its fellow believers and the zero value of the rest of humanity by turning all inhabitants of Western countries into infidels whose harm and killing is a work pleasing to God. He arrogates himself to be the guardian of Islam and the world, which are threatened by a terrible danger from the West that only he can avert. The Koran serves as a quarry for useful arguments that must serve to legitimize and legalize the imperialist implications of Islamism's world domination. In many places, with the public support of Islamic religious representatives, but even more with their clandestine solidarity, what a human life is worth is demonstrated. Kidnappings, beheadings, bombings, suicide bombings, underhanded murder are, in the sense of Islamism, which in turn is based on its interpretation of the Koran and the *Sunna,* legitimate means of getting rid of the forces that oppose the universalism of its claim to rule.

Thereby it is noticeable that with brothers in faith similarly 'short process' is made as with 'infidels'. What receives metaphysical glorification as sacrifice for Allah and Islam is the naked claim to power of Islamism, which believes to embody the world-historical development (as quantitative unfolding), which can be accelerated by the mentioned 'means'. The merciless fight against the West becomes a 'service of God', the greed for power of many religious functionaries or autocratic rulers is camouflaged as God's will and accepted as natural by the people, who only know the Koran, and that from their mouths. There is yet another variant of the globalization of Islamism, "the Europeans are now to be defeated with the weapons of demography" (quoted in Broder, 2006, 151).

The fourth point, the absence of historicism in biology and history, is explained by the cosmology of Islam, the permanent creation of world and life by Allah. There is no place for coincidence, change, self-legislation of nature, historically unique processes, freedom as indeterminism, by whose interaction a creative independence, openness of the results and a self-controlled development of the animate and inanimate nature would be possible. Historically independent developments and the work of world-historical personalities according to their preferences contradict the omnipotence of God The rejection of Western evolutionism in nature and culture is based on the interpretation of the Koran as an "unchangeable treasure of knowledge" (after Prenner 2005, 125 f.). And now follows the already well known thesis that the West, through the philosophy of the Golden Age, had appropriated fragments of the Koran, in which the knowledge for all time was stored pre-existently; and this also future knowledge, especially in the sciences, had been updated by the West rather than by Islam. Thus, development in Islam means the elaboration of the already existing "treasure of knowledge", so that development is at most to be understood as the unfolding of divine potency.

What is the nature of Islamism's political historical utopia? For this purpose, I would like to draw on the analysis *Fundamentalism in Islam* (Tibi 2002, 83-85). The term "Djahiliyya"[92] is to be seen as central to the argument. First, the Islamic historical utopia will be presented as a linear unfolding, which is very similar to the one that already begins with Abraham here.

1. Period of pre-Islam (*Djahiliyya*).
2. Appearance of Islam and struggle with other worldviews (Manichaeism).
3. Victory of Islam, installation of the world domination of the 'true Imam', who, however, has not yet been found.

Islamism reinterprets this utopia for its own purposes:

1. *Neo-Djahiliyya* now refers to the worldwide infection of Islam by decadent Western civilization.
2. Islam is fighting the atheistic West with ever greater success.
3. The *Hakimiyyat Allah*, the rule of Allah on earth[93] , finally ends the infiltration of Islam with corrupted Western modernity and proclaims its comprehensive victory.

Phase 2, the self-reflection of Islam on its traditions and values, has already begun; and under the leadership of Islamism, a total war of liberation is being waged, in which all means are justified because they serve a good cause, that of the worldwide victory of Islam. Thus, the repetition of what happened to Mohammed is being sought on a higher level. Where one obeys, chips fall. The jihad activists are responsible for the latter.

---

[92] It has two meanings: first, it means the pre-Islamic period, and second, "new form of unbelief," "cultural modernity" (84).
[93] The Shiites saw Khomeini as the "Hidden Imam" (Armstrong 2004, 431), through whom a "new age of justice" (431) seemed to dawn. God had influenced history in his sense for the blessing of world Islam. In Iran, the imams behave as God's governors.

One episode may illustrate the ambivalent attitude of Islamism to scientific thinking: Already in the 19th century, the Ottoman Empire was regarded as "the sick man on the Bosporus"; thus, there could no longer be any talk of an Islamic world power. 'What then is the secret of the new Western world power,' the caliph wanted to know. "Science and modern technology" the envoys answered (after Tibi 2001, 35). The author calls the adoption of both cultural technologies an 'illusion' (35), 'the Islamic dream of half modernity' (35). For science and technology cannot be separated from their basic assumptions, so that with this adoption, if it is to lead to own productions, also their implications as "Trojan horses" or "retroviruses", related to the Islamic religious life, must be accepted; unless Islam would face up to the Enlightenment through a historical-critical reflection, allow its political ambitions to be democratically legitimized and take on the existential needs of the faithful as pastoral care.

If Islamism wants to take a world-dominating position, it must, on the one hand, promote the adoption of Western technology and, on the other hand, fiercely fight its worldview assumptions, e.g., secularization. "Koran and Kalashnikov" (as a symbol of non-Muslim technology) must be compatible. Since Islam has come into contact with the superior technology of the West, it has experienced an ambivalent, often hostile relationship between Western science and its undeniable successes and its philosophical premises. As a way out, he has made the principle "the end justifies the means" his maxim in scientific questions of existence (atomic physics), so that everything that promotes Islam is permitted. For the Koran itself states that it is the duty of every Muslim to pursue science and acquire education. It remains permissible to ask why, if Muhammad commanded every Muslim to strive for science, nothing has been handed down of a flourishing Islamic scientific enterprise. Even the reformer Tahtawi (d. 1883) praises the Christians for their scientific enterprise, but restricts his approval to that which does not contradict the Koran. Abduh (1849-1905), a modernist, justifies his positive attitude toward science by arguing that Islam was "friendly to reason" (after Tibi 2001, 46), while Christianity had been "hostile to reason" (46), so that the epoch of Islamic enlightenment had existed only to put dogmatic Christianity in its place-an astonishing intellectual variant from Absurdistan. The reformer Al-Reziq demands the separation of religion and politics, which would have created a free space for the sciences as well, which earned him the destruction of his existence.

Professors Garischa and Zibaq criticize the industrialization of the West because it holds the values of machines higher than those of man. Islam, on the other hand, puts the human being in the first place, he is a "producer" who finds himself in his products (after Tibi 1991, 45). Long live the pleasant self-deceptions! They attribute the actual industrial backwardness of the Islamic world to the alienation from the true faith. There the nonsensical thesis imposes itself that diligent reading in the Koran must release a true industrial innovation rush with the Muslims. Al-Gundi's theses seem even more adventurous and ideologically breakneck. His frequently heard premise that the Koran is the exclusive source of human knowledge leads him to claim that Bacon, the father of inductive natural sciences, in his *Novum Organum* actually only received what was laid down in the Koran. The inductive methodology had been practiced by Islamic scholars before him. Thus, the West, like a thief, had stolen science from Islam, which had to take it back from the West by "re-appropriation" (230).

Here, the ideological effect of ambivalence is particularly glaring. On the one hand, the West is technologically superior to Islam. On the other hand, Muslims believe in their superiority, so that "acceptance thresholds" (233) arise. These are reduced by believing the illusion that Western knowledge actually originated in the minds of Islam. But then orthodox Islam would actually be its own gravedigger, for it should have introduced the Enlightenment. Similarly, the Islamist Al-Ghazali calls for the re-moralization of Islam, for only through this can it achieve scientific success. The scholar Afghani wants to reform Islam in the sense of Luther and then retain it as a belief system and "take over the scientific culture from Europe" (129). He has thus discovered the formula for how a universal scientific culture can emerge in Islam. The Islamic modernist, however, remains dogmatic by belittling the achievements of modern science and seeing in "sacrifice" and "effort" (after Tibi 2001, 187) according to the Qur'an the mastery of science so that it is compatible with the Qur'an. Here it should be briefly interjected that the scientific enterprise demands freedom of the researchers, autonomy with regard to its premises and conclusions, and democratic manners.

Especially in the sciences the dualism I/world is valid in the form of the dichotomy subject/object. How it is formed psychically in man was described very impressively by Konrad Lorenz[94] . This rational everyday function of human thinking is, as already said, changed by its disciplining in such a way that it learns to comprehend the outside world by means of scientific methods. This relation leaves no room for a cognition or intervention of God: the world as presupposed by the positive sciences is 'godless', which is why Islamism, while reaping the fruits of this highly successful relation, does not want to comprehend its ontological implications. Such an attitude has been labeled 'ambivalence' here, which must divide a Muslim's self-understanding, so that emotional overreactions are to be expected as a way out.

The disciplining of the scientific subject has led to its own scientific ethics, called "objectivity postulate" by Monod (1971, 149) and "scientific ethos" by Mohr (1983**). The** latter compares Monod's characterization of the scientist's work to "a self-contained order" (304) and criticizes the scientific asceticism that a scientist must practice. There is a misunderstanding here; for Monod's demand applies only to actual scientific work, in which the empirical subject must purify himself into a pure thinking subject in order to exclude, as far as possible, extraneous influences on the result; otherwise, he is a man who is "constantly dependent [on] the goodwill and material support of the public" (304 f.). This problem aims directly at the issue of "value-free science," see Max Weber in "Werturteilsstreit"[95] . Here the embedding hypothesis applies, that science is embedded in the general activities of society and in the empirical status of the scientist, but must not be influenced by it in the finding of

---

[94] In *The Reverse of the Mirror,* he starts from the observation that "in our experience the inner-conditioned and the outer-conditioned overlap" (1997, 13) and that inner states exert an influence on the perception of outer circumstances (13). Our self-consciousness hovers, as it were, over inner-conditioned and outer-conditioned and tries to judge what about the idea can be attributed to the subject, what to the outer world. Everything that is constantly perceived differently is to be attributed to the subject, everything that is constantly perceived again and again is to be attributed to the object apart from us, to the object. By subtracting the subjective part from the total impression, the idea of an objective external world gains sharper and sharper contours, no matter what subjectively altered states are present. Lorenz calls the process of genesis of the subject-object relation "objectivation" (13). This relation already determines our everyday life; by disciplining the everyday subject to a pure, methodically thinking subject, the undifferentiated perception becomes a constant and concrete object to be described, the practice-related thinking becomes science.

[95] See Meja/Stehr (eds. 1982): *Zum Streit um die Wissenssoziologie.*

results, except for language, technological status and problem definition, which limit the scope of scientific research results. So, is pure knowledge to be realized by an autonomous science or as interest-led[96] inseparable from subjective opinions? It should be added that the exclusion of socio-cultural influences on scientific work only meets a demand in the sense of a regulative idea to strive for it.

The result of scientific work, as the example of "Lyssenko" (a neolamarckist under Stalin) teaches, must not be changed by political-ideological correctness or personal ambition, because then it is useless. So it is in everyone's interest to allow autonomy to the internal scientific enterprise. Here two personalized theories meet, that of the autonomous human being and the autonomous scientist. Both linked, this means for science and the scientist: democratic conditions. Science can only flourish creatively under democratic conditions.[97] This requires a self-given set of rules, against which the sanction of "moral disapproval" of the *scientific community* results.

Being ostentatiously disregarded by one's professional colleagues proves to be an extremely effective means of exerting pressure. However, this only applies if science forms an international, very critically communicating and judging world community. Prescribed provincialism, when compartmentalized, leads to the illusion of enjoying general approval, since all researchers (from the provinces) must agree to the research results because of considerations of expediency. Thus, there can be no scientific Islamist physics, biology or mathematics.

Mohr (1983, 310-313) has codified this universal scientific ethos, which consists of 'basic assumptions', 'basic presuppositions'[98] and 'actual commandments'. The *scientific community* is a model for a basic democratic attitude

---

[96] The best-known example of interest-driven research is provided by Soviet communism, which, by means of Lyssenko's ideological premise of the inheritance of acquired traits (neo-Lamarckism), advocated a party-conformist theory of inheritance that set it back several decades of genetic research.

[97] In the Soviet Union, there were several isolated islands where value-free science was conducted.

[98] Because of the density of the argument, Mohr comes to the floor without comment. "Basic requirements include:
- Freedom of thought (intellectual freedom),
- Freedom of research (the result of a scientific research must not be determined by factors from outside the sciences),

whose consequences mean independence, self-determination, and general discussion of research results, but also 'bloodless' punishment for violations. If the scientific ethos is negated by Islamism, in that the research result must correspond with the statements of the Koran, then it will fare like communism, which left behind a scientific disaster. A universalization of the fundamentalist understanding of science would be tantamount to a reversion to the Stone Age in its effects.

The decree that scientific results must not contradict the Koran, indeed that they must confirm it, leads to an absurd scientific world, which can only bring harm and international disdain to Islam.

- Knowledge is good, i.e. reliable knowledge is better than ignorance under all circumstances.

In other words: Knowledge is a supreme value, the highest good for a human being, as long as he pursues science (primacy of knowledge)" (1983, 310-313).

Subjectivism is thus the condition for the emergence of the subject-object relationship, which not only makes the sciences possible, but also the self-assessment of man as a being in itself, his self-legislation as an autonomous personality, from which human rights can be derived, but also feeds the practical (ethical) background theory of the form of government called "democracy". What is Islamism's relationship to this form of government? The fundamental difference between subjectivism and individualism on the one hand and Quranic objectivism on the other is the reason for the fundamentally different systems of government, "democracy" and "theocracy," which has developed into a feudalistic-oriental despotism in many variations throughout history.

In "In the Shadow of Allah", Tibi (1994) examined the relationship between theocracy (dictatorship of God) and democracy. Here, the arguments of the incompatibility of the two background theories and the forms of government that condition them will be stated. The summary will then explore whether there are compatible segments of both views that are fundamentally opposed to each other.

At first, the fronts are clear: The Islamist Qutb calls supporters of popular sovereignty "infidels," thus excluding democratically minded Muslims from the faith community; Benhadj warns: "Democracy is unbelief" (20). And again Qutb: "After the decline of democracy to bankruptcy, the West has nothing left to give to humanity [...]. It is time for Islam to take the lead" (quoted in Tibi 2001, 330). Enayat resignedly states: "Those Muslim thinkers who face this issue courageously and free from the constraints of their faith [...] usually end up with the open admission that Islam and democracy are incompatible" (334).

Still other doctrines take as their starting point the *shura* (consultation)[99] - mentioned only twice in the Koran - to which the Prophet invited his comrades-in-arms - and, like Abu-Zaid-Fahmi, even see in it the root of democracy:

---

[99] The two Quranic passages that refer to the *shura* read:
"And those who listen to their Lord and establish prayer and whose conduct is (a matter of) mutual consultation, and who spend from what We have given them" Surah (42:38).

The Islamic form of rule is the most advanced political structure that mankind has ever known. Islam has established democracy and established the *shura* as its main argument [...]. With this achievement, Islam has no equal in the history of mankind" (quoted in Tibi 2001, 314 f.).

To develop a theory of Islamic democracy on this basis and to demand its universalization is adventurous and can only be explained by ideological stubbornness. Even more remarkable is that the term "democracy" can take on two completely opposite meanings: as an invention of Islam, it is the 'most progressive' form of rule; as an invention of Kant, it is an 'ugly system' - a failed attempt at Islamist dialectics and a good example of a naive reception of empty words.

Here, Islamism has been guilty of self-contradiction by claiming to be the first to practice this form of government, but then proclaiming "democracy is unbelief" in the same breath. Of course, a distinction must be made here between a 'good' i.e. Muslim democracy and an 'evil' Western one. The ambivalence of Islamism's concept of democracy should always be taken into account when making political decisions.

Maududi calls democracy an "ugly system" (quoted in Tibi 2002, 80). The spectrum of the Islamists' understanding of democracy ranges from demonization to apostasy, decay hypothesis, incompatibility hypothesis to true Islamic invention. The last formulation, as an early Islamic invention, is also meant in an anti-democratic way, because while the West supports a false, rotten, rotten democracy, Islam is the true hoard, the guardian of the Grail of democracy, so that there should be only one democracy in this world: the true Islamic one, which excludes plurality.

Many Islamic scholars living in the West consider the introduction of democratic conditions in Islam, which is dominated by Islamists, to be impossible at present. If one lets the sources of the understanding of democracy speak, rationalism, Kant's subjectivism, theories of natural law, and compares them with the model of an absolute and absolutist rule of God, based on the Koran and Sharia, which grant the believers only an insignificant individual existence in the collective, the researchers must be agreed with. The form of government

---

[...]. So forgive them and ask forgiveness for them; and consult them in matters of administration; but when you have made up your mind, then put your trust in Allah. Allah loves those who trust" Surah (3:159).

that follows from Islam is, with almost naturalistic necessity, that of an "Oriental despotism" of people or parties; however, there are exceptions. Political murder is traditional in Islam because there can be no voting out of office of an unjust imam or system; they are "the shadow of Allah on earth." In general, Islamic representatives cannot be deposed by the people, because they cannot be elected by them either. This also applies to secular dictatorships. Rightly or wrongly, conspiracy groups are formed, which then assassinate the "shadow of Allah" (Tibi 2004), not without first declaring him a religious imperson. According to K. Wittvogel, in order to escape this fate, it is necessary for the ruler to

> as the tiger must possess the physical means to destroy its victims. The despot possesses such means. He has the army, police and intelligence service at his disposal without restriction. He has prison guards, torturers, executioners, and all the tools necessary to arrest, torture, and kill a suspect (quoted in Tibi 2002, 75).

In the wake of such despotisms (Saddam Hussein), corruption, nepotism, social conflicts, political persecution, political murders and political appropriation of Islam occur with almost natural regularity. The 'rule of God' in Islam almost always mutates into a variant of despotism. The cause of fundamentalisms, which cooperate with all authoritarian forms of government, are crisis situations that purport to have a simple and administratively transparent solution to the problem posed. The crisis situation of Islam (see similarity with the crisis situation of the Weimar Republic and the Russian Empire before the October Revolution after World War I) is summarized as follows:

1. Since its founding, Islam has seen itself as a universal cultural system in which politics and religion form an inseparable unit. Its self-image is characterized by feudalistic structures, pre-technological modes of production and unconditional subordination to the will of God. Through the encounter with Western civilization in the 19th century, Muslims are awakened from the centuries-long slumber of a culture frozen in tradition and must concede their inferiority to the West.

2. Demoralized in this way, they have nothing to oppose the imperial and subsequently colonial desires of the West. There are now the arrogant Western occupiers or exploiters who shamelessly exploit the economic

being at the mercy of the West, which is also reflected culturally anthropologically in the contempt of 'Muslim' culture (as a collective term). The reaction of enlightened Muslims is to adapt to the West and its values in order to no longer perceive its hegemony.

3. The unreflective adoption of Western civilization has negative consequences: Mass misery, social unrest, incipient dissolution of traditional family structures, moral unrestraint of liberalism, weak and corrupt governments of their own. The West's internal understanding of democracy does not at all correspond to the external distorted image it realizes in the Muslim world. Islam, as the unifying bond of Muslim identity, is increasingly being called into question and is experiencing a serious crisis of meaning.

4. The import of a Western ideology of liberation, socialism, offers itself as a way out, but its 'godless' conception also meets with resistance from the oppressed masses.

5. The Western-sponsored particularization of universal Islam into rather arbitrarily constructed nation-states with their own regional conflicts prevents a common policy that Pan-Arabism is supposed to revive. The lost Six-Day War also passes the death sentence on this approach to crisis management. The enemy image of "Israel" and "the USA" emerges, to which other Western countries can be assigned at will.

6. The 'victorious' oil crisis does not benefit the people, but corrupt oligarchies who cooperated with the West by using the petrodollars to oppress their own subjects. But from then on, oil becomes a political weapon.

Islam, it can be said, has historically had almost only negative experiences with the West and its democracy. It is only a fig leaf for economic, political and technological hegemonic aspirations, the blessings of which have mostly been shared only by the ruling clique. These corrupt regimes were alimented without moral scruples by the West, which wants to secure sales markets and oil; but it 'forgot' to export its democratic and social principles as well. The double face of Western 'people's rule' can be described as follows: internally and among themselves, democratic practices apply; externally, regimes are supported from which one expects an economic or strategic advantage. Neither socialism nor democratic conditions nor secularization have been able to win over the Islamic countries. So the only way left is to reflect on one's own history and culture. A vacuum had just arisen in world history, which Islamism, already theoretically stabilized, immediately occupied. This seizes the initiative and demands the following counter-reactions:

1. Isolation from the West and its subversive ideas,
2. Rediscovery of Islam with its social power of integration,
3. Rediscovery of own historical flowering phases,
4. Recollection of its own glorious political and religious past and construction of its own historical utopia, which prophesies a renaissance for Islam and a shameful downfall for the West,
5. Construction of a theory of decay of the Western world and its democratic roots, which makes it the duty of Islam to realize its universality predicted by God.

In this way, Islamism's crisis management reactions demonstrate the mechanism by which a new self-confidence can emerge from a despised worldview, which in turn can take on the function of creating identity. One's own deficits are projected onto the opponent, who is now increasingly stylized as the enemy and moral fiend, under powerful ideological argumentation, so that one's own position is strengthened and that of the enemy is weakened.

Finally, the newly emerged **ideology(-)** underlines its mission of redemption, so that the despised become the future masters of the world. Ideological warfare has begun with the artifice of propagating a state utopia that will soon guide reality. The Western democracies are and have become run-down; Islam, as a resurgent religion, has the divine mandate to establish the ideal state globally as the rule of God. With this battle cry, which is eagerly taken up by the underprivileged classes because of their meager existence, the religious message of Islam is to be given world standing politically through Islamism.

By mutually supporting Islam and Islamism, Koran and struggle, God and violence, war to the West and peace to the "House of Islam", the last and final 'small' jihad is to enthrone God's kingdom on earth. Islamism now blows to the attack to achieve the total victory, which then justifies all victims. The offensive towards Germany through targeted immigration and constant interventions of the Islamic protective power "Turkey" with the help of its "Ministry of Religion" has already begun.

From where does Islamism as a winning ideology gain its arguments? We have already been reminded of the social component of Islamism, which takes over schools, hospitals and general welfare for reasons of popular approval, not out of pity for the suffering population (see Hamas in the Palestinian territories and Hezbollah in Lebanon), in order to win popular favor as a "social conscience." Even more important as a cultural stabilizer, however, is the deep religious commitment of Muslims to their religion, so that Islamism pursues two strategies at the same time: internally, a re-Islamization; externally, the creation of a coherent theory of the historical necessity of the new world-dominating function of Islam, which advertises itself as a salvation from the Western system, which has become rotten in itself, even in the Third World.

The myth of a liberation movement, whose goals basically every Muslim can agree with, is first to liberate the oppressed co-religionists living in the West[100] until it can then raise the Green Flag of the Prophet all over the world.

---

[100] Two quotes on this:
"The Islamic World Congress, at its working meeting in Cairo, called for a new strategy for the *dawa/call to* Islam [...], this includes the establishment of Islamic centers in Europe [...] in order to prepare the Muslims living there for their role in the future [...]. The application of the Sharia as a guideline in the lives of Muslims is to be demanded" (document in: al-Sharq al-Ausat of July 28, 1993, quoted from Tibi 1994, 11).
"Islamic laws are not limited to Muslims and their societies. They are created to organize all human relations and are therefore assigned to all humanity, whether Islamic or not yet Islamized; "for Islamic rules create a universal international law" (Sabir Tuayma: *The Islamic Sharia in the Age of Science,* Beirut 1979, 208, quoted in Tibi 2002, 48).

When Chancellor Merkel claims that Islam has arrived in Germany, she is not really saying anything new, because the foundations were laid much earlier.[101] But Islamism can give other and similarly serious reasons for its new world-historical role. Nature as God's creation, as an object *sui generis, which in* Islam is treated with care and respect because it is the image of God's existence and will, is regarded by the West, according to Kant, as an "object of experience," but not as having any value in itself. It is thus subordinated to human availability without limit, so that it is relentlessly exploited by the West according to its commercialized worldview.

The principle of commercialization is taken to the extreme, in that only one value now determines the Western world, the conversion of all values into a market value: human beauty becomes a commercialized sexual object, human intimacy of coexistence the 'grub' of the public through sensational reporting, human precautionary striving the senseless accumulation of often unneeded consumer goods, industrial production the ever more unrestrained exploitation of natural resources, to achieve annual rates of increase, the alleged human self-worth to the function of a 'civilization' based only on material consumption, values become mere usability, the loss of values becomes nihilism, existence secured by social structures becomes ruthless elbow-egocentrism. Even if many arguments are exaggerated, a complacent looking down of the West on the power inherent in Islamic culture is misplaced. Islam, however, must fear that if it accepts the "natural fallacy" as a fallacy and opens itself to enlightenment, it may suffer a fate similar to that of Christianity, so that the harsh regulations by its Islamist superstructure in the sense of insisting on its absolute possession of truth are to be explained, if not at all condoned.

Islamism's idea of the state is directed toward the establishment of a state of God, because both the democratic Occident, with its separation of religion and state, of value and reason, and the despotically ruled Orient, with its instrumentalization and corruption of Islam to secure its own power, do not do justice to man. Common language (Arabic), common thought of a rebirth of the religion "Islam" and its manifestation in a state realizing God's laws, common

---

[101] "The traditions we call 'Western' or 'Islamic' can no longer be identified with specific geographic regions. [...] The rapidity of Muslim immigration [...] suggests that we will soon have to speak not only of Islam *and* the West, but of Islam *in the* West (Kelsay, J.: *Islam and War. The Gulf War and Beyond.* Louisville/KY 1993, 118, quoted in Tibi 2001, 80).

enemy image of a run-down but still dangerous West and corrupt East, common acceptance of violence for the sake of the 'great cause', common 'knowledge' that all this happens on behalf of God, a fervently hoped-for enthronement of the God-sent 'great leader', the 'true' Imam, make a third world war conceivable, predicted by Pflüger (2004), but also by others, in which a God-state or confederation of states determined to the extreme would annihilate each other in the fight against a technically superior secular coalition. This scenario of a negative utopia alone should lead both sides to realize that they will only be losers if they continue to work toward a confrontation.

7. From Islamism to Jihadism

We can distinguish two forms of jihad. As a 'greater' jihad it means "the inner spiritual struggle of the individual against the lower impulses of one's own soul, against vice, passion and ignorance" (Barth 2002, 71). As a 'lesser' jihad, and this is what it is about, it is a "holy war" that "must be waged until all peoples submit to Islam" (71). Both Islam and the West meet when it comes to the contemporary meaning of jihad as 'holy war'. The former main meaning as purification of the life of faith is visibly fading in favor of today's understanding as 'war against the infidels'. However, conventions used to be observed in the conduct of 'holy war'. But this 'chivalrous commentary' it no longer observes today. This 'holy war against the infidels' has undergone an inflationary expansion through Islamic-style fundamentalism, in that it has been extended "to all kinds of armed activities" (72), seizes and justifies any means to destroy the enemy, and transfigures the Islamist terrorists into martyrs who will be rewarded by Allah with the joys of paradise. Nor, for example, can there be any question of the commandment to wage only defensive wars and to observe the rules of war.[102] Here, above all, the murderous action of Islamist horsemen militias against the autochthonous population in the province of Darfur is to be mentioned. (Here clarifying words of the God-believing Islam are missing, which denounce this perversion of the religion as justification of crimes against humanity clearly and credibly for incompatible with the faith in God).

---

[102] The terrorist attacks on the London Underground were explained by the fact that those who would have voted for the British Prime Minister Blair were also to blame for the invasion of Iraq. And what about those who voted for other parties?

The thesis that Islam represents a religion with great potential for ideologization[103] - we need only recall the insistence on the absolute claim to truth, the globality of the claim to rule, the collectivization of Islamic life in the Sharia and the possession of the monopoly on truth -, is to be continued here in the form that Islamism based on Islam, which in turn promotes the militant interpretations of the Koran that suit it, provides the legitimizing justifications for jihad, the uncompromising struggle not only against the West. An **ideology(-)** enters the phase of armed struggle when it wants to realize a totalitarian concept politically. Unfortunately, Islam does not defend itself against its political instrumentation; on the contrary, it believes it can profit from the apparent religious renaissance and is all too willing to be harnessed to the Islamists' cart.

Lieber uses the term "totalitarianism" in two senses (see chap.4, 2.2). What does he specifically understand by the term "totalitarianism"? Its characteristics are to be enumerated here and also recognized as a theory of Islamism, whose practice consists in waging an initially still religious-ideological total war.

The totalitarianism (Islamism)
- is a mass movement,
- demands an uncontrollable claim to exclusivity of rule,
- introduces a centralized state apparatus (still utopia because of the different interests of the individual Muslim states),
- regulates all areas of life so that there is no longer any private freedom (Sharia),
- claims the economic and educational monopoly (Koranic schools),
- organizes permanent control by a terrorist secret police,

---

[103] As an indication of this, one can cite the "hate preachers" who roam Western Europe with their message of extermination of the infidels, i.e. of us, and are prevented from doing so neither by the Islamic communities nor by the state. In the textbooks of the King Fahd Academy, the extermination of those of other faiths was demanded, as it always had been, until the school authorities finally intervened. I assume that in many Islamic countries a textbook investigation with the topic "The image of the non-Muslim in textbook literature" would reveal something similar to the King Fahd Academy. Perhaps an Arabic- or Turkish-speaking colleague will be found to tackle this work, which has now been done at the level of university research.

- produces justification strategies of power to immunize itself from possible changes of rule,
- forms state, religion and society into a unity (still utopia), which is to bring about a comprehensive identification of people and leadership,
- makes total domination over the masses appear as total domination of the masses,
- takes for itself exclusivity of the claim to rule and unlimitedness of the sphere of rule,
- obliges philosophy and the sciences to scientifically justify authoritarian rule,
- makes a dogmatic claim to truth, from which mission consciousness and proselytizing result, and institutionalizes a "providence" that guides and directs the 'true' believers,
- By means of emotionalization, schematization, black-and-white painting, radicalization of feeling, thinking and acting, it puts the masses in a constant state of readiness for aggression,
- produces an **ideology(-)** upstream of the whole life by means of frequent use of friend-foe dichotomies and demonization of enemy images,
- transfigures (religious) leaders and religion into the highest authority of truth because they supposedly possess special knowledge,
- fights other religions and world views because they are dangerous competitors with a different conception of truth.

These criteria, gained from communism and National Socialism, can be applied both to totalitarianism in general and to the specific form of "jihadism. The unifying bond of global Islamism is, on the one hand, this **ideology(-),** and on the other hand, the common language of Arabic as the language of the Koran and of many Muslims, which creates mutual togetherness and makes communication immensely easier.

But one criterion is still missing: concentration on a center of power, a centralist and monolithic center of control. The individual independent Islamic states can be trusted to make truces among themselves and recognize one or more centers of power (Iran, Saudi Arabia after an ouster of the monarchy, Turkey, Pakistan, Indonesia) so that Islamism can begin to dominate Western

Europe and the United States. Ayatollah Khomeini had much of such a 'light figure' that could have assumed such a function in a settlement of the conflict between Shiites and Sunnis, assuming the utopia of a universal and "true Imam or God state" to be re-established. In the previous century, the territorial center of Islam was in Constantinople, then in the Arab world; now Iran is preparing to take on the world heritage of Islam and to impose it militarily by building atomic bombs. But here, too, "the revolution eats its children" (Leonhard), in that, as in Iraq, jihadism, which is not yet centrally controlled, also serves to combat related denominations.

The conflicts smoldering between the individual nation-states of Islamic character make rapid centralization unlikely in the near future. Above all, the permanent conflict between Sunnis and Shiites, which we witness on a daily basis, is currently preventing a stable Muslim attitude toward the West. But a parallel system independent of the individual Islamic states has developed, Al-Qaeda, which forms a decentralized network activated by autonomously acting groups, linked by the media. Barth (2003) explains the emergence of this second Islamist international with the Afghan War, in which 'freedom fighters' from all over the world, where Muslims reside, converged to drive out the infidels, the Soviets, with American weapons assistance. That the USA became a victim of its anti-communism, because the aggression of the Afghan fighters after the victory was directed against it, with the same arguments as against the Soviet Union, cannot give any consolation as an irony of world history.

The Muslim 'freedom fighters' had an experience: like a primal experience, they experienced the solidarity of their fellow fighters because, despite all the differences in their colloquial languages and homelands, they were united by a common bond, Islam. This primal experience[104] of the spiritual unity of Islam created a platform on which the vision of an Islamic world empire was within reach. Even though the old tribal struggles broke out again after the withdrawal of the Soviets, the freedom fighters split into factions again, and the homelands viewed the returned fighters with suspicion because they also made a front against their own, often corrupt, authorities, the frontline experience of international Islamism was sufficient to strive for this unity in the underground. The means of sensitively striking the declared enemies (their own Westernized or dictatorial regimes, Israel and America, the entire decadent West) was the proclamation of "jihad," a total 'holy' war against them. Muslims living in the diaspora have also had the experience of Islamic internationalism, so it can be presumed that their willingness to cooperate transcends any nationality. They can (see London) 'spontaneously' form their own terror cells, which can be sure of great goodwill from radical Muslims.

In doing so, they make use of the notion of the backward-looking historical utopia that there was a pure, godly Islam that made Islam the world religion in the time of Muhammad and the four "rightly guided caliphs. The jihadists use this fundamentalist argument of re-Islamization to justify their irregular actions as terrorists. Islamism in its orthodox form is thus the cue for Islamist terrorism, the extended arm of jihadism. In this context, the life of the prophet is the model, because the times then (*hejira*) and today (apostasy from Islam through secularization) are similar. This reduces Muhammad's role for Islam to that of an irregular warrior, as has already been shown.

But whoever names this fact supposedly sins against the spirit of Islam, although in reality Islamism means a radicalization and militarization of Islam and makes the Prophet the model of political-religious murder and even

---

[104] Muslims also have this "primal experience" of unity in secular foreign countries, where, as brothers in faith, they only emphasize the commonality of their worldview through the diaspora situation. Thus, in addition to a Western-integrative component, "Euro-Islam" can also have the opposite effect. Instead of cultural rapprochement as in the beginning, a sealing off behind one's own uniform identity due to the diaspora situation is striven for (we have to bury the 'hatchet' in the face of the common enemy), through which the traditionally Muslim world also receives the impulse for ideological unification.

praises this as a 'God-pleasing work'. The real enemy of Islam is Islamism, not the West.

Muhammad is not just anyone in the history of Islam. His deeds and sayings are held in almost as high esteem as the Koran itself. Terrorists refer to them when they legitimize their actions. (This 'canonization' of Muhammad's life is not covered by anything). 'It can be no wrong if "in times of great political, social and religious crises" (Barth 2003, 26) we take an example from Muhammad, the man of God, and, when he was in a similar situation, also make use of his methods.' What kind of being does Islamism make of Allah so that he allows innocent and guilty, believers and non-believers, old and children, enemies and friends to be indiscriminately slaughtered in his name just to enforce his will?

God and Mohammed are appropriated by the jihadists as bloody despots to whom no means is sacrosanct in order to expand and secure an absolute rule of God (in reality that of the 'God warriors'). No enlightened person can understand this image of God, by the way also no really believing Muslim, who starts from a sovereign God, who does not let himself be taken in the tow of any **ideologies(-)**. The way to explain the events around Mohammed also in terms of contemporary history is declared apostasy by Islamism, which insists on a literal adaptation of the Koran. "The Islamist tries to correspond as far as possible to Islam as exemplified by the Prophet, and allows only the Koran as well as the *Sunna in* the literal sense to be considered as sources. The rest, the centuries of development and adaptation to the historical situation, he rejects" (143), Barth has to admit.

When it comes to the supposedly uncompromising enforcement of God's will, Islam generally does not attach much importance to subtle differentiations, because this religion does not recognize man as a self-worth and defines man's existence and being only from God. (The official power attributed to him makes him the administrator of God's concerns in the world, but not the creator of worlds of his own).

A person who opposes this order is an imperson, a nothing; and if it is an apostate, it is a praiseworthy act for anyone to kill him. Such a theory and practice of a religion in the 21st century is a scandal!

In the essay *"New Organizational Forms of Terrorism and Order Typologies of Transnational Politics"* (Behr 2002), the author examines the terrorist activities of Al-Qaeda. First, he distinguishes the terms "international," "multinational," and "transnational" from one another (110 f.). "International" means that a body with fixed headquarters is active in many countries, "multinational" that many nations are represented in it in terms of personnel, "transnational" that the organization operates in a decentralized manner in many countries without being controlled by a center. The latter is networked so that it can strike simultaneously in different countries. Such a cell consists of the terrorist core, around which legal companies such as banks, 'charities', individuals, even states are grouped, so that it can only be exposed through insider knowledge. But where does legality end and illegality begin here? It is therefore very difficult to offer solutions here that are also judicially satisfactory.

The term "*war of terrorism*" (113) has come into use here; this is a war fought with terrorist weapons, so that those attacked cannot provide an identifiable opponent. As seen in the war in Lebanon, this is an *asymmetric warfare* that is being waged here. What is despicable is that punitive reactions in response to terror, because the enemy remains invisible, often hit bystanders, which increases the bitterness of those who were supposed to be helped. Conversely, al-Qaeda's terrorist crimes are downplayed and publicly and secretly condoned by those who react with great sensitivity when the enemy attacks. Here, too, the ambivalent behavior of many Muslims is irritating.

Civilized states are characterized by four features:
1. integration of the political actor,
2. sovereignty,
3. National borders,
4. concept of a national security (116-168).

Terrorists are not bound up in the history and tradition of the country in which they operate; as "private individuals," they ignore the ordering function of the state, its legal norm, in which they happen to be. Borders define a certain space of political action. If this is 'de-bordered,' then the contours of nation-states become blurred, which increases the logistical resources of terrorism. The concept of a national security is characterized by predictability, so that the potential attacker knows what he is getting into. Al Qaeda's transnational mode of operation does not meet any of these four criteria, which means that this form of terrorism can no longer be controlled by a national policy. In my opinion, this organization can only be dealt with if the democratic states enable a logistical structuring among themselves similar to that of Al-Qaeda.

The first phase of transnationalization has successfully completed its trial runs (see terrorist acts), the second, in my opinion, will soon start, where many actions will then take place simultaneously, so that every citizen must feel massively threatened. The 'decadent' West will react to this permanent blackmail with good behavior and anticipatory obedience, as it is already doing now, by servilely fulfilling political-religious demands of Al-Qaeda, as it is critically pointed out essayistically by Broder (2006). Now the massive Islamic proselytizing can begin. The dislocation of power, transnationally fluctuating organization, virtual omnipotence, and lack of personalization on the part of al-Qaeda overwhelm the individual nation-state.

Philosophy is powerless here, because the terrorist actors obey an **ideologically(-)** unshakeable 'value background', if one can still use this expression here, which we can put with "inhuman" in descriptive sense. In order to help the Islamization of the world to a breakthrough, the use of any means is permitted, because it serves a 'good' purpose. National Socialism and Soviet Communism, with a similar justification of their 'highest good' "purity of race" and "classless society" respectively, fed the god "ideology" with an unprecedented number of human sacrifices. Jihadism continues this tradition.

It should also have become clear by now that the suicide bombers are not fanatical Muslims, but rationally thinking actors who want to cause maximum destruction. But how do young people come to sacrifice their lives for killing many more innocent people? There must be an apparatus behind these terrorists that provides motivation and training for these young people. The strategy of those behind them is always the same.[105] The young people are not forced to carry out these attacks; they see an honor in being allowed to carry them out because they are granted the "sacrificial death for Allah" (Heiligsetzer

---

[105] Heiligsetzer (2002, 157) summarizes these in five theses:
- "optimizing the precision and targeting of the 'military operation' by eliminating the otherwise necessary protection for the assassins themselves.
- maximum damage, both in terms of material and psychological injury to the enemy,
- the spectacular excitement of international interest,
- the almost complete uselessness of preventive measures,
- a [...] very difficult manhunt for accomplices and backers".

2002, 158) as "martyrs." (Every Muslim should know that suicide and murder are not covered by the Koran).

The strategists who promise the assassins eternal paradise for their deed know that they are lying. The "sacred religious feelings" of the faithful should actually rebel against them. Far from it. The relatives of the sacrificed youths are also proud of their dead children, whom they believe are now living in paradise. Why don't the believers turn against such Koran desecrators who don't get their own hands dirty? In addition, "the religious ideologists are not stingy with promises for the hereafter either: 70 relatives and friends of the perpetrator are allowed into paradise without regard to their way of life; he himself is abundantly provided with virgins, golden palaces and overflowing feasts" (159). This cynicism toward a religion can only come from atheists and nihilists who, for the sake of political calculation, make use of Islam and coolly calculate its symbolic power.

One can only guess how voluntary brainwashing through hate speech against the West turns young people into "living bombs"[106] . Who believes in such a paradise, whose inhibition threshold to 'go over corpses' is strongly lowered. It is given quasi the chance to live in the later life in such a way like many eastern potentates already today. Tolerance cannot be expected with such a strong motivation to become martyrs. Have actually the headscarf-wearing women of Islamic faith taken note of the contents of this Hadith, which promises them also in paradise what is already today, to be pleasure object and servile spirit of the man, but no own person? To what extent popular dreams and motives are reflected in this text is unknown to me.

---

[106] The following text is from Barth (2003, 79), who reveals a profound knowledge of Islam in this book. This hadith, which articulates a Muslim's understanding of the afterlife, has the following content:

"The prospects for the martyr who gives his life in the fight against the non-Muslims are enticing. Immediately after his death, the martyr enters the 'gardens of delight' (paradise), where physical well-being is well provided for: clear water that never goes stale and white milk that does not sour flow there in never-ending streams, as does heavy wine. Clothed in silk, the faithful rest on carpets and dine in silverware. There, the 72 black-eyed huris receive him, who conveniently change back into virgins immediately after each man's attendance; no man has ever touched them. Large and round are their youthful breasts, the rosy buds swell in expectation of the caresses. [...]. They never become loud, only with a gentle voice they speak to their master, for they are always satisfied with him, faithful and devoted. Menstruation and migraine do not know these pure beauties, always they are ready, always willing. [...]. Just in case, immortal boys are also present (beautiful like 'pearls'), who serve as cupbearers. In addition, a meeting with the prophet is arranged for martyrs. And since paradisiacal bliss does not depend on food and women alone, but male friendships are the only things that really matter in life and death, the martyr is allowed to choose 70 friends to accompany him on the day of resurrection. The first drop of blood that a martyr sheds washes away the sins of his earthly existence. [...]. Eternally he will remain 30 years old, no matter how old he was when he passed away. Nor will he ever know the discomfort that old age brings. For in order for him to prove himself a true lord of 72 eternally willing virgins, his potency will increase a hundredfold. When a suicide is sent on his mission, the parting formula is: 'May Allah be with you, may he give you success that you may reach paradise.' Thereupon the death candidate replies 'Inshallah - there we will meet' ".

8. Conclusion

This investigation has shown that two value systems striving for universality dominate our everyday life, subjectivism, which has proven to be very flexible and innovative since Greek antiquity in its confrontation with all European philosophies, and the objectivism of Islam in the form of a mythological-religious world background. While the former can look back on a long history of confrontation with other world-shaping intellectual currents, the latter has crossed blades with the philosophical world only once since Muhammad's codification of Islam in the Qur'an, in the Golden Age, and lost to orthodoxy, so that thereafter doctrinaire Islam was again directive for the Islamic world.

Thus, a philosophy that has developed many times in the course of history is confronted with a value system that has proven to be resistant to evolution since its foundation. Between these two more and more drifting apart value systems the fight has broken out, the fight for global hegemony. This shall now be summarized and an outlook dared, which can civilize this brutal confrontation already in progress.

8.1 Summary

The dualism of both world views, which has already become militant, ignites on the anthropological question: 'What is man?'

The occidental understanding proclaims as the highest value in modernity the self-knowing, standard-setting, creative human being, the subject who, on the basis of a methodical skepticism, separates questionable from undoubted knowledge and thus possesses knowledge that nullifies all skepticism and from this constitutes the knowledge of the objective world; religions assume an existentially conducive but only subordinate status of the subjective holding for-true in order to assist man with the question of meaning in this world.

For the Islamic world, on the other hand, the philosophy of subjectivity, the Enlightenment, is not valid at all; religion administers all truth and objectivity. Behind this religion stands the highest being, God, who in the Koran has handed over the sum of all meaning and being to mankind through the prophet Mohammed as the ultimate truth. The modern subjectivism and the Koranic objectivism stand opposite to each other as value systems, strengthened by the ideology of Islamism to an extremely explosive dichotomy and also demonization, which is called here with Manichaeism. From this basic contradiction of both value systems all other counterpositions can be explained. Man as a value in himself is opposed by an absolute God, for whom the individual human being is a quantity to be neglected. For Allah, the only thing that counts is the *umma*, the community of believers. Allah has eternalized the possession of absolute truth in the Koran for the believers, while the self-critical Western rational view must be satisfied with the possession of only relational truth, which occurs context- and location-bound; there is no theory that could not still be improved by falsification. But with its claim to sole absolute possession of truth, Islam presumes to categorize people: the truth-possessing Muslims are at the top, while the members of the book religions are accorded co-ownership of truth, depending on the political situation. They are people of the second degree or - as Islamism preaches today - devils released for destruction. Basically completely truth- and therefore rightless are the representatives of all other world views. In contrast to this, man as man in the sense of subjectivism is, despite many cultural differences, of the same nature: free, self-determined, self-responsible, self-designing. With its insistence on the absolute possession of truth, Islam gives Islamism the weapons in its hands, according to which it can realize its claim to political and religious sole representation, both in close interaction, vis-à-vis a pluralistic and polycultural world.

This has far-reaching socio-cultural consequences: democratic forms of government on the one hand, dictatorial ones on the other, nomocratic theocracies whose representatives, as "shadows of Allah," pretend to enforce God's will through the state. Islam's fundamental militancy and its division of the world into two spheres result from its self-image as the "best community": the "house of Islam," in which the "great jihad," the struggle for social justice, prevails, and the "house of war," that is, all non-Muslim countries, in which the "small jihad," the struggle against non-Muslims, institutionalized by a set of rules, has been practiced. The "small jihad" has mutated into inhuman terrorism through Islamism, which is supported argumentatively by religious hardliners, the mullahs.

A straight line leads from Islam via Islamism to religiously motivated terrorism; the ideological criteria of "absolute possession of truth," "vertical and horizontal totalitarianism," globalized claim to power" (unfortunately) substantiate this hypothesis of Islam's fundamental militancy, but it has only been activated in times of crisis. Today, we can imagine a web for the relationship between Islam, Islamism and jihadism in which all three levels are interconnected, so that they become increasingly indistinguishable. Islam is not innocent of this present-day low distinguishability of religion, totalitarian ideology of Islamism and terrorist practice by means of jihad, because it has opened itself all too readily to a literal interpretation of its "holy scripture" and has suppressed and still suppresses the thought efforts of the philosophers of the Golden Age. Thereby the religious-political forces were unleashed, which by charging with **ideology(-)** projected all negativities onto a now grimacingly distorted and demonic enemy dummy embodying evil in itself.

The vocabulary with which we are treated on the part of Islam and Islamism exposes all protestations of tolerance. A historical experiment that will soon be completed, the complete expulsion of all Christians from Muslim-ruled countries, anticipates our fate, which 'intellectual' circles and, unfortunately, also many European countries still support with 'anticipatory obedience' or "anticipatory capitulation" (Broder 2006, 42).

The contrary positions resulting from the fundamental opposition "God or man as value in itself" shall now only be mentioned. Explosive emotionality and discursive rationality, the collective, the Umma and the individual subject, the certainty of faith and the certainty of knowledge, God's legal order and 'born' human right, monism and pluralism, holism against the separation of being from ought, the discrimination of women and their equal rights are opposed, the globalization of territorial domination and the domination of world markets, Sharia and positive law, the utopia of the emergence of a global ummah versus self-determined pluralistic forms of government, an archaic society led by mullahs and an enlightened knowledge society. In the political-ideological view of Islamism, a satanic West, a neo-Crusaderism, a decadent Occident, a secularized Christianity as a mixture of all evil, and a divinely inspired, morally good Islam that distributes earthly goods justly are opposed to each other. Every citizen representing Western thought must know that despite all appeasement formulas to the contrary, Islamism, but also Islam, when it has the power, does not tolerate anything else besides itself. The (small) jihad, which was already an instrument of its violent propagation at the beginning of Islam, has developed such a thrust through Islamism that the murder of innocent people is part of its daily rite.

What irritates the West so much about Islam is its ambivalent appearance. It pretends to be peaceful, but increasingly advocates brutal violence through jihad; it sees itself as tolerant, but does not deviate one iota from its absolute claim to truth; it includes the discrimination of women in its program, but pretends to strive for a contemporary image of women; it preaches religious freedom to the West, but suppresses other religions wherever it rules; it claims to be a promoter of science, but fights its secular background premises, He calls those of other faiths infidels, depending on his intentions, and threatens them with extinction, or he calls those who practice the religion close to Islam *djimmi,* second-class citizens. When he speaks of true democracy, he actually means a dictatorship of God, preaches peace to his fellow believers and irregular jihad to those of other faiths who are infidels, and demands equal rights for himself in the diaspora, which he does not grant to his own minorities. The distrust of Islam grows as long as it plays the double role of "doublethink" (Orwell). The serious conflict situation that already exists today will steadily worsen as the discrepancy between a religiously anchored canon of values that has been resistant to change for fourteen centuries and a value system that is open to the world, pluralistic and capable of evolutionary adaptation continues to grow.

The hypothesis of the socio-cultural influence of philosophy on the historical process mentioned at the beginning is compatible with a stratification of reality, the lowest layer of which is determined, often hidden, by basic philosophical, religious or mythical beliefs. It can, if accepted, lead to a way out of the ever-increasing dominance of Islam infected by Islamism. No one should have any illusions about what will happen to him in an Islamic-ruled state if he does not convert to Islam, as did two American journalists in the Gaza Strip. But if the archaic value system of Islam is enriched by a philosophically based one, it is possible that a gradual modification and liberalization of the Islamic belief system can lead to a humanization of the cultural reality of Islamic religiosity. This has happened before, in the Golden Age of Islam from 750-1250 AD, as I cannot emphasize enough.

The general theme of philosophy in the Golden Age is the transcription and reception of the philosophy of ancient Greece, which stimulates discourse in opposition to revealed religion by means of human rationality. It is about "faith seeking insight" (Lerch 1999, 101). Al-Farabi grounds philosophy's claim to truth in the philosophy of Aristotle, specifically his major logical work *Organon.* Here he mainly discusses Aristotle's formalized conclusion form of the syllogism, which also underlies the natural exchange of arguments, but has never been subjected to an examination in its truth value. According to this truth value, Aristotle distinguishes three forms of syllogism, the non-contestable, which starts from two vouched premises and leads to certain truth by linking them, the dialectical conclusion, which starts from probable premises and leads to controversial results, and the fallacious conclusion, which uses questionable premises and leads to grave errors, so that it garnishes them with euphonious rhetoric to help sophistical argumentation to a sham correctness. (Today Aristotle would call this kind of argumentation the political one).

Now Al-Farabi has found a criterion of truth with which he can assign the possession of truth to different disciplines. Philosophy with its true syllogistic conclusions is in possession of the general truth, while the disciplines "theology", "jurisprudence", "linguistics science", since they can represent only a dialectical, i.e. here a particular truth area, are subordinated to it. The poetic conclusion form introduced by Al-Farabi as fourth is reserved for the religion and no science. The beginning of philosophy is thus to be found as with Aristotle in his *Organon.*

Avicenna's method consists in a reduction of corporeality, through which it is made clear that man's self-experience is not mediated by the senses, but, however far man is amputated in thought to limit the possibility of his sensual experience, he always already knows one thing, the existence of his self, his soul. He is aware, insofar as he frees himself from his sensuality step by step, that it is he who performs this act. This self, which is immediately always already 'transcendentally' conscious to us, is called "soul". It is immaterial, individual, independent of the body, thus immortal. It makes man a person, a "thinking subject" (Rudolph 2004, 51), and the rallying point of his indestructible being, which, insofar as it strives for knowledge in life, is the reward "of eternal bliss" (51).

But from the point of view of philosophy, the role of the prophet Mohammed still remains unclear. Just this prophet shows another way to reach the true knowledge. Avicenna calls this way of knowledge "intuition" (52). He attributes it to the philosophers, but also to Mohammed. It means that there are people who do not have to go the rocky way of laboriously gaining knowledge, but by virtue of their natural insight arrive at the right knowledge without lengthy reasoning procedures. Overall, Avicenna deepens the Islamic religion from the point of view of philosophy and thus offers an "offer of integration" (56), but under the primacy of philosophy.

Ibn-Tufail, the world-weary, stands politically in counter position to Islam because he disapproves of the entanglement of the Qur'an, Sunna, and Sharia with worldly rule. He advises every philosopher to withdraw from the public sphere in order to "prove the autonomy of the human intellect" (65). He clothes his doctrine in a Robinsonade to separate what man produces intellectually from knowledge that has been handed down but not always substantiated.

But at the age of fifty, 'Robinson' comes into contact with the neighboring island where a Muslim community lives. "It turns out that the inhabitants of the neighboring island agree on all essential points (the existence of God, the nature of the world, the destiny of man) with the knowledge he has gained on his own" (67). This means, on the one hand, that the thesis that every human being is Muslim by nature is supported by this Isolation experiment. Secondly, it refers to two ways of knowledge, the symbolic one, which owes its knowledge to the Muslim community and the Prophet, and the naturalistic-speculative one, which is achieved through philosophy in pure abstraction. Thus Ibn-Tufail set himself the goal of reconciling Islam and philosophy, Avicenna and Al-Ghazali, practical faith and philosophical speculation in a synthesis. He can be called the representative of a rational theology, because he lets his hero reach knowledge of God as well as the Muslim community of the neighboring island through the Koran.

Averroes, the hermeneuticist, raises the question of the relationship of philosophy to the Koranic revelation. He understands the Koran not as a literal, uninterpretable and supra-temporal utterance of God, but as a scripture, which contains three differently to be understood announcements, so that also a Koran exegesis must be directed accordingly. The first group of suras is evident, i.e. both philosophically and religiously provable like the sentence "There is no God but God", thus to be understood strictly literally. The second must also be understood literally, but can be received differently. Sura (20:5) says: "The Merciful has made Himself right on the throne", which means for the simple believer that God exercises His power like a bodily king, because he knows the kingly rule from the practical life. The philosopher, on the other hand, knows of God's incorporeal existence, so that God cannot disguise himself as a king. The simple believer, then, cannot help but understand this verse allegorically, while the philosopher understands the allegory as such. (The disastrous consequences of a literal interpretation of the Qur'an have, after all, been thoroughly illustrated). The third form of pronouncement is verses where it is not clear whether they are to be understood allegorically or literally. Averroes chooses the example of the resurrection, where it is not certain in which form, bodily or spiritual, it is to be interpreted. No one can provide unequivocal proof for one opinion or the other, so that in these questions different answers do not imply heresy. So there is a philosophical space of contingency in the Qur'an where freedom of opinion must prevail.

Thanks to a philosophically shaped value system, the Golden Age brings about a flourishing of Islamic architecture, Islamic science and mathematics, medicine and religious tolerance, until Islamic zealots and orthodox religious teachers put these philosophers on the Index and thus put an end to intellectual freedom. According to Lerch (2000), the following picture emerges:

1. Islamic philosophers translated the ancient philosophers, mainly Aristotle, and transmitted them to the Christian world.

2. However, the "thinkers of the prophet" (11) also developed independent theories with the aim of synthesizing faith and reason.
3. The philosophy of Islam asks the same questions as Christian philosophy, only rather.
4. The Qur'an is not received in Islam without contradictions, since Muhammad's proclamations did not originate 'from a single source'. It was not until ten years after Muhammad's death that the sayings of the Prophet were recorded in writing in the Koran, not chronologically, but arranged according to the length of the suras. Thus, the suras based on concrete historical events are mixed with those based on pure inspiration. Many theological disputes develop from this, so that the Koran cannot be interpreted in a binding way even today, and so there are *de facto* many currents in Islam. However, because the text of the Koran is not doubted by any Muslim school, the idea of a uniform interpretation is always alive and, as a demand of Islamism, loaded with political explosives. Fundamentalism abridges and mutilates its own religion and culture by putting them at the service of an ideology that abuses religious ties for political demands.
5. The Enlightenment that is underway in Islam today, because such philosophers have to fear for their lives, is either taking place abroad in the West, or in 'internal emigration' because of ostracism.

There are philosophical-religious tendencies in Islam today that want to take up the philosophy of the Golden Age again and then develop it further in order to modify the Qur'an's claim to sole representation and to give room to a rational consideration. The fact that mainly religion-critical voices have had their say here has the purpose of drawing attention to philosophical-religious tendencies that are working towards a change in the present orthodox standstill of Islamic philosophy. The tragedy of this enacted stalemate is that there is no worldwide interfaith competition of ideas, but a compartmentalization of Islam behind the "believer/unbeliever" dichotomy. Here, three analytical ways described by Islamic thinkers are presented to limit Islam's absolute claim to truth in such a way that religious convictions and scientific as well as political postulates remain adversaries, but shed the enemy role and respect each other's sovereignty.

The first, An-Naifar, invokes the history of Christianity, which at the time of Luther offers a similarly desolate state of entanglement of religious and political power as Islam does in many countries today. In that man is justified before God only *sola fide* (by faith alone) and cannot buy heaven by any earthly good works, there is a separation between the secular and the spiritual. Similarly, in Islam, there could be a separation of political claims to power and religious claims, but this is fraught with particular difficulties, since Islam has been a political and religious community at the same time since its inception.

The second, Taha, sees the Koran as a text to be interpreted evolutionarily, whose humanistic original form could only have been realized under Muhammad at the price of historical relativization, and which, in a progressive process up to the present day, has adapted itself to these ideals to such an extent that they have crystallized in a "second message" into a pure supra-temporal truth of faith, so that an instrumentalization of Muhammad for Islamist propaganda becomes impossible.

The third, Abu-Zaid, if the Qur'an is to make a claim to truth that can withstand the sciences, calls on this "holy scripture" to distance itself from its dogmatic and unproven premise of the divinity of this work and to submit to the criteria of science or to separate the profane and theological realms. Thus, he wants to extend hermeneutics to the textual study of the Quran. In doing so, he does not deny that the Qur'an contains transcendent entities, the investigation of which would be a matter for rational theology. Empirically provable, however, are worldview assumptions of its creator Mohammed, whose further background assumption of being inspired by God, however, cannot be verified, but offers historical continuity as a conviction background of a culture *sui generis*. With his scientific hermeneutics program, Abu-Zaid wants to pursue criticism of religion and at the same time criticism of ideology in order to put an end to the instrumentalization of the Qur'an for political interests, to subject the Qur'an to reason in order to make even "prejudices and doubts" (543) subjectively testable. He sees the Qur'an as a "cultural product" that has produced a "civilization of the text" (544); it is the "ruling controlling text" (544) for Islamic civilization. The historical identity of Islam today, he argues, is caught between ossified tradition and cautious secularization. But the Islamic scholars who aspire to the latter have neither a religious nor a political lobby: politicized Islam and Islamized politics have formed an alliance to liquidate anything that merely looks like a Western influence: Ideas and people.

What is needed, on the other hand, is an equivalent to the work of Martin Luther, accompanied by a modernization of Islam that leads to broad acceptance in the Islamic world.

Now that the philosophical-ideological-critical analysis of Islamism has been carried out, the next step is to examine selected literature in the light of these criteria. The selection of literature is determined by topics that occupy a broad space in this work. Because of the scope of the subject matter, it is not possible to aim for completeness; however, different perspectives can enrichingly point to its many manifestations.

A.1 Akbuluth: Islam and its significance for world politics - a misinterpretation and a false interpretation

The starting point of his presentation is a sociology of Islam, its society-changing power within and outside the Islamic world. Insofar as he understands Islam as a world religion, this work sees itself as a sociological examination of religion with Islam, which also affects Europe through migration. Thus, he wants to rationally examine "confusion and perplexity" (9) caused by the encounter with this other religion in order to break down barriers of understanding Islam caused by both. Because "incomplete information [...] results in prejudices and fears towards Islam, the European public partly perceives it as a danger or threat to society" (9). Addressing this problem "sociologically," i.e., by means of the social sciences, suggests a high enlightening value.

But already at the beginning one is puzzled when one reads: "The Koran understands itself as a continuing and supplementary book to other 'holy books', the Torah and the Gospel. (12). In reality, the Qur'an is the original script of his will, residing with God, of absolute truth claim; no room for interpretation is allowed. (But why not throw a crumb of 'recognition' to the Jews and Christians?) In reality, this is also how the author sees it when he writes:

> "This [the cultural-historical interpretation of the Qur'an - the author] is countered by the argument that Islam cannot be changed by history and also by the margins of in-

terpretation, since the Qur'an as the highest authority (God's word) forms the unchanging basis for all questions relating to Islam and has not lost its originality since its writing until today" (21).

The passive voice used here is meant to indicate generality without subjective variations of interpretation. So nothing with 'addition' and 'continuation'. But he has to admit "that also in the case of Islam ambiguities of the initial teachings and reinterpretations of them in the course of history are to be found" (21) - a not easily resolvable contradiction between claim to unchangeable truth and a reality of many forms of interpretation of different faiths.

Thus, as an Islamist (which remains to be proven), he keeps the way open to arrive at an unambiguous and true interpretation of the Koran by linking it to the founding period of Islam, because different interpretations would weaken the one sacred claim to truth. We are cleverly taught plurality of opinion with fundamental unity of Islam.

The statement that "for the politicization of Islam the Koran [offers] no basis" cannot be agreed with. (22), so that no particular political order can be derived from it. But this argument is wrong on several counts, first because the *shura is, after* all, described as the nucleus of democracy, and second because Muhammad founded an Islamic state at the same time as Islam, and its rules, the *Sunna,* established by the Prophet, constitute "a binding basis for Islamic doctrine and belief" (Barth 2003, 62). Thus, through the side door of the *Sunna,* politics has become linked to Islam again after all; "in the example of the person of Muhammad [the Prophet] became a political leader at the same time; and Islam entered history as a religion and at the same time as a political factor" (Akbuluth 2002, 23). And it is the stated goal of the Islamists to 're-enact' history by directly referring to Muhammad. Therefore, this author projects ideas borrowed from Marxism directly onto the Prophet, who "demands just remuneration for workers" (26) and whose "exploitation" (26) he criticizes. (It should be noted here that in Muhammad's day, workers do not exist in our current parlance, so with this terminological mischaracterization, the author reveals himself as belonging to the social, formerly Marxist wing of Islamism). Mohammed is thus the first Marxist and Islam a theory of the abolition of the barriers between rich and poor and the inequality of people. It fits perfectly that in the succession of the Prophet "slavery began to dissolve[107]" (26), so Islam as a religion of humanized social justice' helped to triumph. Half-truths include the statement:

> "In order to build new social structures, he [the Prophet - the author] was anxious to raise the knowledge level of the people. Therefore, he made it obligatory for every Muslim to educate himself and engage in science "(30).

This author forgets here that the one who makes this demand is illiterate himself. What kind of concept of science is the basis here? Surely that of 'acquiring knowledge of something ... acquire' and not that of a methodical knowledge acquisition, although here and also in other places the impression of the science veneration[108] of the Islam is to be aroused. Except for the

---

[107] This author seems particularly sympathetic to the socialist camp of Islam: "The new religion became the means of struggle of the poor against the rich and ruling classes [here the ruling practice of the Kuraish tribe - the author]" (24). But the claim that through Muhammad's work slavery was overcome step by step, like the class struggle slogans, is based on a projective objectification of how Akbuluth wants to see the beginnings of Islam. This is precisely the official dogma of Islamic fundamentalism, to look back to the transfigured beginnings (here with a Marxist undertone) of Islam in order to pretend to be the perfector of these ideas. The portrayal of the relationship between Islam and slavery can be exposed as a deliberate deception. While Christianity is above all ashamed of the slave trade with the New World and seeks to deal with this crime so that it is stored in our cultural memory, on the part of Islam there is persistent silence about its own involvement in this barbarity - the method of concealing one's own misdeeds is a thoroughly common method of Islam's 'coming to terms with the past'. Since the Arab slave traders operated in areas remote from world politics, this terrible event was not publicly perceived, so that this cognitive deficit must serve to claim the opposite even for itself. But in *The History of Slavery* (Delacampagne 2004), this historical clutter that so fits the picture is cleared up. Slavery was common in the three book religions, also the Arab tradition before Mohammed used it, the religion of the blacks, the animism, was and is demonized, so that there were good reasons of the use of slavery in Islam. The palace of the "Caliph of Baghdad" (119) was populated by "no less than 11000 slaves in the 10th century" (120). According to Delacampagne, the Arab slave trade in Africa claimed "11 million victims" (126), as many as the "transatlantic slave trade" (126) of the 'Christian West'. To deliberately ignore the historical facts in order to construct a historically unprovable continuity is a political propaganda tool; for a sociology of religion appearing with scientific pretensions it simply means untruth.

[108] With justified pride, Akbuluth points to medical, mathematical and astronomical discoveries of this period, as well as to the 'translation', assimilation and transmission of ancient philosophy. He also states the real reason, namely because "the sciences [could] work freely on their own, without political and religious limitations and prohibitions" (57-62). And **this**

Golden Age (750-1258), Islam has distinguished itself by hostility to science, as far as the basic scientific-ontological decisions are concerned, especially towards the positive sciences. Here, too, Akbuluth projects a wish "This is how it should be" onto the cognitive level of "This is how it is, too," in order to pretend something to Western man.

The author does not even attempt to empirically refute the widespread practice of subjugating women in Islam, which I assume. By means of a "Qur'anic sociology" he wants to prove the progressiveness of the legal status of women proclaimed by the Qur'an, which has developed further until today, in that "Islam [has] set a historically highly significant impulse in favor of a social equality of women." (31). An impulse is a push with consequences for the object that has been pushed, which is now moving in a certain direction. That is, Islam has set in motion the Qur'an's provisions about women as legal persons in the direction of women's emancipation. This cannot be at all if, as here, this author is convinced of the time-independent truth of the Quran. What the Koran says about the 'nature' of women is anthropologically valid for all time. It is true that Mohammed represented a progressive image of women for his time, but by preserving it in patriarchal and dictatorial systems of rule, it has led to the almost complete disenfranchisement of women up to the present. There were already views on women's rights in theory and practice in Roman law that were much more progressive. But far worse is the position of women today in many Islamic countries, where she is deprived of the most important thing, her own identity, and is only allowed to shed her impersonality as a creature disguised in public when she is within the walls of the family. But even there, she does not live freely, but must seek out the intimacy of the home when male visitors come. By means of the "Koran sociology" the author evades the verifiable proof of the lawless existence of many women in Islam. Is this the enlightenment of a competent sociologist of religion about the social position of women in Islam? What may have been progress in Muhammad's time has regressed over time into a politically sanctioned patriarchal instrument of women's oppression. The method of "Quranic sociology", which presents the legal provisions of women's position in society, which are limited in

---

is **exactly** my demand for a new reflection and determination of Islam under the guidance of philosophy!

comparison to men's rights[109] , as if they represent reality, is to be sharply criticized.

Generally speaking, the argumentation schemes of Islamists are deductive, in that what is presented in the Koran is inferred to be true and therefore empirically real (strong correspondence). The more Koranic a Muslim state is, the more lawless and thus masked a woman appears (see the Wahabi state in Saudi Arabia, the Iranian 'God state', the Taliban in Afghanistan), to name only the most common Islamic 'women's rights' advocates. It is a pity that the author leaves out the social position of women in contemporary Islam. Instead of empiricism, he provides Koranic ideology.

Akbuluth has taken a liking to the method of "Koranic sociology," which deductively derives from the Koran a social order that is claimed to apply in reality. This gives rise to the possibility of a trivializing interpretation. Behind this is the value system of the Islamist author, whose absolute assertion of truth already leads the pen in advance, so that the result that Islam is the best community on this earth only needs to be 'discovered' sociologically.

This brings me to the most sensitive chapter of Islam: its relationship to other religions. Here, too, Akbuluth has the same recipe for downplaying at the ready, claiming that "The Qur'an unequivocally demands tolerance toward members of other religions," "It forbids any coercive practice as far as religion is concerned," and "In the religious sphere, the provision of the free exercise of religion applies" (38 f.). For this purpose, he cites the Quranic verses (5:48), (2:62) and (42:15). However, as already proven in the chapter "Criteria of Ideology," the position of Islam in relation to the other book religions is highly ambivalent.[110] It is wrong to praise the Koran as a document of tolerance (tolerance is often based on weakness) toward those of other faiths, but also to accuse it of constant aggression toward non-Muslims. Empirically, historical epochs can be assigned to one version or the other; insofar as in the Golden

---

[109] Even the Quran admits, "And as women have duties, so have they rights, according to custom; but men have a certain precedence [which is constantly being extended by patriarchy - the author] over them; and Allah is all-powerful; all-wise" Sura (2:228).

[110] Here is a collection of Quranic quotations: "Those who disbelieve and die as disbelievers, upon them the curse of Allah and the angels and mankind at large" (2:161), "And fight against them [the disbelievers - the author] until there is no more persecution and all faith is directed toward Allah. But if they stand off, then, verily Allah sees well what they do" (8:39), "And when the forbidden months have passed, then kill the idolaters wherever you meet them [...]" (9:5).

Age an Islam enlightened by philosophy guaranteed tolerance and freedom of thought, this religion proved to be relatively peaceable toward other faiths, but only because its absolute claim to truth was claimed by philosophy. Today, however, one has to wear oversized blinders in order to see a tolerant side to Islam in its current presentation. The permanent missionary task that follows from the claim to the monopoly on truth is superimposed on the history of Islam as a constantly present religious imperialism.

In the chapter "Islamic Understanding of War and the Law of War" we witness the presentation of the conceptual game "just and unjust war". Akbuluth first summarizes when a war is justified: namely, to protect the Islamic community from enemies who want to destroy religion and people. Then, however, a slogan from the mothballs of communist liberation ideology appears, the imperialist doctrine[111] , that "wars to overthrow 'unjust' systems of rule in other countries that oppress, persecute, or kill people (including Muslims) through tyrannical methods" may be called 'just wars' (44).

And further: "Islam sees itself entitled to work for this 'justice' not only within its own borders, but also in other areas, since this is the will of God and the Koran has instructed the Muslims to do so" (44).[112] Thus the criteria for a 'just' war are universalized - a Marxist heritage -; if the Muslim idea of "justice" has to apply in all countries, as well as that of "unjust systems of rule", which have to be fought by means of war, then this means nothing else that the Koran with the quoted Sura blatantly legitimizes its believers to strive for world domination; and this will probably not be able to proceed differently than it did already at the beginning of Islam by "fire and sword". This interpretation reminds fatally of the communist liberation doctrine, in which one first appropriated the empty formulas "justice" "just war" and "unjust form of rule" with class struggle slogans. Given the polyphony of Islam, who is at all entitled to present unambiguously valid definitions of the aforementioned empty formulas? With this communist-Koranian imperialism claim trivialized by trivializing interpretation, the credibility of Akbuluth's 'enlightener' about

---

[111] We mirror this thesis so that all 'unjust' Islamic systems of government may and should be fought by the West. What is then left of the Islamic world?

[112] Islamic imperialism is justified by sura (8:75): "Those who have believed and emigrated and fought in the cause of Allah, and those who gave (them) shelter and help - these are indeed true believers. To them be forgiveness and honorable provision."

the nature of Islam can only be classified as very low. His goal is not socio-logical information about the social impact of Islam: the Koran, with its claim of absolute possession of truth, becomes a political weapon for fundamental-ism, in this case in the variety of Islamic fundamentalism, which is also sup-posed to find our applause.

The author's premise then is: "However, the term 'fundamentalism' is a cat-egory foreign to Islam" (74). According to Pörksen (1989), he calls it a "plastic word," which has a similar meaning as a catchword or empty formula. It has associative negative connotations and is therefore suitable for discriminating against the political opponent without precise indication of content. In order to protect Islam from this discrimination, the author asks about the history of this term.

In 1910-1915, a series of writings entitled *The Fundamentals* appears in the United States, preaching a religious renewal and giving rise to a Protestant "revival movement" in the Anglo-Saxon world. It follows three basic princi-ples:

"1. The literal infallibility of the Scriptures,
2. the nullity of all modern theologies and sciences, as far as they contradict the Bible faith,
3. the conviction that no one who does not share the fundamentalist point of view can be a true Christian" (Akbuluth 2002, 76).

(If we use "Koran" for holy scripture and "Muslim" for "Christian," an Is-lamic fundamentalism inevitably results[113] , which the author does not seem to notice). Since the Christian fundamentalism sketched here takes an anti-modern attitude toward science and personal lifestyle, altogether therefore as unteachable sectarianism is felt, it has acquired the connotation of backward-ness, hostility to progress and limitedness. A second source of meaning lies in the term itself: Basis. Fundamentalism means according to it the search for that, which gives the true reason for a complex reality, which can be analyzed only with difficulty. Fundamentalism means after it, however, also that some-thing, which one led back to its true reasons, must be reorganized accordingly.

---

[113] See Tepe: *Fundamentalism as a Form of Thought,* where this concept is presented as a "form of thought": http://wwwalt.phil-fak.uni-duesseldorf.de/germ4/tepe/tepeSite/mim/edi-tionMIM/a01_pt_fund/pt_funda.pdf

Fundamentalism means however also the security of the own point of view of the last certainty.

Now the inflation and negation of this term begins in the form of the term "fundamentalism", e.g. with the Green party (Fundis and Realos) (Fundamentalists and Realists), with the West against the Iranian fundamentalist Khomeini, with the Marxists against the orthodox wing. This is why Akbuluth calls for this term to be given scientific criteria (rightly so), but only to be applied to Protestant fundamentalism (wrongly, as has been shown). He wants fundamentalism to apply only as a "Western phenomenon" (Hemminger 1991, 10). His justification consists in a categorization of Christians into a Bible-critical and a fundamentalist wing. The latter want to convince these critics that only a literally understood Bible contains the whole truth and that the positive sciences are not capable of solving the life problems of the 'now'. There would be no such religious differentiation in Islam. He asserts:

> "In Islam, there is no such tendency that would question an immediate validity of the Koran. Therefore, there is no fundamentalist trend that would seek to assert the infallibility of the Qur'an [...]" (Akbuluth 2002, 81).

What happens when the claim of infallibility of the Koran is doubted? There are certainly reform forces in Islam who do not want to interpret the Koran in an orthodox way. But this is where Akbuluth's powers of perception go on strike; for he wants the pejorative meaning to be attributed to Christian fundamentalism, and the valorizing meaning as "Islamic worldview" to Islamism, so that there can be no criticism of the Koran. He is not entirely wrong; for manifold threats and reprisals have silenced many critics. Here is a case: The Egyptian university teacher Abu Zaid (see Tibi, FAZ, 03.07.1996) had developed a Koran exegesis with a literary approach, which came to the conclusion that this hermeneutic approach would shake the absolute truth claim of the Koran. He was condemned as an apostate and ordered to divorce[114].

It is shameful that a scientist who calls himself an 'enlightener' pretends not to know what threatens those who deny the absolute truth of the Koran. What should not be, must not be. Tibi (1985) presents a case that can explain why there are no reform forces in Islam, citing Muhammad Muslehuddin, a Pakistani Islamist:

---

[114] Reported according to Müller (1996, 148 f.).

"Those who think of reforming or modernizing Islam are misguided and their efforts are doomed to failure. [...]. For why should Islam be modernized, which is already perfectly pure and universal for all time. [...]. They overlook the fact that [...] God alone can know what is truly good for human beings" (96).

Likewise, he finds an argument to turn the hostility to science in orthodox Islam, especially when it comes to hermeneutic interpretations of the Koran, almost into the opposite. We already know it: "Islam namely demands to take note of all sciences and to apply them in society. Even if this science is only taught 'in faraway China'" (Koranic quote, Akbuluth 2002). To apply Muhammad's concept of science to modern sciences and their ontological premises is scientifically adventurous. Akbuluth's hope of thus escaping the negative tint of the term fundamentalism has not been fulfilled. [115]

He calls the renaissance of Islam "Islamism," a "new political ideology" (83) (in the sense of social theory). To avoid the charge that Islamism is basically fundamentalism, he posits, "Islamism is first and foremost a social movement." (83). This version, however, contradicts the usual conceptions of "isms" as worldviews whose content is formed by the corresponding root term, according to which Islamism means first of all a worldview shaped by the religion Islam. In the West, however, the concept of Islam would become increasingly negatively charged, so it would have been better to use the word "social Islamism" to neutralize its negative connotation.

Qutb, the theorist of Islamism, names as the basis of this worldview, which represents the truth alone, "the Koran, Sunna (words and way of life of the Prophet) and the 'era of the right-guided caliphs' ".[116] Thus Akbuluth agrees with the recognized theorist of Islamism that Islamism does not mean a further development of Islam in the sense of its past history of salvation, but a return to the true sources of the beginning of the Islamic era, the era of the 'liberation of workers, slaves and women', which has not been falsified by history. These "models for the Islamic system [...] are not meant to be a 'restoration' of that time, but, based on it, a response to the challenges of the 20th century" (97). The author theorizes to develop Islam as a social theory, so that he believes he

---

[115] His goal is to assign fundamentalism as an "Winkelried term" to the West. Just as the latter (Winkelried) drew the enemy's lances upon himself to give air to the others, this very negatively toned term is intended to transport the negative connotations to the Western variant so that Islamism can become a beacon of hope as a progressive worldview.

[116] Quoted from Akbuluth (2002, 97).

can attribute the discredited term "fundamentalism" to the United States, but surround himself with a social and humane aura of Islamism.

Akbuluth's analysis lays out the reasons for the rise of Islamism: Muslims' disenchantment with the Western ideologies of Soviet communism and capitalism, Westernization of many societies, dissolution of traditional structures in families, feelings of inferiority in the face of the superiority of colonial economy and industry, warlike humiliation of the Arab world by Israel. Islamism is not only to contain these wrong developments, but to develop positive alternatives to these pernicious influences. One of these positive alternatives is: " [...] to install a new social order based on Islam" (84) in order to create "new social, political and cultural conditions acceptable to the masses" (84).

This results in a causal hierarchy. From the religion of Islam, certain general norms of behavior can be deduced that are supposed to produce a new Islamic identity to be formed, which he initially denies. Now, these norms date from the 'founding era' of Islam; to what extent they can still support a modern society remains questionable. Islam's credibility is based on the normative acceptance of its established rules of life, so that an attack on its credibility would also shake its social impact.

This author is of the opinion, also held by the author, that "with the end of the East-West system competition, Islamism [took] the place of Marxism in a certain way by developing an international and at the same time 'anti-colonialist' thrust" (96 f). The language of Islamism has also made use of communist ideology, and "imperialism, anti-imperialism, the Third World, people's war, revolution, socialism" (101) have occupied its contents. The potential universalism of Islam already mentioned thus corresponds to an Islamism that goes beyond the borders of Islam and sees itself as a competitor of world capitalism. This "Islamic internationalism" (89) is intended to cause all Muslims, including those in non-Islamic countries, to form an *ummah*. Furthermore, Islamists hold the doctrine that "Islam [is] understood to be an all-social system based entirely on itself, based on the Qur'an and *Sunnah, and to be* practicable at any time and in any place" (90). Accordingly, the world can only be saved by Islam because, according to Qutb, "all other worldviews and models have failed" (99).

The further one follows Akbuluth's text, the clearer it becomes that he himself is an Islamist and is engaged in fundamentalist propaganda instead of sociological science. When he describes the role of women in Islam today, one cannot help but see in him the true stronghold of feminism. Although a Turk himself, there is no mention of the scandalous 'honor killings' that are justified by 'family honor' and un-Islamic behavior and are therefore not prosecuted in the courts. He quotes the 'feminist' by his own grace, Mernissi:

> "I have found a feminist prophet and brought him to mind from the darkness of the past. In my book, dozens of suras from the Quran and statements of the Prophet can be read, in which human rights and equal rights for men and women are expressed." [117]

So here again a 'sura sociology' instead of facts. The author's answer in 'sura sociology':

> "Allah decrees you concerning your children: one boy has as much share as two girls." [...] (4:11).

> "And if any of your women commit unseemly deeds, then call four of you as witnesses against them; if they testify to it, then lock them up in the houses until death overtakes them or Allah opens a way out for them" (4:15).

> "And if two men among you commit such a thing, punish them both. Then if they repent and mend their ways, leave them for yourselves [...]." (4:16).

> " Men are in charge of women because Allah has honored some over others and because they give of their wealth. Therefore, virtuous women are the obedient ones [...]" (4:34).

In the chapter "Democracy and Human Rights", the reader knows in advance what to expect: namely, that both have always been practiced by Islam, but have been 'betrayed' in the course of history. So, back *ad fontes,* as our sociologist Mernissi has already shown with women's rights. "Islam was the first to 'invent' democracy and to put it into practice" (Akbuluth 2002, 130), so resounds the chorus of the Islamists. Of course, democracy here does not mean "rule by the people," but rather the backward rule of religious leaders using Allah as an instrument.

This is justified by sura (3:159): "[...] and consult with them about this matter!" and sura (42:38): "And those who listen to their Lord, establish prayer,

---

[117] See *Die Zeit*: Der Prophet war ein Feminist (Dec. 22, 1995, 26). It is true that a neutral interpretation of the Koran actually gives women in Islam greater leeway than they have in most Islamic countries today. However, the Islamist fundamentalists who are all too happy to invoke this tolerance "clearly express in their writings, political speeches, and conversations that headscarves and veiling are desired" (Akbuluth 2002, 114), and he does not object. Here the frequent double standard of Islamism becomes clear.

consult among themselves, and from what We have given them." It is a truly thin ice on which the Islamists build their claim to have been the first democrats according to the Koran. Akbuluth's attempt at enlightenment is directed at all those who have only a rough knowledge of Islam, because they are judged to be easily indoctrinated.

Again, the author 'forgets' to point to the core of any democracy worthy of the name, the image of man, which provides the reason for such a form of government. Instead, criteria of an "Islamic ideal state" (130), i.e. a fiction with a non-binding utopian character, are taken for real coin-with well-known results. For the democratic form of government, the condition is the free subject as sovereign, because this subject, as an autonomous personality, can exercise the possibility of self-determination and self-legislation. Democracy consists in the free exercise of this right, whereby for practical considerations a representative democracy is recommended, in which elected representatives exercise sovereignty instead of the individual subjects of a people. In order to guarantee universality of human rights, one assumes a "pre-state natural state" (Müller 1996) of man, so that the validity of human rights is not to be made dependent on human culture. The author rejects this quite plausible argument because it is not human 'nature' but humanity in its cultural diversity itself that must establish its universal rights. In the development of human rights, Christianity, Enlightenment, liberalism and natural law theories have been the inspiration. Müller's summary of the justification of human rights looks like this:

> "Man is self-determined because he is capable of reason and thus of insight into what is good and evil. He has an ethical consciousness that can exist independently of religious and governmental guidelines. He has a dignity which, unlike honor, does not follow from his behavior but solely from his being human" (53).

In Islam, which means "surrender to the will of Allah," the sovereign is Allah, the lawgiver, to whose will the Muslim must submit. An "absolute dictatorship of God" applies. If it is so, it is nonsense that "Islam was the first to 'invent' democracy" (Akbuluth 2002, 130). As is so often the case, Islamists understand democracy and human rights to mean something different from the West, namely:

> "Islamic human rights are laid down directly by God, and the observance of these rights is a duty prescribed by the Koran. For this reason, human rights are better enshrined in an Islamic state because of their 'sanctity,' since they are God's commands" (132).

In Islam, sanctity means uncriticizability. Indisputably, someone for whom human rights are God-given will assign them a more stringent value, since he bears responsibility not only to people but also to God, so that rights and duties endowed with 'higher' consecrations can make it easier for the individual to comply with them. However, they must be equally valid in their scope if metaphysical justification is dispensed with. But if they are only metaphysically (religiously) founded, they also apply only to the believers of this religion. If universal human rights, which are in fact duties owed only to God, can be justified solely on the basis of the Koran, then a compulsion to follow precisely these religious premises without contradiction and to proselytize those of other faiths can be derived from the observance of human rights.

The universalization of Islamic human rights means the fulfillment of a mission in the direction of the universalization of Islam's claim to rule. "Equality before the law" "between Muslim and non-Muslim", "man and woman", "black and white" (133) is only eyewash, because whoever of those mentioned is not a believer in God, i.e. cannot comprehend the reasoning of God's will, these rights of obligation do not apply to him either.

But what rights apply to atheists, for example? The Islamist model of a state justified by religion is the grave of liberality and its atheist, materialist and rationalist representatives.

Which 'Islamist model of democracy' realized in the present is the author likely to exemplify? It can't be any other, the Iranian one. For a newspaper-reading contemporary, it is a pleasure to read Akbuluth's work:

> "In Iran, Islamists [...] accept a republic functioning according to democratic principles, with 'general elections, a constituent assembly, a parliament where real debates take place, with a president, a council of ministers, political groups, a constitution, and a kind of supreme court'" (120). [118]

Is Khomeini's death fatwa against the writer Rushdie also such an invention of 'fundamentalist democracy'? According to Rotter (1993), Article 25 of the Iranian constitution reads:

> "The formation of political parties, societies political and professional associations as well as religious societies is permitted provided they do not violate the principles of independence, freedom and national unity, the principles of Islam or the basis of the Islamic Republic."

---

[118] Quoted in Rotter (1993, 177).

What, then, are political parties still allowed to do in Iran? Performing Friday prayers together in the mosque. The truly 'democratic' Iranianocracy deserves special praise for publicly flogging women who do not want to wear the headscarf.

Today, it is a generally accepted premise that the author of a treatise on religious studies need not be considered a believer in God; on the contrary, as a scientist, he is not there to provide evidence of God's existence and to be a practicing believer himself to do so. In the book The *Islam,* the author starts from the thesis of the religious scientist's faith. For this purpose, he criticizes the demand that "church free" (9), i.e. not religiously bound, religious studies must be proceeded. As a justification he mentions "that even faith-based neutrality presupposes a (admittedly negative) decision of faith", so that it too "is based on a certain worldview" (9). But this is not the point, insofar as this "negative faith decision" does not influence the scientific work.

It is true that also 'pure' science has to start from certain background premises. As an example the theories of evolution may be considered, which assume a platonic nature in wide areas; because in a chaos without constants life is not possible, which depends on the presence of the self-same. But they themselves cannot give any proof for this 'prejudice', they can, however, strengthen their argumentation power with this hypothesis. Since today the natural sciences are the model of all sciences, it is clearly defined what scientific work means.

Scientific work does not require a "negative decision of faith", but an agnosticism of any kind, namely not to put theological or metaphysical premises before their work, because they are not capable of falsification in the sense of Popper. Thus, scientificity does not require a "negative faith decision"; for then it would itself be a form of worldview. Any belief in values, excluded the objectivity postulate of Monod and the scientific ethos in the sense of Salamun (1975) and Mohr (1982) is 'indifferent' for the sciences. The empirical subject must discipline itself with its methods and statements to the 'pure subject', so that the 'pure' object, without all personal additions can have its say. Whether atheist, Christian, Muslim, animist - the consequently pursued science makes them equal subjects, who must come to the same result with the same problem, because the kind of method must not determine the result: they now belong to the *scientific community.* The religious understanding of values remains out of the game, is therefore not addressed at first. Thus, if a religion is to be investigated culturally-historically, sociologically or psychologically, the causal chain runs from metaphysical presuppositions, which themselves cannot be investigated objectively, but which constitute the conditions of an empirical reality, to the consequences resulting from them, so that the consequences of, e.g., a conception of God can be investigated objectively, but this does not allow any conclusion about the existence of God. The author uses a straight opposite methodology:

> "If we make it clear in advance that we want to approach Islam from the standpoint of the Christian revelation of salvation, then this approach seems to us no less scientific and, moreover, clearer and more realistic and helpful. For as a believing person I am also closer to a foreign faith [but see religious wars among related religions - the author] than the one who rejects the faith or is indifferent to it" (Kellerhals 1969, 9f.).

Man alone is thus incapable of arriving at truly scientific knowledge by virtue of his ratiocination, God is to decide in the end. "That means: only when God himself opens our eyes, we see the right way" (162). This sounds similar to the praise of Allah in an Islamic scientific work. In 1966 - the book had already been published in Switzerland in 1956 - such a man was awarded the "Science Prize of the City of Basel" (6).

This kind of interpretation, the "projective-appropriating procedure"[119] confirms the premises projected into it, so that they can be rediscovered in the 'object'. Islam confirms the scientific proof of the truth of Christianity, this confirms Islam as a scientifically founded faith. Faith and knowledge confirm and legitimize each other.

The religion from whose perspective the other is examined naturally stands higher, is more correct:

> "For it is only from the cross that the whole depth, the whole seriousness, the whole weight of human sin becomes recognizable - and it is precisely the cross as a work of redemption that Islam radically rejects, obviously because its understanding of sin is different from the Christian one. What is right here, what is wrong here? God alone, before whom we both stand, the Christian and the Muslim, has to decide here" (Kellerhals 1969, 159).

---

[119] However, this notion, introduced to literary studies by Tepe (2001), applies not only there but to hermeneutic texts as a whole. It states:
"Projective-appropriative interpretations of text massively carry one's own worldview framework onto the text and strive to interpret the text according to this system, which involves 'translating' it into the conceptuality of one's own framework, as it were. The interpretation *de facto* amounts to *projecting* one's own belief system onto the text, thereby making the text a confirmatory instance for one's own worldview framework" (126).

This is a typical strategy of the post-war period, to bring about a synthesis of faith and knowledge on a 'scientific' basis. One can be a believer and a scientist at the same time, know and believe, evaluate and proceed descriptively, live religiosity practically and investigate it theoretically. This "and" then also prejudices a mutual compatibility of rational arguments and felt values; harmony floats around the opposites - but it only creates a false appearance.

In his lecture "Islam - Religion of Peace" in the context of the BKA - Autumn Conference 2001, an answer is already given by the title, which - as Elyas admits - can also remain questionable at first. His lecture serves not so much to deepen the knowledge of religious studies, but to present the practical Muslim religiosity and the mentality that can be derived from it, in order to give the German authorities an argumentation aid in assessing the possible terrorist potential of Islam and the preventive measures that can be derived from it. Since the term "peace" occurs fifty times in the Koran, and "Islam" (*salam* - peace) is also derived from this word, for the Muslim "Islam" means "to realize peace in the world" (Elyas 2001, 31). Theologically, this peacefulness is associated with Allah's will for peace, to which every Muslim must conform. But the word "peace" belongs to the "essential empty formulas" (Salamun), which pretend to have meaning already stored in the term, so to speak, which one only needs to extract. If one claims it for oneself, one believes to be in possession of its meaning. However, every world view has occupied this term differently, but only seldom explicates its criteria, so that it has to be valid for the thing par excellence, because its high prestige can serve in each case the purposes of the own world view, although it has been provided with an often even opposite meaning. Therefore, the question of its meaning must be asked here. Here I adhere to the well-documented biography of the prophet, to which Elyas says:

> Prophet Muhammad used to make a supplication every day saying, "O God, You are peace, from You comes peace, so grant that we may live in peace" (32).

This peaceful attitude, which, so to speak, flows over from God to Muhammad, does not correspond at all to the Prophet's vita already presented here. In his case, peace applies only to his followers. Barth (2003) draws the following conclusion: "And especially disturbing is his ambivalent attitude toward violence" (23). (Ambivalence in many areas is precisely a hallmark of Islam.) Examples of violence by the Prophet: He carries out raids to weaken his opponents, liquidates the Jewish quarter of Medina, raids a Meccan caravan in Ramadan, has "apostates" killed at night (23-25). He is legitimized by God for the raid, because:

> They ask you about fighting in the Holy Month. Say, "Then fighting is distressing, but turning away from Allah's way and expelling him and the Sacred Mosque and its inhabitants is even more distressing in the sight of Allah. [...]" (2:218).

Here the end justifies the means, so that just in Islam man threatens to become the instrument of God. I read from this that the concept of peace in Islam is used ambiguously according to the motto "peace to the huts" means at the same time "war to the palaces": for one's own co-religionists it guarantees a largely conflict-solving way; for the non-Muslims it can justify trusting cooperation, only temporarily tolerated existence, even persecution up to killing without punishment, the Koran provides evidence for all these possibilities. That is why Islam has such a 'peaceful beginning' with "fire and sword". Elyas sweeps this part of the truth under the carpet. He forgets that violence already played a prominent role in the founding of the religion of Islam, which, fortunately interspersed with phases of liberality, can be effortlessly documented through the history of Islam. Allah's life-enhancing commandments do not apply to "pagans" (Elyas 2001, 33), so atheists, positivists, liberals do not fall under Islam's peace obligation - further evidence that the term "peace" realizes its positive connotations only within the Muslim community. Elyas brought the same argument structure as Akbuluth. It is noticeable that he does not seek to question the reality of Islam as we also experience it firsthand, but distills an ideal Islam from the Quran that does not correspond with reality. In this way, we learn a great deal about the idealistic claim of this religion on its representatives, but almost nothing about its representation in reality, so that "claim equals reality" is suggested. What reality can now no longer be covered up falls under the heading of "un-Islamic" (39).

The method of omitting the not-so-beneficial alternatives of Koranic maxims serves a similar purpose: Elyas cannot repeat enough how peaceable, how tolerant Islam is as a religion and as a way of life for individual Muslims. He counters the reference to suras that can be interpreted in completely opposite ways with the assertion:

> Islam and Islamic scholars have laid down rules according to which an interpretation is interpreted as Islamic or not. [...]. If a contradiction to various fundamental further texts is worked out from a text, this interpretation is refuted because it contradicts so many other principles (39).

To what extent there is such a set of rules is not known to me. However, this sends a message to even critical non-Muslims: Everyone should believe that there is *a* binding interpretation of the Koran that can be relied upon. This belief is shaken, however, if one has to measure the Koran's claim to truth "Thus God is the guarantor of the correctness of its [the book's - the author's] content; he declares it binding and demands obedience and allegiance from people" (Khoury 2001, 34) against the possible rules of interpretation, which perhaps feign harmony where essential contradictions are involved. Elyas opposes a reinterpretation of Islam, which is inherently peaceful and which some people "suddenly make into a militant, inhuman religion" (2001, 38). Doesn't it (Islam) do that itself when it plays with the term "holy war" almost daily? Historically, it is easy to prove the expansionist urge of Islam "with fire and sword" in the direction of founding great empires; and it is not by chance that the wars of the Ottoman Empire have burned themselves into the cultural memory of Central and Eastern Europeans, and also the green flag of the Prophet as a symbol of subjugation and slavery remains unforgotten.

Islamism makes it easy for a warlike interpretation by practicing a cult of martyrdom.[120] What we see almost daily are Muslim terrorist acts that injure or kill many innocent victims. These "martyrs" invoke the Koran by claiming to be fighters in Allah's cause. (Khomeini even promises them the kingdom of heaven.) In reality, they are political tools of a policy that instrumentalizes Islamism for its own ends. And the Koran, which can often be interpreted ambivalently and therefore in a very misleading way, provides the justification for religious-political murder free of charge, so that the terrorists are allowed to feel like God's warriors. A clear and unambiguous word from the religious and political dignitaries of the Islamic world would be desirable here.

The term "un-Islamic" (39) is used to comment on the facts in a very restrained manner. In addition to heaven, there is also a hell in Islam; why is this not threatened to the terrorists by the Islamic clergy with the aid of the Koran? What follows from this lukewarm attitude? Many Muslims are accused of secretly harboring a certain sympathy for the 'freedom heroes'. The asymmetry of the behavior that can often be observed: If a Muslim assassin also kills many Muslims in his action, this is quickly dismissed with the "argument" "Allah's will"; if a Muslim kills Christians, he receives thunderous applause from the Islamists' lodge; if a non-Muslim kills Muslims, then the entire Islamic world demonstrates.

---

[120] As an example of this, Surah (3:170): "Indeed, do not consider those who were slain in the cause of Allah as dead - but alive with their Lord; they will be granted bounties."

The increasing distance between the two religions would be promoted in Germany by some groups out of opportunism, "in order to deny Muslims certain rights" (39). I repeat here: There are 2500 newly opened mosques in Germany, not a single newly opened Christian church in Turkey. How stupid does Elyas think we are? Here any self-criticism and insight is missing. I get the impression that the author is not entirely opposed to the idea of a Muslim state within the German state.

The chapter "Human Rights as an Indication of the Peacefulness [of Muslims - the author]" represents a cynicism that can almost no longer be surpassed. (34 ff.). According to this, the Koran and Sunna guarantee human rights - it is as simple as that - and something like human rights violations in practice and in the commandments do not occur.

Elyas sees the Germans here as blind greens or green blind people to whom he can tell fairy tales from "A Thousand and One Nights" and sell them as cognitive reasoning.

Again, he uses the method of quoting suras, according to which, of course, it is for the best as far as the observance of human rights is concerned.[121] Human rights in Islam are especially authenticated and secured "because they are part of our faith" (Elyas 2001, 35), i.e. from God, the actual sovereign. A part of this sovereignty has been leased to the religious functionaries, who are now supposed to be the guardians of human rights? An Ayatollah Khomeini as the guardian of human rights - a truly absurd idea!

On freedom of religion in Islam, Elyas quotes the Quranic verses:

> Sura (2:256): *There is no compulsion in religion.* Sura (109:6): *Your religion to you and my religion to me.*

---

[121] There are two clearly different versions of human rights, on the one hand those developed by Kant from the autonomy of the human person and his self-determined and self-determining reason, which are practiced as self-legislation in democratic systems and are supposed to apply universally, and on the other hand those of Islam, which are also supposed to apply universally and are given to man by the Koran, i.e. by God. Man in Islam is not a self-determined person, but is subject to the law of God, which, however, because God only wants man's salvation, guarantees him free development within the framework of these laws. This, however, conceals the problem of Islamic human rights; for to whom is the control of the observance of these rights incumbent? Because of the inseparability of politics and religion in many Islamic states and the political idea of a state of God on earth, religious functionaries are the real guarantors of human rights - a horror vision for the non-Islamic world.

Just this method, to strengthen one's own premises by quoting the Koran, is sharply criticized, if it is a 'western' scientist, especially if he takes a counter-position. I will let reality speak here. It is true that Islam *must* not hinder the free practice of religion; but such a principle is ignored by local conditions in Muslim countries as a whole. This example can be generalized: Wherever Christians and Muslims live in one state and the latter form the majority, Christians are oppressed, even in the formally secular country of Turkey. How can a Turk talk about religious freedom when not a *single* Christian church has been allowed to be built in his country for a long time, where church property has been confiscated, where no priests are allowed to be trained? What an outcry goes through the Muslim world when citizens refuse to grant permission to build a mosque, of which there are two and a half thousand in Germany. Immediately, religious freedom is in danger. Here, too, the aforementioned asymmetry of behavior, which makes many people suspicious of Islam, becomes visible: in one's own country, people of other faiths are oppressed and disadvantaged in all respects, which is not perceived at all by the Islamic majority or is suppressed or even approved of, while a possible singularly erroneous behavior on the part of the West is acknowledged with angry protests and insistence on fundamental rights.

(Imagine if there was a courageous party in Germany that would enforce the demand for reciprocal action, "We treat Muslims the way they treat Christians.") [122]

We do not hear a word here from the author Elyas, who claims to speak for Islam as a whole. People of other faiths may convert to Islam, but in many Muslim countries it is strictly forbidden for a Muslim to adopt another religion: a violation of this prohibition can be punished by death. If a Muslim marries a Christian, she must convert to Islam.

The rationale for this 'double standard'? Article 6b of the Draft Declaration of Human Rights concerning freedom of religion says:

> It is incumbent upon the Muslim - who has already been guided to the right path by confessing God and His Unity - to maintain Islam. [123]

---

[122] In 2013, such a party was founded: the AFD [editor's note].
[123] Quoted in Müller (1996, 144).

This 'Islamic' interpretation of the human right is also very contradictory, so great suspicion is called for when Islam comments on them. The author interprets this contradictory attitude towards them in the way that when Muslims live in Western foreign countries, they know to insist on the observance of the liberal Western human right 'freedom of religion', but 'forget' to let these standards apply to their own country as well. But let us listen further for repetition:

> "This must not be confused with the punishment of the apostate, that is, the punishment of the Muslim who leaves Islam. Because this is one thing and what we have said about freedom of religion is another thing. The Muslim, by submitting to God, has committed himself to abide by the rules of Islam and its creed. And if he goes apostate, he violates his commitment, harms the state and rebels against it. This requires punishment [...]." [124]

This example shows very succinctly the Orwellian doublethink of the Islamists, who demand that others observe human rights, but for themselves can refrain from doing so at will for reasons of faith. Now, Elyas cannot excuse himself by saying that he knows nothing about this ambiguous interpretation of human rights by Islam. His addressee is the Federal Criminal Police Office, whose organs he accuses of erroneous behavior toward Muslims, instead of disclosing the value system that determines the actions of many Muslims and also of the Muslim public, so that German authorities can react in a differentiated manner. Whoever reads his chapter "Human Rights as an Indication of the Peaceableness [of Muslims - the author]" cannot help but be deeply moved inside by the profound tolerance of the Muslim world. (This is meant ironically!)

The peak of demagogy, however, is the Koran quotation used by Elyas: "Women are twin siblings of men" (2001, 35) as proof of the equal rights[125] of women in Islam. With this, he considers the entire German public to be

---

[124] Ibidem 144 f.

[125] The phenomenon of "asymmetry," which we have often encountered in perception and reality, seems to be based on a cultural perception specific to Islam. Against the dominance and omnipresent presence of the man, the woman hardly appears in public life, the man is not constricted by any dress code, while the women have to keep their bodies covered for reasons of tradition, religion, family honor, sending out sexual charms, and in the case of sexual assaults, the perpetrator-victim relationship is reversed in that the violated women are also supposed to be to blame for the male assaults. This also explains the naïve formulation: "Nor are people preferred or disadvantaged on the basis of gender" (Elyas 2001, 35).

stupid, which, after all, comes into contact with this topic on a daily basis. In order to make the asymmetry and difference between Koranic exegesis and reality conspicuous, the gender roles are reversed in the following, which would not be noticeable at all in the case of symmetry:

'A female witness is more credible than two male witnesses; women are allowed to beat their husbands if they rebel in marriage; a woman inherits twice as much as her husband; a woman is allowed to marry four men, women have priority over men; all professions are open to women; women are allowed to show their faces; compulsory education is also compulsory for women; sexual self-determination is also compulsory for them, as is the right to vote and to stand for election'.

An outcry in the Islamic world would be the result. Elyas simply does not want to take note of this asymmetry; I call this deliberate deception of a body that wants to get to know Islam in order to also have the necessary sensitivity in the fight against terror.

He does not see forced marriages, 'honor killings', tolerated physical violence against women, family paternalism, 'compulsory mummery' because 'family honor' wants it that way, locking women away from the public.

Are these deficits, although they are frequently discussed in the press, perceived by him but deliberately concealed in order to idealize Islam or really not noticed because they are part of the Islamic 'cultural understanding'? As a religious-political representative, he stands for the first alternative. Too bad.

The author already differentiates the appearance of Islam in his preface. On the one hand, he sees in it an "offer of spiritual values that enable and promote a deep religious life" (9), but also "a state order that lays claim to totality for the whole person and to universality for the whole of humanity" (9). Thus, he must act in a dual role: as a scholar of religion and as a political scientist, because Islam shows both faces. He keeps his work free of immanent and explicit creeds, interprets undogmatically and does not conceal the contradictions of this religion.

However, he makes it clear in many places that he is convinced of the existence of God or Allah. His work is based on the working hypothesis: "Christianity and Islam are administrators of a "religious truth"" (207) and defines this as "truth that one does" (207). In doing so, he moves away from the concept of truth in the Western sciences in the direction of intuitive religious truth. Insofar as Khoury does religious studies, however, his statements are to be classified as cognitive and thus as true in the descriptive sense; but when he speaks of convictions, beliefs, values, of the "transcendence of God as the object of religious truth" (201), his projective-appropriative interpretation can only be salvaged by positing the triad "conviction, belief, values" for the conception of truth pathetically understood here. Parts I - III of his work deal cognitively with Muslim beliefs. The quality of the presentation leads not only to an informative knowledge of Islam, but to a deeper understanding of this religion as a whole, Part IV confronts it with the conditions of a secularized world, and Part V pleads for a fair dialogue between Islam and Christianity on the basis of their common but relative possession of truth, i.e. he urges equal eye level between both religions.

In Part IV, Khoury presents Islam's claim to its triple universality, which has already been discussed in detail: absolute claim to truth, totality of this claim for all areas of life, establishment of a globally valid state of God. In modern terms, Islam politically implies an imperialist claim, which is conceded only coyly or not at all by 'connoisseurs of Islam'. After an initial peaceful phase of Islam, Mohammed changes his mind about people of other faiths because they reject this faith. His followers war and fight the dissenters until they are liquidated or converted. This fight is godly, because the God of Islam, Allah, wants

Islam to rule worldwide. The expression of this imperialism, according to Khoury, is the division of the world into "the territory of Islam" and "the territory of war (115), to which two legal forms correspond: the Islamic kingdom of God and thus of peace, and the dominion of the dissenters and unbelievers, in which "numerous points contradict the provisions of divine law" (115). The ultimate goal of Islam is the complete incorporation of the "territory of war." As long as the sole rule of Islam has not encompassed the entire world, the "holy war" (*jihad*) remains a permanent state.[126] In contrast, Christianity's claim to universality ("Go into all the world and teach all nations") seems harmless. Therefore, in the minds of Islamists, only temporary agreements apply to non-Islamic states. (This substantial disrespect for Western state institutions is documented in the formation of Islamic parallel societies, which distance themselves so strongly from the institutional and civilizational conception of their non-Islamic country of residence that, for example, in the French suburbs of Paris, the *Code Napoleon* no longer applies, but the *Sharia*). However, this kind of forced acquiescence to other systems also implies great diplomatic caution in the drafting of treaties with Islamic countries, because they are guided more by the idea of jihad than by the legal principle *pacta sunt servanda vis-à-vis the* interpretation of these treaties. (The best example of disrespect for international treaties is provided by the President of Iran).

In contrast to all assertions of religious freedom, as Akbuluth (2001), although he should know better, presents as fact, "the classical legal system of Islam provides for the formation of a society with two classes of citizens" (Khoury 2001, 119), the subjugated subjects (*Djimmi*), second-class citizens, and the ruling Muslims with the consequences visible everywhere today. Furthermore, the author lectures critically on the religious freedom derived from the Koran and existing in reality, on apostasy, on the religious rights of the *Djimmi, in* order to then present critical arguments from the Muslims' point of view against the pluralistic way of life of the Western world. Khoury contrasts what Islam wants to adopt from the West and what it strictly rejects.

---

[126] To clarify the term: Although the term "holy war" originates from the Christian crusades, its content is used today as "jihad" in the Muslim world in a similar way, only with reversal of the warring parties at that time ("holy war" against "crusaders"). Its meaning in today's usage of Islamism is understood as the perception of a means, legitimized in the Koran, to achieve the universal rule of Islam, which includes terrorist, but also political and diplomatic actions.

He considers compatible with his doctrine:
- Introducing science and technology to assert itself and then outperform the West technically, scientifically and organizationally,
- Striving for material prosperity,
- Establish a modern infrastructure.

He condemns in the religious sphere:
- The atheistic ideology of communism,
- the separation of religion and state,
- methodical atheism in research, science; materialism as philosophy and worldview, rationalism, existentialism.

He condemns in the social sphere:
- The Anglo-European economic order with preference for capital,
- the gap between commerce and morality,
- the Western state as an instrument of prosperity and need satisfaction,
- the deep chasm between moral claims to justice and superficial materialism,
- the spiritual bleakness, aimlessness and meaninglessness of Western worldviews,
- the excessive will to power, which lacks human measure.

He condemns in the moral realm:
- The relativization of norms in order to live out without limits,
- the cost-benefit thinking of capitalism,
- the degradation of the human being to a means and a tool,
- the fetish character of money around which a decadent society revolves,
- the turn to a sexism that destroys families,
- prostitution as a perversion of love,
- Alcoholism, drugs, homosexuality, pornography, adultery, and the exchange of partners.

He condemns the Western double standard:
- in matters of human rights,

- in advancing moral arguments in order to represent one's own interests more effectively,
- in the realization of equality, which applies only between people of the Western Hemisphere.

He condemns the pursuit of hegemony even after the colonial period:
- Concerns of Islamic countries are not taken into account at international conferences,
- Islamic countries are constantly threatened by constant armament,
- the West is not living up to its claimed leadership role,
- the democratic form of rule with its emphasis on unrestricted subjectivity and freedom is in reality an illusion (135-139).

This compilation will not be commented on further, but the possibilities of de-escalation and dialogue between the two opponents described in Book V will be discussed. Here Khoury leaves the religious-scientific and religious-sociological level of the controversy and mutates into a theologian and moralist. His work can therefore no longer fulfill the scientific criteria; but that is not why it is useless in its entirety, but on the basis of everyday realism it is determinative for the life and culture of two great religions.

Even our everyday life (fortunately) rarely runs on purely scientific tracks, but is determined by everyday things, the mastering of which often requires no less rational argumentation than scientific work.

Khoury once finds the enabling of a fruitful dialogue in the verse similar to the Ring Parable:

> For each of you, We have set a direction and a path. And if God had wanted, He would have made you one community. But He wants to test you in what He has given you. So hasten to the good things. To God you will all return, then He will make known to you what you disagreed about (5:48),

and on the other hand in the verse:

> "Grow in the grace and knowledge of our Lord Jesus Christ" (2 Pet. 3:18).

Both religions are certain that God is the absolute truth and that people do not possess it, but their knowledge is relative, provisional, with regard to God. Under these conditions, both religions cannot justify their claim to absoluteness in this world, but they can compete for it, so that non-orthodox Christians and Muslims find a way to understand the other in the transcendence of God or Allah. But only for these two groups there is appreciative tolerance and ability for dialogue.

His work is guided by the rule: 'It is inevitable to look at Europe from the outside, to see its failures as well as its successes through the eyes of the very large part of humanity taken by the peoples of Asia and Africa' (2001, 29). He does not quite succeed in maintaining this perspective taken from the outside, because his value system that shapes him is Marxism, that is, a European 'invention'.

His opening assertion, "Originating in the heart of the West as a positive and proud self-determination, this category [fundamentalism - the author] is now used to label the 'barbarians' located outside the West, who in fact prefer to call themselves Islamists" (5). This dialectical formulation does not live up to its promise, however, because even at the time of the founding of the biblical renewal movement, liberal-minded Americans felt repelled by this anti-science, fundamentalist ideology and its musty morality.

Losurdo develops from the ideology-critical criterion "dichotomy" the fundamentalization that can be observed everywhere in the world. It appears in religions as sacred divine against secular law, as "unshakable contraposition between the 'universal' interests of the West and the equally 'universal' interests of Islam" (6), as 'sacred' human rights against the legislation of individual states, as Manichaeism, the struggle between good and evil, as the creation of an "immovable identity" (13) between two cultures, as the "repulsive reaction of one culture against another" (14), as the "imperial conflict between the great powers" (24), as the "clash of two mentalities" (33), as the "crusade of the 'secular' and 'civilized' West against the 'barbaric' and 'clerical' Islam" (48).

This author shows with many examples that the accusation of fundamentalism can not only apply to the Others, but that this ideology has been exported worldwide from Europe. Here, too, it is good to show by examples the emergence of such antagonisms, which can grow into fundamentalist movements. In the process, it regularly becomes clear that one's own position is affirmed, but the contrary position is negated, so that ultimately it is believed that the struggle is between good and evil:

[Bacon's "*sacrum bellum* against infidels and savages" (45), extermination of Indians and other primitive peoples, legitimization of World War I by Wilson's "will of God that brought us to war" (46), George Busch's "'crusade' against evil" (48), bin Laden's "war of evil against good" (44)].

How does Losurdo define fundamentalism? For religious fundamentalism, he finds the formula of "deriving political principles from a text considered sacred" (5). This binding instruction for action, understood as intersubjective and objective, has a destructive effect on one's own culture, because deviating traditions, non-religious legislation and value systems that are not congruent are sanctioned.

According to Losurdo, fundamentalism is generally characterized by "building an immovable identity" (18). It is no longer the encounter with other cultures that also shapes one's own, but a self-reflection frozen in stereotypes and clichés that naturalizes one's own culture, but also the counterculture.

This can go so far as to preoccupy an anthropological opposition of "Westerners" and Muslims, as Qutb, one of the fathers of Islamism, actually does.[127] Therefore, the characteristic of fundamentalism as a "repulsive reaction of one culture towards another" (14) is understandable.

Fundamentalism therefore applies not only to different religions, but also to great powers with a claim to universalization, as this author demonstrates with Francophilia and Germanophilia in the period before and after the First World War.

The history of World War II is a prime example of fundamentalist movements: The *American way of life,* National Socialism, Communism, National-

---

[127] Qutb projects his contemporary image of an Islamist as the member of a "noble ancient tribe," onto "Noah ... Jacob ... Moses ... Mohammed" (12) and allows a line of development to become visible up to the present time. Already at the beginning of this line there is also the enemy, to whom Qutb ascribes "an innate will of aggression" (12). Through this, Islam has strayed from its true path and got into many crises, which are coming to a head more and more today. A "business as usual" would plunge Islam into an abyss, so it is necessary to return to the true roots of Islam, to the time of Mohammed and the "right caliphs," when the enemies lay in the dust. Islam today must undergo a "cultural cleansing" (12) to end centuries of infiltration with corrupt unculture. This "cultural cleansing" (12), with the exception of the sciences, whose origins are placed in the Qur'an, aims not only to restore Islamic identity, but also to have a value-enhancing effect on Islamic self-confidence as a "golden age" that has been and will be again.

ism. But these "forms of thought" (Tepe) can appear in two variants, the militant and the moderate. Fundamentalism can dispense with both universalism and its religious ornamentation, like the "freedom wars" with their "Teutoman" (39) underpinnings.

Losurdo, however, does not only engage in a description and ideological analysis of fundamentalism in general and Islamic fundamentalism in particular, but also shows that fundamentalization is not an unalterable natural phenomenon, but can be explained rationally and is therefore avoidable in principle. We must self-critically note that the West as a whole has pursued an intellectual as well as political and economic hegemony over the Islamic world since the Enlightenment. The answers to this are increasing nationalism, anticolonialism, economic socialism. The West and Christianity as the causative agent grow together into an enemy image: the "crusaderism," which becomes the focal point of all negative Islamic projections and is endowed with a naturalistic-historical continuity.

With this popanza, whose value-enhancing effect must not be underestimated because Saladin defeated the Crusaders who despised Islam, political Islam has created a construct for itself that encourages 'final victory' as a model. It is gratifying that the defeat of the Ottoman Empire before Vienna is not invoked today as constant proof of the superiority of the Occident over the Orient. When the West responds to this battle rhetoric and stages a counter-crusade, it retroactively legitimizes Islamic fundamentalism. Then what Losurdo calls "immobile identity" happens (13), the competing cultures no longer fertilize each other, but seal themselves off and develop a momentum of mutual alienation, which in the sense of ideology perceives in the other culture only what it projects into it in terms of negativity.

The author discussed here assumes a "balance between criticism of the West and adoption of its achievements" (43), through which cultural exchange is possible. Criticizability and recognition of civilizational achievements on both sides act as culture-opening forces. When this simultaneous attraction and repulsion no longer works, when the systems isolate themselves, "all that remains is the holy war of the West against the holy war of Islam" (43).

Here ends the analysis of the selected literature. For the outlook (8.2), please go back to page 173. The author's closing words can be found there at the end of page 178.

Bibliography

Clarifying translations from German to English are in [Parentheses].

Abdullah, Muhammad Salim: *Der Koran*. In: Zewell, Rudolf (Publisher): *Islam – Die missbrauchte Religion*. München 2001.

Affoldenbach, Martin: *Die „Islamische Charta" – Ein Meilenstein für den Islam in Deutschland*? [*The "Islamic Charter" - A Milestone for Islam in Germany*? In: *Christians and Muslims. Responsibility for Dialogue*.] In: *Christen und Muslime. Verantwortung zum Dialog*. Evangelische Akademien in Deutschland (Publisher), Darmstadt 2006.

Akbuluth, Duran: *Der Islam und seine Bedeutung für die Weltpolitik*. [*Islam and its Significance for World Politics*.] Ulm 2002.

Alboga, Bekir et.al.: *Christen und Muslime*, Evangelische Akademie Deutschland (Publisher), 2006.

al-Farabi: *Falsafah Aristutalis (Philosophy of Aristotle)*, trans. M. Mahdi in *Alfarabi's Philosophy of Plato and Aristotle*, Ithaca, NY: Cornell 1969.

Al-Ghazali, Muhammed: *Die Nische der Lichter*. Hamburg 1987.

Armstrong, Karen: *Im Kampf um Gott. Fundamentalismus im Christentum, Judentum und Islam*. [*In the Struggle for God. Fundamentalism in Christianity, Judaism and Islam*.] München 2004.

Bacon, Francis: *Novum Organum*. 1620.

Barr, James: *Fundamentalismus*. München 1981.

Barth, Peter: *Islam und Islamismus*. München 2003.

Bayertz, Kurt: *Naturphilosophie als Ethik. Zur Vereinigung von Natur und Moralphilosophie im Zeichen der ökologischen Krise*. [*On the Unification of Nature and Moral Philosophy in the Sign of the Ecological Crisis*.] Philosophia naturalis 24. 1987.

Behr, H.: *Neue Organisationsformen des Terrorismus und Ordnungstypologien transnationaler Politik*. In: Bendel, Petra / Hildebrandt, Mathias (Publisher): *Im Schatten des Terrorismus*. Wiesbaden 2002.

Beltz, Walter: *Die Mythen des Koran*. [*The Myths of the Koran*.] Berlin 1980.

Bendel, Petra / Hildebrandt, Mathias (Publisher): *Im Schatten des Terrorismus*. Wiesbaden 2002.

Bendel, Petra / Hildebrandt, Mathias: *Der 11. September 2001*. In: Bendel, Petra / Hildebrandt, Mathias (Publisher): *Im Schatten des Terrorismus*. Wiesbaden 2002.

Beyaz, Zekeriya: *Christen und Muslime. Verantwortung zum Dialog*. [*Christians and Muslims. Responsibility for Dialogue*.] Sammelband der Evangelischen Akademien (Publisher) in Deutschland. Darmstadt 2006.

Birnbacher, Dieter (Publisher): *Ökophilosophie*. Stuttgart 1997.

Birnbacher, Dieter (Publisher): *Ökologie und Ethik*. Stuttgart 1980.

Birnbacher, Dieter: *Sind wir für die Natur verantwortlich?* [*Are We Responsible for Nature?*] In: Birnbacher, D. (Publisher): *Ökologie und Ethik*. Stuttgart 1980.

Birnbacher, Dieter: *Schopenhauer als Ideologiekritiker*. In: Birnbacher, D. (Publisher): *Schopenhauer in der Philosophie der Gegenwart*. Würzburg 1996.

Birnbacher, Dieter: *Natur als Maßstab menschlichen Handelns*. In: Birnbacher, D. (Publisher): *Ökophilosophie*. Stuttgart 1997.

Birnbacher, Dieter: *Analytische Einführung in die Ethik*. Berlin 2003.

BKA (Publisher): *Islamistischer Terror*. Neuwied 2001.

Broder, Henryk M.: *Hurra, wir kapitulieren!* Berlin 2006.

Cassirer, Ernst: *Philosophie der symbolischen Formen II*. Darmstadt 1969.

Colli, Giorgio / Montinari, Mazzino (Publisher): Friedrich Nietzsche. Kritische Studienausgabe in 14 Bänden. Berlin und New York 1988.

Dawkins, Richard: *Das egoistische Gen*. [*The Selfish Gene*.] Heidelberg 1994.

Dawkins, Richard: *Der blinde Uhrmacher*. [*The Blind Watchmaker*.] München 1996.

Delacampagne, Christian: *Die Geschichte der Sklaverei*. [*The History of Slavery*.] Düsseldorf und Zürich 2004.

Dittmar, Peter: *Ost gut – West schlecht.* [*East good - West bad.*] Köln 1977.

Djassemi, Mohammed: *Macht und Staat im Islam.* [*Power and State in Islam.*] Niebüll 2002.

Elyas, Nadeem: *Islam – Religion des Friedens.* [*Islam - Religion of Peace.*] In: BKA (Publisher) *BKA Herbsttagung 2001: Islamistischer Terrorismus.* Neuwied und Kriftel 2002.

Esposito, John L.: *Unholy War: Terror in the Name of Islam.* New York 2003.

Feuerbach, Ludwig: *Das Wesen des Christentums.* Berlin 1956.

Frisch, Max: *Andorra.* 1961.

Galter, Hannes D.: *Eine Religion im Ausnahmezustand.* In: Salamun, K. (Publisher): *Fundamentalismus "interdisziplinär".* Wien 2005.

Gehlen, Arnold: *Die Seele im technischen Zeitalter,* Gesamtausgabe Bd. 6, V. Klostermann, Frankfurt am Main 2004.

Geiger, Theodor: *Ideologie und Werturteil.* In: Lenk, Kurt (Publisher): *Ideologie.* Frankfurt am Main 1984.

Goldziher, Ignaz: *Vorlesung über den Islam.* [*Lecture on Islam.*] Heidelberg 1963.

Haeckel, Ernst: *Die Welträtsel.* Stuttgart 1905.

Hegel, Georg Wilhelm Friedrich: Werke in 20 Bänden. Frankfurt am Main 1969–1971.

Heiligsetzer, Edda: *Extremismus, Terrorismus, ,Heiliger Krieg': Zur Soziologie religiöser Terroristen.* [*Extremism, Terrorism, 'Holy War': On the Sociology of Religious Terrorists.*] In: Bendel, Petra / Hildebrandt, Mathias (Publisher): *Im Schatten des Terrorismus.* Wiesbaden 2002.

Heine, Peter: *Islam zur Einführung.* Hamburg 2003.

Helferich, Christoph: *Geschichte der Philosophie.* Stuttgart 2001.

Hemminger, Hansjörg: *Fundamentalismus, ein vielschichtiger Begriff.* In: Hemminger, Hansjörg (Publisher): *Fundamentalismus in der verweltlichten Kultur.* Stuttgart 1991.

Hildebrand, K. (Publisher): *Zwischen Religion und Politik.* München 2003.

Hildebrandt, Mathias (Publisher): *Im Schatten des Terrorismus.* Wiesbaden 2002.

Hitler, Adolf: Mein Kampf. München Teil 1 in 1925, Teil 2 in 1926.

Huntington, Samuel: *Kampf der Kulturen*. [*Clash of Civilizations*.] Wien 1996.

Hurgronje, Snouck: *Verspreide Geschriften*. Bd. 3. Leiden 1923, Netherlands.

Horovitz, Josef: *Das koranische Paradies*. In: Paret, Rudi (Publisher): *Der Koran*. Darmstadt 1975.

Hübner, Kurt: *Die Wahrheit des Mythos*. [*The Truth of Myth*.] München 1984.

Hübner, Kurt: *Mythische und wissenschaftliche Denkform*. In: Poser, Hans (Publisher): *Philosophie und Mythos*. Berlin 1979.

Ibn-Tufail, Abu-Bakr Muhammad Ibn Abd al-Malik Muhammad al-Qaisi: *Robinsonade*.

Kalikow, Theodora June: (Dean of Plymouth State College in New Hampshire), 1984.

Kant, Immanuel: Works in Twelve Volumes. Publisher: Weischedel, Wilhelm. Frankfurt am Main 1964.

Kellerhals, Emanuel: *Der Islam. Seine Geschichte, seine Lehre und sein Wesen*. [*Der Islam. Its history, its doctrine and its essence*.] Basel 1945.

Kellerhals, Emanuel: *Der Islam. Geschichte, Lehre, Wesen*. [*The Islam. History, Doctrine, Essence*.] Siebenstern Verlag. Hamburg und München 1969.

Khalil, Imalduldin: *Die Refutation des Säkularismus*. Beirut 1979.

Khoury, Adel Theodor, Hagemann, L., Heine, Peter: *Islam-Lexikon*. Freiburg 1991.

Kienzler, Klaus (Publisher): *Der neue Fundamentalismus*. Düsseldorf 1990.

Kocsis, Isabel: *Mohammed und die Gewalt*. München 2001.

Lenk, Hans: *Von Deutungen zu Wertungen*. Frankfurt am Main 1994.

Lenk, Hans: *Schemaspiele*. Frankfurt am Main 1995.

Lenk, Kurt: *Ideologie*. Frankfurt am Main 1984.

Leonhard, Wolfgang: *Die Revolution entlässt ihre Kinder*. 1965.

Lerch, Wolfgang Günter: *Denker des Propheten*. [*Thinkers of the Prophet*.] Düsseldorf 2000.

Lerch, Wolfgang Günter: *Muhammeds Erben: die unbekannte Vielfalt des Islam.* [*Muhammed's Heirs: The Unknown Diversity of Islam.*] Düsseldorf 1999.

Lieber, Hans-Joachim: *Ideologie.* Paderborn 1985.

Lorenz, Konrad: *Die Rückseite des Spiegels.* München 1973.

Lorenz, Konrad: a) *Kants Lehre vom Apriorischen im Lichte gegenwärtiger Biologie.* [*Kant's Doctrine of the Apriori in the Light of Contemporary Biology.*] In Lorenz, Konrad / Wuketis, Franz (Publisher): *Die Evolution des Denkens.* München 1983.

Lorenz, Konrad: b) *Der Abbau des Menschlichen.* [*The degradation of the human.*] München 1983.

Lorenz, Konrad: *Evolution und Apriori.* In: Riedl, R. / Wuketis, Fr. (Publisher): *Die Evolutionäre Erkenntnistheorie – Bedingungen, Lösungen, Kontroversen.* Wien 1987.

Losurdo, Domenico: *Was ist Islamismus?* [*What is Islamism?*] Essen 2001.

Maetzig, Kurt: Ernst Thälmann – Sohn seiner Klasse. [Ernst Thälmann - Son of his Class.] DEFA Film 1954.

Maududi, Abu al-: *Der Islam und die moderne Zivilisation.* [*Islam and Modern Civilization.*] Cairo, no year given.

Mannheim, Karl: *Die Methoden der Wissenssoziologie.* [*The Methods of the Sociology of Knowledge.*] In: Lenk, K. (Publisher): *Ideologie.* Frankfurt am Main 1984.

Mannheim, Karl: *Ideologische und soziologische Interpretation der geistigen Gebilde.* In: Meja, Volker / Stehr, Nico (Publisher): *Der Streit um die Wissenssoziologie.* Bd. 1. Frankfurt am Main 1982.

Mohr, Hans: *Ist das Ethos der Wissenschaften mit der evolutionären Erkenntnistheorie vereinbar?* [*Is the Ethos of Science Compatible with Evolutionary Epistemology?*] In: Lorenz, Konrad / Wuketis, F. M, (Publisher): *Die Evolution des Denkens.* München 1983.

Monod, Jacques: *Zufall oder Notwendigkeit?* [*Chance or Necessity?*] München 1996.

Moore, George Edward: *Principia ethica.* Stuttgart 1970.

Müller, Lorenz: *Islam und Menschenrechte.* Hamburg 1996.

Nagel, Tilman: *Geschichte der islamischen Theologie*. München 1994.

Orwell, George: ***1984***. Frankfurt am Main 1976.

Paley, William: Natural Theology, 1802.

Paret, Rudi (Hg.): *Der Koran*. Darmstadt 1975.

Pelz, Heidrun: *Linguistik*. Hamburg 1996.

Pflüger, Friedbert: *Ein neuer Weltkrieg*? [*A New World War*?] München 2004.

Popper, Karl R.: *Objektive Erkenntnis.* Hamburg 1974.

Pörksen, Uwe: *Plastikwörter. Die Sprache einer internationalen Diktatur.* [*Plastic Words. The Language of an International Dictatorship.*] Stuttgart 1989.

Portmann, Adolf: *Zoologie und das neue Bild des Menschen. Biologische Fragmente zu einer Lehre vom Menschen.* [*Zoology and the New Image of Man. Biological Fragments on a Doctrine of Man.*] Hamburg 1956.

Poser, Hans (Publisher): *Philosophie und Mythos.* Berlin 1979.

Prenner, Karl: *Islamischer Fundamentalismus und Koraninterpretation.* In: Salamun, Kurt (Publisher): *Fundamentalismus „interdisziplinär".* Wien 2005.

Qutb, Sayyid: *Ma'alim fi al-Tariq* (English title: *Milestones*), Egypt 1964.

Rapoport, Anatol: *Allgemeine Systemtheorie* [*General Systems Theory*], Darmstadt 1988.

Russell, Bertrand: *Philosophie des Abendlandes* [*Philosophy of the Occident.*], München 1950.

Rotter, Gernot: *Der Islam hat die Demokratie erfunden.* In: Rotter, Gernot (Publisher): *Die Welten des Islam.* Frankfurt am Mai 1993.

Rudolph, Ulrich: *Islamische Philosophie.* München 2004.

Salamun, Kurt: *Ideologie, Wissenschaft, Politik.* Graz 1975.

Salamun, Kurt (Publisher): *Fundamentalismus "interdisziplinär".* Wien 2005.

Salamun, Kurt: *Ist mit dem Verfall der Großideologien auch die Ideologiekritik zu Ende?* In: Salamun, Kurt (Publisher): *Ideologien und Ideologiekritik.* Darmstadt 1992.

Sarrazin, Thilo: *Deutschland schafft sich ab. Wie wir unser Land aufs Spiel setzen.* [*How we are putting our country at risk.*] München 2010.

Schmidt, Alfred: *Das Phänomen des Fundamentalismus in Geschichte und Gegenwart.* In: Kienzler, Klaus (Publisher): *Der neue Fundamentalismus.* Düsseldorf 1990.

Schnädelbach, Herbert: *Erkenntnistheorie zur Einführung.* Hamburg 2002.

Schimmel, Annemarie: *Im Namen Allahs, des Allbarmherzigen.* [*In the Name of Allah, the All-Merciful.*] Düsseldorf 1996.

Schupp, Franz: *Mythos und Religion.* In: Poser, Hans (Publisher): *Philosophie und Mythos.* Berlin 1979.

Schwer, T., (Publisher): *Der Koran.* München 2003.

Serauky, Eberhard: *Geschichte des Islam.* Berlin 1991.

Tepe, Peter: *Theorie der Illusionen.* Essen 1988.

Tepe, Peter: *Illusionskritischer Versuch über den historischen Materialismus.* Essen 1989.

Tepe, Peter: *Postmoderne, Poststrukturalismus.* Wien 1992.

Tepe, Peter: *Mein Nietzsche.* Wien 1993.

Tepe, Peter und May, Helge: *Mythisches, Allzumythisches – Theater um alte und neue Mythen.* Ratingen 1995.

Tepe, Peter: *Nietzsche / Erkennen.* Essen 1995.

Tepe, Peter: *Nationalsozialismus und Mythos.* In: Mythologica 5 (1997). See also http://www.petertepe.de/texte/texte.htm *Fundamentalismus als Denkform.* [*Fundamentalism as a Form of Thought.*]

Tepe, Peter: *Mythos & Literatur.* Würzburg 2001.

Tepe, Peter: *Grundsätzliches über Feindbilder.* [*Fundamental Things about Images of the Enemy.*] In: *Aufklärung und Kritik – Zeitschrift für freie und humanistische Philosophie.* Publisher: Gesellschaft für kritische Philosophie 2/2002b Nürnberg 2002.

Tibi, Bassam: *Der neue Totalitarismus.* [*The New Totalitarianism.*] Darmstadt 2004.

Tibi, Bassam: *Der Islam und das Problem der kulturellen Bewältigung sozialen Wandels*. [*Islam and the Problem of the Cultural Management of Social Change*.] Frankfurt 1985.

Tibi, Bassam: *Fundamentalismus und die Quellen des Terrorismus im politischen Islam*. [*Fundamentalism and the Sources of Terrorism in Political Islam*.] In: Bundeskriminalamt (BKA) (Publisher): *Islamistischer Terrorismus*. Neuwied 2001.

Tibi, Bassam: *Der Islam und die westliche Welt*. [*Islam and the Western World*.] Darmstadt 2001.

Tibi, Bassam: *Die Krise des modernen Islams*. [*The Crisis of Modern Islam*.] München 1991.

Tibi, Bassam: *Fundamentalismus im Islam*. Darmstadt 2002.

Tibi, Bassam: *Im Schatten Allahs. Der Islam und die Menschenrechte*. [*In the Shadow of Allah. Islam and Human Rights*.] München1994.

Topitsch, Ernst: *Gemeinsame Grundlage mythischen und philosophischen Denkens*. In: Poser, H. (Publisher): *Philosophie und Mythos*. Berlin 1979.

Topitsch, Ernst: *Erkenntnis und Illusion*. Hamburg 1979.

Vernant, Jean-Pierre: *Griechische Mythen, neu erzählt*. [*Greek Myths, Retold*] Köln 2000.

Vollmer, Gerhard: *Evolutionäre Erkenntnistheorie*. [*Evolutionary Epistemology*.] Stuttgart / Leipzig 1998.

Von Ditfurth, Hoimar: *Der Geist fiel nicht vom Himmel*. Hamburg 1976.

Von Kutschera, Franz: *Vernunft und Glaube*. Berlin 1991.

Wielandt, Rotraut: *Zeitgenössischer islamischer Fundamentalismus*. [*Contemporary Islamic Fundamentalism*.] In: Kienzler, K. (Publisher): *Der neue Fundamentalismus*. Düsseldorf 1990.

Zewell, Rudolf (Publisher): Islam – *Die missbrauchte Religion oder Keimzelle des Terrorismus*? München 2001.